MYSELF WITH OTHERS

MYSELF
WITH OTHERS
SELECTED ESSAYS

CARLOS
FUENTES

FARRAR, STRAUS AND GIROUX
NEW YORK

First published 1988 by
André Deutsch Limited
105–106 Great Russell Street, London WC1B 3LJ
Printed in the United States of America
Published simultaneously in Canada by
Collins Publishers, Toronto

Designed by Debby Jay
ISBN 0-374-2237-5

Portions of this book have appeared, in somewhat
different form, in *Granta*, *TriQuarterly*, *Vanity Fair*,
and *World Literature Today*. A longer and somewhat
different version of *Cervantes, or The Critique
of Reading* was originally published under
the same title by the Institute of Latin American
Studies, the University of Texas at Austin;
copyright © 1976 by
the Institute of Latin American Studies,
the University of Texas, Austin

Acknowledgment is made to New Directions
Publishing Corporation for permission
to reprint an excerpt from
"In the middle of this phrase . . ."
from *Octavio Paz: Selected Poems*.
Copyright © 1975 by Octavio Paz
and Eliot Weinberger

To Philip Roth and Claire Bloom

CONTENTS

PART ONE
MYSELF

How I Started to Write

I

I was born on November 11, 1928, under the sign I would have chosen, Scorpio, and on a date shared with Dostoevsky, Crommelynck, and Vonnegut. My mother was rushed from a steaming-hot movie house in those days before Colonel Buendía took his son to discover ice in the tropics. She was seeing King Vidor's version of *La Bohème* with John Gilbert and Lillian Gish. Perhaps the pangs of my birth were provoked by this anomaly: a silent screen version of Puccini's opera. Since then, the operatic and the cinematographic have had a tug-of-war with my words, as if expecting the Scorpio of fiction to rise from silent music and blind images.

All this, let me add to clear up my biography, took place in the sweltering heat of Panama City, where my father was beginning his diplomatic career as an attaché to the Mexican legation. (In those days, embassies were established only in the most important capitals—no place where the mean average year-round temperature was perpetually in the nineties.) Since my father was a convinced Mexican nationalist, the problem of where I was to be born had to be resolved under the sign, not of Scorpio, but of the Eagle and the Serpent. The Mexican legation, however, though it had extra-territorial rights, did not have even a territorial midwife; and the Minister, a fastidious bachelor from Sinaloa by the name of Ignacio Norris, who resembled the poet Quevedo as one pince-nez resembles another, would have none of me suddenly appearing on the

3

legation parquet, even if the Angel Gabriel had announced me as a future Mexican writer of some, albeit debatable, merit.

So if I could not be born in a fictitious, extraterritorial Mexico, neither would I be born in that even more fictitious extension of the United States of America, the Canal Zone, where, naturally, the best hospitals were. So, between two territorial fictions—the Mexican legation, the Canal Zone—and a mercifully silent close-up of John Gilbert, I arrived in the nick of time at the Gorgas Hospital in Panama City at eleven that evening.

The problem of my baptism then arose. As if the waters of the two neighboring oceans touching each other with the iron fingertips of the canal were not enough, I had to undergo a double ceremony: my religious baptism took place in Panama, because my mother, a devout Roman Catholic, demanded it with as much urgency as Tristram Shandy's parents, although through less original means. My national baptism took place a few months later in Mexico City, where my father, an incorrigible Jacobin and priest-eater to the end, insisted that I be registered in the civil rolls established by Benito Juárez. Thus, I appear as a native of Mexico City for all legal purposes, and this anomaly further illustrates a central fact of my life and my writing: I am Mexican by will and by imagination.

All this came to a head in the 1930s. By then, my father was counselor of the Mexican Embassy in Washington, D.C., and I grew up in the vibrant world of the American thirties, more or less between the inauguration of Citizen Roosevelt and the interdiction of Citizen Kane. When I arrived here, Dick Tracy had just met Tess Truehart. As I left, Clark Kent was meeting Lois Lane. You are what you eat. You are also the comics you peruse as a child.

At home, my father made me read Mexican history, study Mexican geography, and understand the names, the dreams and defeats of Mexico: a nonexistent country, I then thought, invented by my father to nourish my infant imagination with yet another marvelous fiction: a land of Oz with a green cactus road, a landscape and a soul so different from those of the United States that they seemed a fantasy.

A cruel fantasy: the history of Mexico was a history of crushing defeats, whereas I lived in a world, that of my D.C. public school, which celebrated victories, one victory after another, from York-town to New Orleans to Chapultepec to Appomattox to San Juan

Hill to Belleau Wood: had this nation never known defeat? Sometimes the names of United States victories were the same as the names of Mexico's defeats and humiliations: Monterrey. Veracruz. Chapultepec. Indeed: from the Halls of Montezuma to the shores of Tripoli. In the map of my imagination, as the United States expanded westward, Mexico contracted southward. Miguel Hidalgo, the father of Mexican independence, ended up with his head on exhibit on a lance at the city gates of Chihuahua. Imagine George and Martha beheaded at Mount Vernon.

To the south, sad songs, sweet nostalgia, impossible desires. To the north, self-confidence, faith in progress, boundless optimism. Mexico, the imaginary country, dreamed of a painful past; the United States, the real country, dreamed of a happy future.

The French equate intelligence with rational discourse, the Russians with intense soul-searching. For a Mexican, intelligence is inseparable from maliciousness—in this, as in many other things, we are quite Italian: *furberia*, roguish slyness, and the cult of appearances, *la bella figura*, are Italianate traits present everywhere in Latin America: Rome, more than Madrid, is our spiritual capital in this sense.

For me, as a child, the United States seemed a world where intelligence was equated with energy, zest, enthusiasm. The North American world blinds us with its energy; we cannot see ourselves, we must see *you*. The United States is a world full of cheerleaders, prize-giving, singin' in the rain: the baton twirler, the Oscar awards, the musical comedies cannot be repeated elsewhere; in Mexico, the Hollywood statuette would come dipped in poisoned paint; in France, Gene Kelly would constantly stop in his steps to reflect: *Je danse, donc je suis.*

Many things impressed themselves on me during those years. The United States—would you believe it?—was a country where things worked, where nothing ever broke down: trains, plumbing, roads, punctuality, personal security seemed to function perfectly, at least at the eye level of a young Mexican diplomat's son living in a residential hotel on Washington's Sixteenth Street, facing Meridian Hill Park, where nobody was then mugged and where our superb furnished seven-room apartment cost us 110 pre-inflation dollars a month. Yes, in spite of all the problems, the livin' seemed easy during those long Tidewater summers when I became

perhaps the first and only Mexican to prefer grits to guacamole. I
also became the original Mexican Calvinist: an invisible taskmaster
called Puritanical Duty shadows my every footstep: I shall not
deserve anything unless I work relentlessly for it, with iron dis-
cipline, day after day. Sloth is sin, and if I do not sit at my
typewriter every day at 8 a.m. for a working day of seven to eight
hours, I will surely go to hell. No *siestas* for me, alas and alack
and *hélas* and *ay-ay-ay*: how I came to envy my Latin brethren,
unburdened by the Protestant work ethic, and why must I, to this
very day, read the complete works of Hermann Broch and scribble
in my black notebook on a sunny Mexican beach, instead of lolling
the day away and waiting for the coconuts to fall?

But the United States in the thirties went far beyond my personal
experience. The nation that Tocqueville had destined to share
dominance over half the world realized that, in effect, only a
continental state could be a modern state; in the thirties, the U.S.A.
had to decide *what to do* with its new worldwide power, and Franklin Roosevelt taught us to believe that the first thing was for the
United States to show that it was capable of living up to its ideals.
I learned then—my first political lesson—that this is your true
greatness, not, as was to be the norm in my lifetime, material
wealth, not arrogant power misused against weaker peoples, not
ignorant ethnocentrism burning itself out in contempt for others.

As a young Mexican growing up in the U.S., I had a primary
impression of a nation of boundless energy, imagination, and the
will to confront and solve the great social issues of the times without
blinking or looking for scapegoats. It was the impression of a
country identified with its own highest principles: political democracy, economic well-being, and faith in its human resources,
especially in that most precious of all capital, the renewable wealth
of education and research.

Franklin Roosevelt, then, restored America's self-respect in this
essential way, not by macho posturing. I saw the United States in
the thirties lift itself by its bootstraps from the dead dust of Okla-
homa and the gray lines of the unemployed in Detroit, and this
image of health was reflected in my daily life, in my reading of
Mark Twain, in the images of movies and newspapers, in the North
American capacity for mixing fluffy illusion and hard-bitten truth,
self-celebration and self-criticism: the madcap heiresses played by

Carole Lombard coexisted with the Walker Evans photographs of hungry, old-at-thirty migrant mothers, and the nimble tread of the feet of Fred Astaire did not silence the heavy stomp of the boots of Tom Joad.

My school—a public school, nonconfessional and coeducational—reflected these realities and their basically egalitarian thrust. I believed in the democratic simplicity of my teachers and chums, and above all I believed I was, naturally, in a totally unselfconscious way, a part of that world. It is important, at all ages and in all occupations, to be "popular" in the United States; I have known no other society where the values of "regularity" are so highly prized. I was popular, I was "regular." Until a day in March—March 18, 1938. On that day, a man from another world, the imaginary country of my childhood, the President of Mexico, Lázaro Cárdenas, nationalized the holdings of foreign oil companies. The headlines in the North American press denounced the "communist" government of Mexico and its "red" president; they demanded the invasion of Mexico in the sacred name of private property, and Mexicans, under international boycott, were invited to drink their oil.

Instantly, surprisingly, I became a pariah in my school. Cold shoulders, aggressive stares, epithets, and sometimes blows. Children know how to be cruel, and the cruelty of their elders is the surest residue of the malaise the young feel toward things strange, things other, things that reveal our own ignorance or insufficiency. This was not reserved for me or for Mexico: at about the same time, an extremely brilliant boy of eleven arrived from Germany. He was a Jew and his family had fled from the Nazis. I shall always remember his face, dark and trembling, his aquiline nose and deep-set, bright eyes with their great sadness; the sensitivity of his hands and the strangeness of it all to his American companions. This young man, Hans Berliner, had a brilliant mathematical mind and he walked and saluted like a Central European; he wore short pants and high woven stockings, Tyrolean jackets and an air of displaced courtesy that infuriated the popular, regular, feisty, knickered, provincial, Depression-era little sons of bitches at Henry Cooke Public School on Thirteenth Street N.W.

The shock of alienation and the shock of recognition are sometimes one and the same. What was different made others afraid,

less of what was different than of themselves, of their own incapacity to recognize themselves in the alien.

I discovered that my father's country was real. And that I belonged to it. Mexico was my identity yet I lacked an identity; Hans
Berliner suffered more than I—headlines from Mexico are soon
forgotten; another great issue becomes all-important for a wonderful
ten days' media feast—yet he had an identity as a Central European
Jew. I do not know what became of him. Over the years, I have
always expected to see him receive a Nobel Prize in one of the
sciences. Surely, if he lived, he integrated himself into North
American society. I had to look at the photographs of President
Cárdenas: he was a man of another lineage; he did not appear in
the repertory of glossy, seductive images of the salable North American world. He was a mestizo, Spanish and Indian, with a faraway,
green, and liquid look in his eyes, as if he were trying to remember
a mute and ancient past.

Was that past mine as well? Could I dream the dreams of the
country suddenly revealed in a political act as something more
than a demarcation of frontiers on a map or a hillock of statistics
in a yearbook? I believe I then had the intuition that I would not
rest until I came to grips myself with that common destiny which
depended upon still another community: the community of time.
The United States had made me believe that we live only for the
future; Mexico, Cárdenas, the events of 1938, made me understand
that only in an act of the present can we make present the past as
well as the future: to be a Mexican was to identify a hunger for
being, a desire for dignity rooted in many forgotten centuries and
in many centuries yet to come, but rooted here, now, in the instant,
in the vigilant time of Mexico I later learned to understand in the
stone serpents of Teotihuacán and in the polychrome angels of
Oaxaca.

Of course, as happens in childhood, all these deep musings had
no proof of existence outside an act that was, more than a prank,
a kind of affirmation. In 1939, my father took me to see a film at
the old RKO–Keith in Washington. It was called *Man of Conquest*
and it starred Richard Dix as Sam Houston. When Dix/Houston
proclaimed the secession of the Republic of Texas from Mexico,
I jumped on the theater seat and proclaimed on my own and from
the full height of my nationalist ten years, "Viva México! Death

to the gringos!" My embarrassed father hauled me out of the theater, but his pride in me could not resist leaking my first rebellious act to the *Washington Star*. So I appeared for the first time in a newspaper and became a child celebrity for the acknowledged ten-day span. I read Andy Warhol *avant l'air-brush*: Everyone shall be famous for at least five minutes.

In the wake of my father's diplomatic career, I traveled to Chile and entered fully the universe of the Spanish language, of Latin American politics and its adversities. President Roosevelt had resisted enormous pressures to apply sanctions and even invade Mexico to punish my country for recovering its own wealth. Likewise, he did not try to destabilize the Chilean radicals, communists, and socialists democratically elected to power in Chile under the banners of the Popular Front. In the early forties, the vigor of Chile's political life was contagious: active unions, active parties, electoral campaigns all spoke of the political health of this, the most democratic of Latin American nations. Chile was a politically verbalized country. It was no coincidence that it was also the country of the great Spanish-American poets Gabriela Mistral, Vicente Huidobro, Pablo Neruda.

I only came to know Neruda and became his friend many years later. This King Midas of poetry would write, in his literary testament rescued from a gutted house and a nameless tomb, a beautiful song to the Spanish language. The Conquistadors, he said, took our gold, but they left us their gold: they left us our words. Neruda's gold, I learned in Chile, was the property of all. One afternoon on the beach at Lota in southern Chile, I saw the miners as they came out, mole-like, from their hard work many feet under the sea, extracting the coal of the Pacific Ocean. They sat around a bonfire and sang, to guitar music, a poem from Neruda's *Canto General*. I told them that the author would be thrilled to know that his poem had been set to music.

What author? they asked me in surprise. For them, Neruda's poetry had no author, it came from afar, it had always been sung, like Homer's. It was the poetry, as Croce said of the *Iliad*, "d'un popolo intero poetante," of an entire poetizing people. It was the document of the original identity of poetry and history.

I learned in Chile that Spanish could be the language of free men. I was also to learn in my lifetime, in Chile in 1973, the fragility of both our language and our freedom when Richard Nixon, unable to destroy American democracy, merrily helped to destroy Chilean democracy, the same thing Leonid Brezhnev had done in Czechoslovakia.

An anonymous language, a language that belongs to us all, as Neruda's poem belonged to those miners on the beach, yet a language that can be kidnapped, impoverished, sometimes jailed, sometimes murdered. Let me summarize this paradox: Chile offered me and the other writers of my generation in Santiago both the essential fragility of a cornered language, Spanish, and the protection of the Latin of our times, the lingua franca of the modern world, the English language. At the Grange School, under the awesome beauty of the Andes, José Donoso and Jorge Edwards, Roberto Torretti, the late Luis Alberto Heyremans, and myself, by then all budding amateurs, wrote our first exercises in literature within this mini-Britannia. We all ran strenuous cross-country races, got caned from time to time, and recuperated while reading Swinburne; and we were subjected to huge doses of rugby, Ruskin, porridge for breakfast, and a stiff upper lip in military defeats. But when Montgomery broke through at El Alamein, the assembled school tossed caps in the air and hip-hip-hoorayed to death. In South America, clubs were named after George Canning and football teams after Lord Cochrane; no matter that English help in winning independence led to English economic imperialism, from oil in Mexico to railways in Argentina. There was a secret thrill in our hearts: our Spanish conquerors had been beaten by the English; the defeat of Philip II's invincible Armada compensated for the crimes of Cortés, Pizarro, and Valdivia. If Britain was an empire, at least she was a democratic one.

In Washington, I had begun writing a personal magazine in English, with my own drawings, book reviews, and epochal bits of news. It consisted of a single copy, penciled and crayonned, and its circulation was limited to our apartment building. Then, at age fourteen, in Chile, I embarked on a more ambitious project, along with my schoolmate Roberto Torretti: a vast Caribbean saga that was to culminate in Haiti on a hilltop palace (Sans Souci?) where a black tyrant kept a mad French mistress in a garret. All this was set in the early nineteenth century and in the final scene (Shades of

Jane Eyre! Reflections on Rebecca! Fans of Joan Fontaine!) the palace was to burn down, along with the world of slavery.

But where to begin? Torretti and I were, along with our literary fraternity at The Grange, avid readers of Dumas *père*. A self-respecting novel, in our view, had to start in Marseilles, in full view of the Chateau d'If and the martyrdom of Edmond Dantès. But we were writing in Spanish, not in French, and our characters had to speak Spanish. But, what Spanish? My Mexican Spanish, or Roberto's Chilean Spanish? We came to a sort of compromise: the characters would speak like Andalusians. This was probably a tacit homage to the land from which Columbus sailed.

The Mexican painter David Alfaro Siqueiros was then in Chile, painting the heroic murals of a school in the town of Chillán, which had been devastated by one of Chile's periodic earthquakes. He had been implicated in a Stalinist attempt on Trotsky's life in Mexico City and his commission to paint a mural in the Southern Cone was a kind of honorary exile. My father, as chargé d'affaires in Santiago, where his mission was to press the proudly independent Chileans to break relations with the Berlin–Rome Axis, rose above politics in the name of art and received Siqueiros regularly for lunch at the Mexican Embassy, which was a delirious mansion, worthy of William Beckford's follies, built by an enriched Italian tailor called Fallabella, on Santiago's broad Pedro de Valdivia Avenue.

This Gothic grotesque contained a Chinese room with nodding Buddhas, an office in what was known as Westminster Parliamentary style, Napoleonic lobbies, Louis XV dining rooms, Art Deco bedrooms, a Florentine loggia, many busts of Dante, and, finally, a vast Chilean vineyard in the back.

It was here, under the bulging Austral grapes, that I forced Siqueiros to sit after lunch and listen to me read our by then 400-page-long opus. As he drowsed off in the shade, I gained and lost my first reader. The novel, too, was lost; Torretti, who now teaches philosophy of science at the University of Puerto Rico, has no copy; Siqueiros is dead, and, besides, he slept right through my reading. I myself feel about it like Marlowe's Barabbas about fornication: that was in another country, and, besides, the wench is dead. Yet the experience of writing this highly imitative melodrama was not lost on me; its international setting, its self-conscious search for language (or languages, rather) were part of a constant attempt at a breakthrough in my life. My upbringing taught me that cultures are not isolated, and perish when deprived of contact with what is different and challenging. Reading, writing, teaching, learning, are all activities aimed at introducing civilizations to each other. No culture, I believed unconsciously ever since then, and quite consciously today, retains its identity in isolation; identity is attained in contact, in contrast, in breakthrough.

Rhetoric, said William Butler Yeats, is the language of our fight with others; poetry is the name of our fight with ourselves. My passage from English to Spanish determined the concrete expression of what, before, in Washington, had been the revelation of an identity. I wanted to write and I wanted to write in order to show myself that my identity and my country were real: now, in Chile, as I started to scribble my first stories, even publishing them in school magazines, I learned that I must in fact write in Spanish.

The English language, after all, did not need another writer. The English language has always been alive and kicking, and if it ever becomes drowsy, there will always be an Irishman . . .

In Chile I came to know the possibilities of our language for giving wing to freedom and poetry. The impression was enduring; it links me forever to that sad and wonderful land. It lives within me, and it transformed me into a man who knows how to dream, love, insult, and write only in Spanish. It also left me wide open to an incessant interrogation: What happened to this universal language, Spanish, which after the seventeenth century ceased to be a language of life, creation, dissatisfaction, and personal power and became far too often a language of mourning, sterility, rhetorical applause, and abstract power? Where were the threads of my tradition, where could I, writing in mid-twentieth century in Latin America, find the direct link to the great living presences I was then starting to read, my lost Cervantes, my old Quevedo, dead because he could not tolerate one more winter, my Góngora, abandoned in a gulf of loneliness?

At sixteen I finally went to live permanently in Mexico and there I found the answers to my quest for identity and language, in the thin air of a plateau of stone and dust that is the negative Indian image of another highland, that of central Spain. But, between Santiago and Mexico City, I spent six wonderful months in Argentina. They were, in spite of their brevity, so important in this reading and writing of myself that I must give them their full worth. Buenos Aires was then, as always, the most beautiful, sophisticated, and civilized city in Latin America, but in the summer of 1944, as street pavements melted in the heat and the city smelled of cheap wartime gasoline, rawhide from the port, and chocolate éclairs from the *confiterías*, Argentina had experienced a succession of military coups: General Rawson had overthrown President Castillo of the cattle oligarchy, but General Ramírez had then overthrown Rawson, and now General Farrell had overthrown Ramírez. A young colonel called Juan Domingo Perón was General Farrell's up-and-coming Minister of Labor, and I heard an actress by the name of Eva Duarte play the "great women of history" on Radio Belgrano. A stultifying hack novelist who went by the pen name Hugo Wast was assigned to the Ministry of Education under his real name, Martínez Zuviría, and brought all his anti-Semitic, undemocratic, pro-fascist phobias to the Buenos Aires high-school system, which I had suddenly been plunked into. Coming from the America of the New Deal, the ideals of revolutionary Mexico, and the politics of the Popular Front in Chile, I could not stomach this, rebelled, and was granted a full summer of wandering around Buenos Aires, free for the first time in my life, following my preferred tango orchestras—Canaro, D'Arienzo, and Anibal Troilo, alias Pichuco—as they played all summer long in the Renoir-like shade and light of the rivers and pavilions of El Tigre and Maldonado. Now the comics were in Spanish: Mutt and Jeff were Benitín y Eneas. But Argentina had its own comic-book imperialism: through the magazines *Billiken* and *Patorozú*, all the children of Latin America knew from the crib that "las Malvinas son Argentinas."

Two very important things happened. First, I lost my virginity. We lived in an apartment building on the leafy corner of Callao and Quintana, and after 10 a.m. nobody was there except myself, an old and deaf Polish doorkeeper, and a beautiful Czech woman, aged thirty, whose husband was a film producer. I went up to ask her for her *Sintonía*, which was the radio guide of the forties, because I wanted to know when Evita was doing Joan of Arc. She said that had passed, but the next program was Madame Du Barry. I wondered if Madame Du Barry's life was as interesting as Joan of Arc's. She said it was certainly less saintly, and, besides, it could be emulated. How? I said innocently. And thereby my beautiful apprenticeship. We made each other very happy. And also very sad: this was not the liberty of love, but rather its libertine variety: we loved in hiding. I was too young to be a real sadist. So it had to end.

The other important thing was that I started reading Argentine literature, from the gaucho poems to Sarmiento's *Memories of Provincial Life* to Cané's *Juvenilia* to Güiraldes's *Don Segundo Sombra* to . . . to . . . to—and this was as good as discovering that Joan of Arc was also sexy—to Borges. I have never wanted to meet Borges personally because he belongs to that summer in B.A. He belongs to my personal discovery of Latin American literature.

II

Latin American extremes: if Cuba is the Andalusia of the New World, the Mexican plateau is its Castile. Parched and brown, inhabited by suspicious cats burnt too many times by foreign invasions, Mexico is the sacred zone of a secret hope: the gods shall return.

Mexican space is closed, jealous, and self-contained. In contrast, Argentine space is open and dependent on the foreign: migrations, exports, imports, words. Mexican space was vertically sacralized thousands of years ago. Argentine space patiently awaits its horizontal profanation.

I arrived on the Mexican highland from the Argentine pampa when I was sixteen years old. As I said, it was better to study in a country where the Minister of Education was Jaime Torres Bodet than in a country where he was Hugo Wast. This was not the only contrast, or the most important one. A land isolated by its very nature—desert, mountain, chasm, sea, jungle, fire, ice, fugitive mists, and a sun that never blinks—Mexico is a multi-level temple that rises abruptly, blind to horizons, an arrow that wounds the sky but refuses the dangerous frontiers of the land, the canyons, the sierras without a human footprint, whereas the pampa is nothing if not an eternal frontier, the very portrait of the horizon, the sprawling flatland of a latent expansion awaiting, like a passive lover, the vast and rich overflow from that concentration of the transitory represented by the commercial metropolis of Buenos Aires, what Ezequiel Martínez Estrada called Goliath's head on David's body.

A well-read teenager, I had tasted the literary culture of Buenos Aires, then dominated by *Sur* magazine and Victoria Ocampo's enlightened mixture of the cattle oligarchy of the Pampas and the cultural clerisy of Paris, a sort of Argentinian cosmopolitanism. It then became important to appreciate the verbal differences between the Mexican culture, which, long before Paul Valéry, knew itself to be mortal, and the Argentine culture, founded on the optimism of powerful migratory currents from Europe, innocent of sacred stones or aboriginal promises. Mexico, closed to immigration by the TTT— the Tremendous Texas Trauma that in 1836 cured us once and for all of the temptation to receive Caucasian colonists because they had airport names like Houston and Austin and Dallas—devoted its population to breeding like rabbits. Blessed by the Pope, Coatlicue, and Jorge Negrete, we are, all eighty million of us, Catholics in the Virgin Mary, misogynists in the stone goddesses, and *machistas* in the singing, pistol-packing *charro*.

The pampa goes on waiting: twenty-five million Argentinians today; scarcely five million more than in 1945, half of them in Buenos Aires.

Language in Mexico is ancient, old as the oldest dead. The eagles of the Indian empire fell, and it suffices to read the poems of the defeated to understand the vein of sadness that runs through Mexican literature, the feeling that words are identical to a farewell: "Where shall we go to now, O my friends?" asks the Aztec poet of the Fall of Tenochtitlán: "The smoke lifts; the fog extends. Cry, my friends. Cry, oh cry." And the contemporary poet Xavier Villaurrutia, four centuries later, sings from the bed of the same lake, now dried up, from its dry stones:

> In the midst of a silence deserted as a street before the crime
> Without even breathing so that nothing may disturb my death
> In this wall-less solitude
> When the angels fled
> In the grave of my bed I leave my bloodless statue.

A sad, underground language, forever being lost and recovered. I soon learned that Spanish as spoken in Mexico answered to six unwritten rules:

- Never use the familiar *tu*—thou—if you can use the formal you—*usted*.
- Never use the first-person possessive pronoun, but rather the second-person, as in "This is *your* home."
- Always use the first-person singular to refer to your own troubles, as in "Me fue del carajo, mano." But use the first-person plural when referring to your successes, as in "During our term, we distributed three million acres."
- Never use one diminutive if you can use five in a row.
- Never use the imperative when you can use the subjunctive.
- And only then, when you have exhausted these ceremonies of communication, bring out your verbal knife and plunge it deep into the other's heart: "Chinga a tu madre, cabrón."

The language of Mexicans springs from abysmal extremes of power and impotence, domination and resentment. It is the mirror of an overabundance of history, a history that devours itself before extinguishing and then regenerating itself, phoenix-like, once again. Argentina, on the contrary, is a tabula rasa, and it demands a passionate verbalization. I do not know another country that so fervently—with the fervor of Buenos Aires, Borges would say—opposes the silence of its infinite space, its physical and mental pampa, demanding: Please, *verbalize* me! Martin Fierro, Carlos Gardel, Jorge Luis Borges: reality must be captured, desperately, in the verbal web of the gaucho poem, the sentimental tango, the metaphysical tale: the pampa of the gaucho becomes the garden of the tango becomes the forked paths of literature.

What is forked? What is said.

What is said? What is forked.

Everything: Space. Time. Language. History. Our history. The history of Spanish America.

I read *Ficciones* as I flew north on a pontoon plane, courtesy of Pan American Airways. It was wartime, we had to have priority; all cameras were banned, and glazed plastic screens were put on our windows several minutes before we landed. Since I was not an Axis spy, I read Borges as we splashed into Santos, saying that the best proof that the Koran is an Arab book is that not a single camel is mentioned in its pages. I started thinking that the best proof that Borges is an Argentinian is in everything he has to evoke because it isn't there, as we glided into an invisible Rio de Janeiro. And as we flew out of Bahia, I thought that Borges invents a world because he needs it. I need, therefore I imagine.

By the time we landed in Trinidad, "Funes the Memorious" and "Pierre Ménard, Author of Don Quixote" had introduced me, without my being aware, to the genealogy of the serene madmen, the children of Erasmus. I did not know then that this was the most illustrious family of modern fiction, since it went, backwards, from Pierre Ménard to Don Quixote himself. During two short lulls in Santo Domingo (then, horrifyingly, called Ciudad Trujillo) and Port-au-Prince, I had been prepared by Borges to encounter my wonderful friends Toby Shandy, who reconstructs in his miniature cabbage patch the battlefields of Flanders he was not able to experience historically; Jane Austen's Catherine Moreland and Gustave Flaubert's Madame Bovary, who like Don Quixote believe in what they read; Dickens's Mr. Micawber, who takes his hopes to be realities; Dostoevsky's Myshkin, an idiot because he gives the benefit of the doubt to the good possibility of mankind; Pérez Galdós's Nazarín, who is mad because he believes that each human being can daily be Christ, and who is truly St. Paul's madman: "Let him who seems wise among you become mad, so that he might truly become wise."

As we landed at Miami airport, the glazed windows disappeared once and for all and I knew that, like Pierre Ménard, a writer must always face the mysterious duty of literally reconstructing a spontaneous work. And so I met my tradition: *Don Quixote* was a book waiting to be written. The history of Latin America was a history waiting to be lived.

III

When I finally arrived in Mexico, I discovered that my father's imaginary country was real, but more fantastic than any imaginary land. It was as real as its physical and spiritual borders: Mexico, the only frontier between the industrialized and the developing worlds; the frontier between my country and the United States, but also between all of Latin America and the United States, and between the Catholic Mediterranean and the Protestant Anglo-Saxon strains in the New World.

It was with this experience and these questions that I approached the gold and mud of Mexico, the imaginary, imagined country, finally real but only real if I saw it from a distance that would assure me, because of the very fact of separation, that my desire for reunion with it would be forever urgent, and only real if I wrote it. Having attained some sort of perspective, I was finally able to write a few novels where I could speak of the scars of revolution, the nightmares of progress, and the perseverance of dreams.

I wrote with urgency because my absence became a destiny, yet a shared destiny: that of my own body as a young man, that of the old body of my country, and that of the problematic and insomniac body of my language. I could, perhaps, identify the former without too much trouble: Mexico and myself. But the language belonged to us all, to the vast community that writes and talks and thinks in Spanish. And without this language I could give no reality to either myself or my land. Language thus became the center of my personal being and of the possibility of forming my own destiny and that of my country into a shared destiny.

But nothing is shared in the abstract. Like bread and love, language and ideas are shared with human beings. My first contact with literature was sitting on the knees of Alfonso Reyes when the Mexican writer was ambassador to Brazil in the earlier thirties. Reyes had brought the Spanish classics back to life for us; he had written the most superb books on Greece; he was the most lucid of literary theoreticians; in fact, he had translated all of Western culture into Latin American terms. In the late forties, he was living in a little house the color of the *mamey* fruit, in Cuernavaca. He would invite me to spend weekends with him, and since I was eighteen and a night prowler, I kept him company from eleven in the morning, when Don Alfonso would sit in a café and toss verbal bouquets at the girls strolling around the plaza that was then a garden of laurels and not, as it has become, of cement. I do not know if the square, ruddy man seated at the next table was a British consul crushed by the nearness of the volcano; but if Reyes, enjoying the spectacle of the world, quoted Lope de Vega and Garcilaso, our neighbor the *mescal* drinker would answer, without looking at us, with the more somber *stanze* of Marlowe and John Donne. Then we would go to the movies in order, Reyes said, to bathe in contemporary epic, and it was only at night that he would start scolding me: You have not read Stendhal yet? The world didn't start five minutes ago, you know.

He could irritate me. I read, against his classical tastes, the most modern, the most strident books, without understanding that I was learning his lesson: there is no creation without tradition; the "new" is an inflection on a preceding form; novelty is always a variation on the past. Borges said that Reyes wrote the best Spanish prose of our times. He taught me that culture had a smile, that the intellectual tradition of the whole world was ours by birthright, and that Mexican literature was important because it was literature, not because it was Mexican.

One day I got up very early (or maybe I came in very late from a binge) and saw him seated at five in the morning, working at his table, amid the aroma of the jacaranda and the bougainvillea. He was a diminutive Buddha, bald and pink, almost one of those elves who cobble shoes at night while the family sleeps. He liked to quote Goethe: Write at dawn, skim the cream of the day, then you can study crystals, intrigue at court, and make love to your kitchen maid. Writing in silence, Reyes did not smile. His world, in a way, ended on a funereal day in February 1913 when his insurrectionist father, General Bernardo Reyes, fell riddled by machinegun bullets in the Zócalo in Mexico City, and with him fell what was left of Mexico's Belle Epoque, the long and cruel peace of Porfirio Díaz.

The smile of Alfonso Reyes had ashes on its lips. He had written, as a response to history, the great poem of exile and distance from Mexico: the poem of a cruel Iphigenia, the Mexican Iphigenia of the valley of Anáhuac:

> I was another, being myself;
> I was he who wanted to leave.
> To return is to cry. I do not repent of this wide world.
> It is not I who return,
> But my shackled feet.

My father had remained in Buenos Aires as Mexican chargé d'affaires, with instructions to frown on Argentina's sympathies toward the Axis. My mother profited from his absence to enroll me in a Catholic school in Mexico City. The brothers who ruled this institution were preoccupied with something that had never entered my head: sin. At the start of the school year, one of the brothers would come before the class with a white lily in his hand and say: "This is a Catholic youth before kissing a girl." Then he would throw the flower on the floor, dance a little jig on it, pick up the bedraggled object, and confirm our worst suspicions: "This is a Catholic boy after . . ."

Well, all this made life very tempting. Retrospectively, I would agree with Luis Buñuel that sex without sin is like an egg without salt. The priests at the Colegio Francés made sex irresistible for us; they also made leftists of us by their constant denunciation of Mexican liberalism and especially of Benito Juárez. The sexual and political temptations became very great in a city where provincial mores and sharp social distinctions made it very difficult to have normal sexual relationships with young or even older women.

All this led, as I say, to a posture of rebellion that for me crystallized in the decision to be a writer. My father, by then back from Argentina, sternly said, Okay, go out and be a writer, but not at my expense. I became a very young journalist at the weekly *Siempre*, but my family pressured me to enter law school, or, in the desert of Mexican literature, I would literally die of hunger and thirst. I was sent to visit Alfonso Reyes in his enormous library-house, where he seemed more diminutive than ever, ensconced in a tiny corner he saved for his bed among the Piranesi-like perspective of volume piled upon volume. He said to me: "Mexico is a very formalistic country. If you don't have a title, you are nobody: *nadie, ninguno*. A title is like the handle on a cup; without it, no one will pick you up. You must become a *licenciado*, a lawyer; then you can do whatever you please, as I did."

So I entered the School of Law at the National University, where, as I feared, learning tended to be by rote. The budding explosion in the student population was compounded by cynical teachers who would spend the whole hour of class taking attendance on the two hundred students of civil law, from Aguilar to Zapata. But there were great exceptions of true teachers who understood that the law is inseparable from culture, from morality, and from justice. Foremost among these were the exiles from defeated Republican Spain, who enormously enriched Mexican universities, publishing houses, the arts, and the sciences. Don Manuel Pedroso, former dean of the University of Seville, made the study of law compatible with my literary inclinations. When I would bitterly complain about the dryness and boredom of learning the penal or mercantile codes by heart, he would counter: "Forget the codes. Read Dostoevsky, read Balzac. There's all you have to know about criminal or commercial law." He also made me see that Stendhal was right that the best model for a well-structured novel is the Napoleonic Code of Civil Law. Anyway, I found that culture consists of connections, not of separations: to specialize is to isolate.

Sex was another story, but Mexico City was then a manageable town of one million people, beautiful in its extremes of colonial and nineteenth-century elegance and the garishness of its exuberant and dangerous nightlife. My friends and I spent the last years of our adolescence and the first of our manhood in a succession of cantinas, brothels, strip joints, and silver-varnished nightclubs where the bolero was sung and the mambo danced; whores, mariachis, magicians were our companions as we struggled through our first readings of D. H. Lawrence and Aldous Huxley, James Joyce and André Gide, T. S. Eliot and Thomas Mann. Salvador Elizondo and I were the two would-be writers of the group, and if the realistic grain of *La Región Más Transparente* (*Where the Air Is Clear*) was sown in this, our rather somnambulistic immersion in the spectral nightlife of Mexico City, it is also true that the cruel imagination of an instant in Elizondo's *Farabeuf* had the same background experience. We would go to a whorehouse oddly called El Buen Tono, choose a poor Mexican girl who usually said her name was Gladys and she came from Guadalajara, and go to our respective rooms. One time, a horrible scream was heard and Gladys from Guadalajara rushed out, crying and streaming blood. Elizondo, in the climax of love, had slashed her armpit with a razor.

Another perspective, another distance for approximation, another possibility of sharing a language. In 1950 I went to Europe to do graduate work in international law at the University of Geneva.

Octavio Paz had just published two books that had changed the face of Mexican literature, *Libertad Bajo Palabra* and *El Laberinto de la Soledad*. My friends and I had read those books aloud in Mexico, dazzled by a poetics that managed simultaneously to renew our language from within and to connect it to the language of the world.

At age thirty-six, Octavio Paz was not very different from what he is today. Writers born in 1914, like Paz and Julio Cortázar, surely signed a Faustian pact at the very mouth of hell's trenches; so many poets died in that war that someone had to take their place. I remember Paz in the so-called existentialist nightclubs of the time in Paris, in discussion with the very animated and handsome Albert Camus, who alternated philosophy and the boogie-woogie in La Rose Rouge. I remember Paz in front of the large windows of a gallery on the Place Vendôme, reflecting Max Ernst's great postwar painting "Europe after the Rain," and the painter's profile as an ancient eagle; and I tell myself that the poetics of Paz is an art of civilizations, a movement of encounters. Paz the poet meets Paz the thinker, because his poetry is a form of thought and his thought is a form of poetry; and as a result of this meeting, an encounter of civilizations takes place. Paz introduces civilizations to one another, makes them presentable before it is too late, because behind the wonderful smile of Camus, fixed forever in the absurdity of death, behind the bright erosion of painting by Max Ernst and the crystals of the Place Vendôme, Octavio and I, when we met, could hear the voice of *el poeta Libra*, Ezra, lamenting the death of the best, "for an old bitch gone in the teeth, for a botched civilization."

Octavio Paz has offered civilizations the mirror of their mortality, as Paul Valéry did, but also the reflection of their survival in an epidemic of meetings and erotic risks. In the generous friendship of Octavio Paz, I learned that there were no privileged centers of culture, race, or politics; that nothing should be left out of literature, because our time is a time of deadly reduction. The essential orphanhood of our time is seen in the poetry and thought of Paz as a challenge to be met through the renewed flux of human knowledge, of *all* human knowledge. We have not finished thinking, imagining, acting. It is still possible to know the world; we are unfinished men and women.

                I am not at the crossroads;
                                              to choose
                is to go wrong.

For my generation in Mexico, the problem did not consist in
discovering our modernity but in discovering our tradition. The
latter was brutally denied by the comatose, petrified teaching of
the classics in Mexican secondary schools: one had to bring Cervantes back to life in spite of a school system fatally oriented
toward the ideal of universities as sausage factories; in spite of the
more grotesque forms of Mexican nationalism of the time. A Marxist
teacher once told me it was un-Mexican to read Kafka; a fascist
critic said the same thing (this has been Kafka's Kafkian destiny
everywhere), and a rather sterile Mexican author gave a pompous
lecture at the Bellas Artes warning that readers who read Proust
would proustitute themselves.

To be a writer in Mexico in the fifties, you had to be with Alfonso
Reyes and with Octavio Paz in the assertion that Mexico was not
an isolated, virginal province but very much part of the human
race and its cultural tradition; we were all, for good or evil, contemporary with all men and women.

In Geneva, I regained my perspective. I rented a garret overlooking the beautiful old square of the Bourg-du-Four, established
by Julius Caesar as the Forum Boarium two millennia ago. The
square was filled with coffeehouses and old bookstores. The girls
came from all over the world; they were beautiful, and they were
independent. When they were kissed, one did not become a sullied
lily. We had salt on our lips. We loved each other, and I also
loved going to the little island where the lake meets the river, to
spend long hours reading. Since it was called Jean-Jacques Rousseau Island, I took along my volume of the *Confessions*. Many
things came together then. A novel was the transformation of experience into history. The modern epic had been the epic of the
first-person singular, of the I, from St. Augustine to Abélard to
Dante to Rousseau to Stendhal to Proust. Joyce de-Joyced fiction:
Here comes everybody! But H.C.E. did not collectively save the
degraded Ego from exhaustion, self-doubt, and, finally, self-for-
getfulness. When Odysseus says that he is nonexistent, we know

and he knows that he is disguised; when Beckett's characters proclaim their nonbeing, we know that "the fact is notorious": they are no longer disguised. Kafka's man has been forgotten; no one can remember K the land surveyor; finally, as Milan Kundera tells us, nobody can remember Prague, Czechoslovakia, history.

I did not yet know this as I spent many reading hours on the little island of Rousseau at the intersection of Lake Geneva and the Rhône River back in 1951. But I vaguely felt that there was something beyond the exploration of the self that actually made the idea of human personality possible if the paths beyond it were explored. Cervantes taught us that a book is a book is a book: Don Quixote does not invite us into "reality" but into an act of the imagination where all things are real: the characters are active psychological entities, but also the archetypes they herald and always the figures from whence they come, which were unimaginable, unthinkable, like Don Quixote, before they became characters first and archetypes later.

Could I, a Mexican who had not yet written his first book, sitting on a bench on an early spring day as the *bise* from the Jura Mountains quieted down, have the courage to explore for myself, with my language, with my tradition, with my friends and influences, that region where the literary figure bids us consider it in the uncertainty of its gestation? Cervantes did it in a precise cultural situation: he brought into existence the modern world by having Don Quixote leave his secure village (a village whose name has been, let us remember, forgotten) and take to the open roads, the roads of the unsheltered, the unknown, and the different, there to lose what he read and to gain what we, the readers, read in him.

The novel is forever traveling Don Quixote's road, from the security of the analogous to the adventure of the different and even the unknown. In my way, this is the road I wanted to travel. I read Rousseau, or the adventures of the I; Joyce and Faulkner, or the adventures of the We; Cervantes, or the adventures of the You he calls the Idle, the Amiable Reader: you. And I read, in a shower of fire and in the lightning of enthusiasm, Rimbaud. His mother asked him what a particular poem was about. And he answered: "I have wanted to say what it says there, literally and in all other senses." This statement of Rimbaud's has been an inflexible rule for me and for what we are all writing today; and the present-day vigor of the literature of the Hispanic world, to which I belong, is not alien to this Rimbaudian approach to writing: Say what you mean, literally and in all other senses.

I think I imagined in Switzerland what I would try to write someday, but first I would have to do my apprenticeship. Only after many years would I be able to write what I then imagined; only years later, when I not only knew that I had the tools with which to do it, but also, and equally important, when I knew that if I did not write, death would not do it for me. You start by writing to live. You end by writing so as not to die. Love is the marriage of this desire and this fear. The women I have loved I have desired for themselves, but also because I feared myself.

IV

My first European experience came to a climax in the summer of 1950. It was a hot, calm evening on Lake Zurich, and some wealthy Mexican friends had invited me to dinner at the elegant Baur-au-Lac Hotel. The summer restaurant was a floating terrace on the lake. You reached it by a gangplank, and it was lighted by paper lanterns and flickering candles. As I unfolded my stiff white napkin amid the soothing tinkle of silver and glass, I raised my eyes and saw the group dining at the next table.

Three ladies sat there with a man in his seventies. This man was stiff and elegant, dressed in double-breasted white serge and immaculate shirt and tie. His long, delicate fingers sliced a cold pheasant, almost with daintiness. Yet even in eating he seemed to me unbending, with a ramrod-back, military bearing. His aged face showed "a growing fatigue," but the pride with which his lips and jaws were set sought desperately to hide the fact, while the eyes twinkled with "the fiery play of fancy."

As the carnival lights of that summer's night in Zurich played with a fire of their own on the features I now recognized, Thomas Mann's face was a theater of implicit, quiet emotions. He ate and let the ladies do the talking; he was, in my fascinated eyes, a meeting place where solitude gives birth to beauty unfamiliar and perilous, but also to the perverse and the illicit. Thomas Mann had managed, out of this solitude, to find the affinity "between the personal destiny of [the] author and that of his contemporaries in general." Through him, I had imagined that the products of this solitude and of this affinity were named art (created by one) and civilization (created by all). He spoke so surely, in *Death in Venice*, of the "tasks imposed upon him by his own ego and the European soul" that as I, paralyzed with admiration, saw him there that night I dared not conceive of such an affinity in our own Latin American culture, where the extreme demands of a ravaged, voiceless continent often killed the voice of the self and made a hollow political monster of the voice of the society, or killed it, giving birth to a pitiful, sentimental dwarf.

Yet, as I recalled my passionate reading of everything he wrote, from *Blood of the Walsungs* to *Dr. Faustus*, I could not help but feel that, in spite of the vast differences between his culture and ours, in both of them literature in the end asserted itself through a relationship between the visible and the invisible worlds of narration. A novel should "gather up the threads of many human destinies in the warp of a single idea"; the I, the You, and the We were only separate and dried up because of a lack of imagination. Unbeknownst to him, I left Thomas Mann sipping his demitasse as midnight approached and the floating restaurant bobbed slightly and the Chinese lanterns quietly flickered out. I shall always thank him for silently teaching me that, in literature, you know only what you imagine.

The Mexico of the forties and fifties I wrote about in *La Región Más Transparente* was an imagined Mexico, just as the Mexico of the eighties and nineties I am writing about in *Cristóbal Nonato* (*Christopher Unborn*) is totally imagined. I fear that we would know nothing of Balzac's Paris and Dickens's London if they, too, had not invented them. When in the spring of 1951 I took a Dutch steamer back to the New World, I had with me the ten Bible-paper tomes of the Pléiade edition of Balzac. This phrase of his has been a central creed of mine: "Wrest words from silence and ideas from obscurity." The reading of Balzac—one of the most thorough and metamorphosing experiences of my life as a novelist—taught me that one must exhaust reality, transcend it, in order to reach, to try to reach, that absolute which is made of the atoms of the relative: in Balzac, the marvelous worlds of *Séraphita* or *Louis Lambert* rest on the commonplace worlds of *Père Goriot* and *César Birotteau*.

Likewise, the Mexican reality of *Where the Air Is Clear* and *The Death of Artemio Cruz* existed only to clash with my imagination, my negation, and my perversion of the facts, because, remember, I had learned to imagine Mexico before I ever knew Mexico.

This was, finally, a way of ceasing to tell what I understood and trying to tell, behind all the things I knew, the really important things: what I did not know. *Aura* illustrates this stance much too clearly, I suppose. I prefer to find it in a scene set in a cantina in *A Change of Skin*, or in a taxi drive in *The Hydra Head*. I never wanted to resolve an enigma, but to point out that there *was* an enigma.

I always tried to tell my critics: Don't classify me, read me. I'm a writer, not a genre. Do not look for the purity of the novel according to some nostalgic canon, do not ask for generic affiliation but rather for a dialogue, if not for the outright abolition, of genre; not for one language but for many languages at odds with one another; not, as Bakhtin would put it, for unity of style but for *heteroglossia*, not for monologic but for dialogic imagination. I'm afraid that, by and large, in Mexico at least, I failed in this enterprise. Yet I am not disturbed by this fact, because of what I have just said: language is a shared and sharing part of culture that cares little about formal classifications and much about vitality and connection, for culture itself perishes in purity or isolation, which is the deadly wages of perfection. Like bread and love, language is shared with others. And human beings share a tradition. There is no creation without tradition. No one creates from nothing.

I went back to Mexico, but knew that I would forever be a wanderer in search of perspective: this was my real baptism, not the religious or civil ceremonies I have mentioned. But no matter where I went, Spanish would be the language of my writing and Latin America the culture of my language.

Neruda, Reyes, Paz; Washington, Santiago de Chile, Buenos Aires, Mexico City, Paris, Geneva; Cervantes, Balzac, Rimbaud, Thomas Mann: only with all the shared languages, those of my places and friends and masters, was I able to approach the fire of literature and ask it for a few sparks.

How I Wrote One of My Books

ONE, yes, one girl, twenty years of age, in the summer of '61, over twenty-five years ago, crossed the threshold between the small drawing room of an apartment on the Boulevard Raspail and entered the bedroom where I was waiting for her.

There was a rumor of discontent and a smell of explosives in the French capital. These were the years when de Gaulle was finding a way out from Algeria and the OAS, the Secret Army Organization, was indiscriminately blowing up Jean-Paul Sartre and his concierge: the bombs of the generals were egalitarian.

But Paris is a double city; whatever happens there possesses a mirage which seems to reproduce the space of actuality. We soon learn that this is a form of deceit. The abundant mirrors of Parisian interiors do more than simply reproduce a certain space. Gabriel García Márquez says that with their army of mirrors the Parisians create the illusion that their narrow apartments are double the real size. The true mystery—Gabriel and I know this—is that what we see reflected in those mirrors is always *another* time: time past, time yet to be. And that, sometimes, if you are lucky, a person who is *another* person also floats across these quicksilver lakes.

I believe that the mirrors of Paris contain something more than their own illusion. They are, at the same time, the reflection of something less tangible: the light of the city, a light I have attempted to describe many times, in political chronicles of the events of May 1968 and of May 1981 and in novels such as *Distant Relations*, where I say that the light of Paris is identical to "the expectation that every afternoon . . . for one miraculous moment, the phenomena of the day—rain or fog, scorching heat or snow—[will] disperse and reveal, as in a Corot landscape, the luminous essence of the Île de France."

A second space: a second person—the other person—in the mirror is not born *in* the mirror: she comes from the light. The girl who wandered in from her living room into her bedroom that hot afternoon in early September more than twenty years ago was another *because* six years had gone by since I first met her, in the budding grove of her puberty, in Mexico.

But she was also another because the light that afternoon, as if it had been expecting her, defeated a stubborn reef of clouds. That light—I remember it—first stepped through timidly, as if stealing by the menace of a summer's storm; then it transformed itself into a luminous pearl encased in a shell of clouds: finally it spilled over for a few seconds with a plenitude that was also an agony.

In this almost instantaneous succession, the girl I remembered when she was fourteen years old and who was now twenty suffered the same changes as the light coming through the windowpanes: that threshold between the parlor and the bedroom became the lintel between all the ages of this girl: the light that had been struggling against the clouds also fought against her flesh, took it, sketched it, granted her a shadow of years, sculpted a death in her eyes, tore the smile from her lips, waned through her hair with the floating melancholy of madness.

She was another, she had been another, not she who was going to be but she who, always, was being.

The light possessed the girl, the light made love to the girl before I could, and I was only, that afternoon, "a strange guest in the kingdom of love" ("en el reino del amor huésped extraño"), and knew that the eyes of love can also see us with—once more I quote Quevedo—"a beautiful Death."

The next morning I started writing *Aura* in a café near my hotel on the rue de Berri. I remember the day: Khrushchev had just proclaimed his Twenty-Year Plan in Moscow, where he promised communism and the withering away of the state by the eighties—here we are now—burying the West in the process, and his words were reproduced in all their gray minuteness in the *International Herald Tribune*, which was being hawked by ghostly girls, young lovers jailed in brief prisons of passion, the authors of *Aura*: the dead girls.

TWO, yes, two years before, I was having a few drinks with Luis Buñuel in his house on the Street of Providence, and we talked about Quevedo, a poet the Spanish film director knew better than most academic specialists on baroque poetry of the seventeenth century.

You have already noticed, of course, that the true author of *Aura* (including the dead girls I have just mentioned) is named Francisco de Quevedo y Villegas, born on September 17, 1580, in Madrid and supposedly deceased on September 8, 1645, in Villanueva de los Infantes; the satirical and scatological brother of Swift, but also the unrivaled poet of our death and love, our Shakespeare, our John Donne, the furious enemy of Góngora, the political agent for the Duke of Osuna, the unfortunate, jailed partisan of fallen power, the obscene, the sublime Quevedo dead in his stoical tower, dreaming, laughing, searching, finding some of the truly immortal lines in the Spanish language:

> Oh condición mortal Oh dura suerte
> Que no puedo querer vivir mañana
> Sin la pensión de procurar mi muerte.

> (Oh mortal state Oh man's unyielding fate
> To live tomorrow I can have no hope
> Without the cost of buying my own death.)

Or maybe these lines, defining love:

> Es yelo abrasador, es fuego helado,
> es herida que duele y no se siente,
> es un soñado bien, un mal presente,
> es un breve descanso muy cansado.

> (It is a freezing fire, a burning ice,
> it is a wound that hurts yet is not felt,
> a happiness desired, a present evil,
> a short but, oh, so tiring rest.)

Yes, the true author of *Aura* is Quevedo, and I am pleased to represent him here today.

This is the great advantage of time: the so-called author ceases to be such; he becomes an invisible agent for him who signed the book, published it, and collected (and goes on collecting) the royalties. But the book was written—it always was, it always is— by others. Quevedo and a girl who was almost dust in love, *polvo enamorado*. Buñuel and an afternoon in Mexico City, so different from an afternoon in Paris but so different also, in 1959, from the afternoons in Mexico City today.

You could see the two volcanoes, Popocatepetl the smoking mountain and Iztaccihuatl the sleeping lady, as you drove down Insurgentes Avenue, and the big department store had not yet been erected at the corner of Buñuel's house. Buñuel himself, behind a mini-monastery of very high brick walls crowned by crushed glass, had returned to the Mexican cinema with *Nazarín* and was now playing around in his head with an old idea: a filmic transposition of Géricault's painting *Le Radeau de la Méduse*, which hangs in the Louvre and which describes the drama of the survivors of a naval disaster in the eighteenth century.

The survivors of the good ship *Medusa* at first tried to behave like civilized human beings as they floated around in their raft. But then, as the days went by, followed by weeks, finally by what seemed like an eternity, their imprisonment on the sea cracked the varnish of good manners and they became salt first, then waves, finally sharks: in the end they survived only because they devoured each other. They needed one another to exterminate one another.

Of course, the cinematic translation of the terrible gaze of the Medusa is called *The Exterminating Angel*, one of Buñuel's most beautiful films, in which a group of society people who have never truly needed anything find themselves mysteriously incapable of leaving an elegant salon. The threshold of the salon becomes an abyss and necessity becomes extermination: the shipwrecks of Providence Street only need each other to devour each other.

The theme of necessity is profound and persistent in Buñuel, and his films repeatedly reveal the way in which a man and a woman, a child and a madman, a saint and a sinner, a criminal and a dreamer, a solitude and a desire need one another.

Buñuel was inventing his film *The Exterminating Angel* and crossing back and forth, as he did so, over the threshold between

the lobby and the bar of his house, looking for all the world like
a pensioned picador from old Cagancho's cuadrilla. Buñuel's com-
ings and goings were, somehow, a form of immobility.

> A todas partes que me vuelvo veo
> Las amenazas de la llama ardiente
> Y en cualquier lugar tengo presente
> Tormento esquivo y burlador deseo.
>
> (Everywhere I turn I see
> The menace of the burning flame
> And everywhere I am aware
> Of aloof torment and mocking desire.)

Since we had been talking about Quevedo and a portrait of the
young Buñuel by Dali in the twenties was staring at us, Eluard's
poetic formula imposed itself on my spirit that faraway Mexican
afternoon of transparent air and the smell of burned tortilla and
newly sliced chiles and fugitive flowers: "Poetry shall be recip-
rocal"; and if Buñuel was thinking of Géricault and Quevedo and
the film, I was thinking that the raft of the *Medusa* already contained
two eyes of stone that would trap the characters of *The Exterminating Angel* not only in the fiction of a shadow projected on the
screen but within the physical and mechanical reality of the camera
that would, from then on, be the true prison of the shipwrecks of
Providence: a camera (why not?) on top of Lautréamont's poetical
meeting of an umbrella and a sewing machine on a dissecting
table.

Buñuel stopped midway between lobby and bar and asked aloud:
"And if on crossing a doorsill we could instantly recover our youth;
if we could be old on *one* side of the door and young as soon as
we crossed to the *other* side, what then . . . ?"

THREE, yes, three days after that afternoon on the Boulevard
Raspail, I went to see a picture that all my friends, but especially
Julio Cortázar, were raving about: *Ugetsu Monogatari: The Tales
of the Pale Moon After the Rain*, by the Japanese filmmaker Kenji
Mizoguchi. I was carrying around with me the first feverish pages
of *Aura*, written in that café near the Champs-Elysées as I let my
breakfast of coffee and croissants grow cold and forgot the headlines
of the morning *Figaro*. "You read the advertisement: this kind of

offer is not made every day. You read it and then reread it. It seems addressed to you and to nobody else."

Because "You are Another," such was the subjacent vision of my meetings with Buñuel in Mexico, with the girl imprisoned by the light in Paris, with Quevedo in the freezing fire, the burning ice, the wound that hurts yet is not felt, the happiness desired, the present evil which proclaims itself as Love but was first of all Desire. Curiously, Mizoguchi's film was being shown in the Ursulines Cinema, the same place where, more than thirty years before, Buñuel's *Un Chien Andalou* had first been screened to a vastly scandalized audience. You remember that Red Cross nurses had to be posted in the aisles to help the ladies who fainted when Buñuel, on the screen, slashes the eye of a girl with a razor as a cloud bisects the moon.

The evanescent images of Mizoguchi told the beautiful love story adapted by the Japanese director from the tale "The House among the Reeds," from the collection of the *Ugetsu Monogatari*, written in the eighteenth century by Ueda Akinari, born in 1734 in the red-light district at Sonezaki, the son of a courtesan and an unknown father. His mother abandoned him when he was four years old; he was adopted and raised by a family of paper and oil merchants, the Ueda, with infinite love and care, but also with a profound sense of nostalgia and doom: the happy merchants were unclassed by commerce from their former military tradition; Akinari contracted the pox and was saved perhaps by his adoptive mother's contracting of the disease: she died, he was left crippled in both hands until the God of Foxes, Inari, permitted him to hold a brush and become a calligraphist and, thus, a writer.

But first he inherited a prosperous business; it was destroyed by fire. Then he became a doctor: a little girl whom he was treating died, yet her father continued to have faith in him. So he gave up medicine. He could only be a lame writer, somehow a character in his own stories, persecuted by bad luck, poverty, illness, blindness. Abandoned as a child, Akinari spent his late years dependent on the charity of others, living in temples or the houses of friends. He was an erudite. He did not commit suicide, yet died in 1809.

So with his sick hand miraculously aided by the God of Foxes, Ueda Akinari could take a brush and thus write a series of tales that are unique because they are multiple.

"Originality" is the sickness of a modernity that wishes to see itself as something new, always new, in order continually to witness its own birth. In so doing, modernity is that fashionable illusion which only speaks to death.

This is the subject of one of the great dialogues by the magnificent Italian poet and essayist of the nineteenth century Giacomo Leopardi. Read Leopardi: he is in the wind. I was reading him with joy in the winter of '81, then met Susan Sontag in New York the following spring. She had been surprised by a December dawn in Rome reading Leopardi: like Akinari, infirm; unlike him, a disillusioned romanticist turned pessimistic materialist and maybe, because he knew that in mankind, "outside of vanity, all is pain," he could write some of the most burning lyrical marvels in the Italian language and tell us that life can be unhappy when "hope has disappeared but desire remains intact." For the same reason, he could write the biting dialogue of Fashion and Death:

FASHION: Lady Death! Lady Death!
DEATH: I hope that your hour comes, so that you shall have no further need to call me.
FASHION: My Lady Death!
DEATH: Go to the Devil! I'll come looking for you when you least desire me.
FASHION: But I am your sister, Fashion. Have you forgotten that we are both the daughters of decadence?

Ancient peoples know that there are no words that do not descend from other words and that imagination only resembles power because neither can reign over *Nada*, Nothing, *Niente*. To imagine Nothing, or to believe that you rule over Nothing, is but a form— perhaps the surest one—of becoming mad. No one knew this better than Joseph Conrad in the heart of darkness or William Styron in the bed of shadows: the wages of sin are not death, but isolation.

Akinari's novella is set in 1454 and tells the story of Katsushiro, a young man humiliated by his poverty and his incapacity for work in the fields who abandons his home to make his fortune as a merchant in the city. He leaves his house by the reeds in the care of his young and beautiful wife, Miyagi, promising he will return as the leaves of autumn fall.

Months go by; the husband does not return; the woman resigns herself to "the law of this world: no one should have faith in tomorrow." The civil wars of the fifteenth century under the Ashikaga shoguns make the reencounter of husband and wife impossible. People worry only about saving their skins, the old hide in the mountains, the young are forcibly drafted by the competing armies; all burn and loot; confusion takes hold of the world and the human heart also becomes ferocious. "Everything," says the author, reminding us that he is speaking from memory, "everything was in ruins during that miserable century."

Katsushiro becomes prosperous and manages to travel to Kyoto. Once settled there, seven years after he bid farewell to Miyagi, he tries to return home but finds that the barriers of political conflict have not fallen, nor has the menace of assault by bandits disappeared. He is fearful of returning to find his home in ruins, as in the myths of the past. A fever takes hold of him. The seven years have gone by as in a dream. The man imagines that the woman, like himself, is a prisoner of time and that, like himself, she has not been able to stretch out her hand and touch the fingers of the loved one.

The proofs of precarious humanity surround Katsushiro; bodies pile up in the streets; he walks among them. Neither he nor the dead are immortal. The first form of death is an answer to time: its name is forgetting, and maybe Katsushiro's wife (he imagines this) has already died; she is but a denizen of the subterranean regions.

So it is death that, finally, leads Katsushiro back to his village: if his wife has died, he will build a small altar for her during the night, taking advantage of the moon of the rainy season.

He returns to his ruined village. The pine that used to identify his house has been struck by lightning. But the house is still there. Katsushiro sees the light from a lamp. Is a stranger now living in his house? Katsushiro crosses the threshold, enters, and hears a very ancient voice say, "Who goes there?" He answers, "It is I, I have come back."

Miyagi recognizes her husband's voice. She comes near to him, dressed in black and covered with grime, her eyes sunken, her knotted hair falling down her back. She is not the woman she had been. But when she sees her husband, without adding a word, she bursts out crying.

The man and the woman go to bed together and he tells her the reason why he has been so late in returning, and of his resignation; she answers that the world had become full of horror, but that she had waited in vain: "If I had perished from love," she concludes, "hoping to see you again, I would have died of a lovesickness ignored by you."

They sleep embraced, sleep deeply. As day breaks, a vague impression of coldness penetrates the unconsciousness of Katsushiro's dream. A rumor of something floating by awakens him. A cold liquid falls, drop after drop, on his face. His wife is no longer lying next to him. She has become invisible. He will never see her again.

Katsushiro discovers an old servant hidden in a hut in the middle of a field of camphor. The servant tells the hero the truth: Miyagi died many years ago. She was the only woman who never quit the village, in spite of the terrible dangers of war, because she kept alive the promise: we shall see each other once again this autumn. Not only the bandits invaded this place. Ghosts also took up their lodgings here. One day Miyagi joined them.

Mizoguchi's images told a story similar yet different from Akinari's tale. Less innocent, the contemporary filmmaker's story transformed Miyagi into a sort of tainted Penelope, a former courtesan who must prove her fidelity to her husband with greater conviction than a virgin.

When the village is invaded by the troops of Governor Uesugui sent from Kamakura to fight a ghostly and evasive shogun in the mountains, Miyagi, to save herself from the violence of the soldiers, commits suicide. The soldiers bury her in her garden, and when her husband finally returns, he must appeal to an old witch in order to recover the spectral vision and spectral contact with his dead wife.

FOUR, no, four years after seeing the film by Mizoguchi and writing *Aura*, I found in an old bookshop in the Trastevere in Rome, where I had been led by the Spanish poets Rafael Alberti and María Teresa León, an Italian version of the Japanese tales of the *Togi Boko*, written by Hiosuishi Shoun and published in 1666. My surprise was quite great when I found there, written two hundred years before Akinari's tale and three hundred before Mizoguchi's film, a story called "The Courtesan Miyagino," where this same narrative is told, but this time with an ending that provides direct access to necrophilia.

The returning hero, a Ulysses with no heroism greater than a recovered capacity for forgetting, does not avail himself of a witch to recover his embodied desire, the courtesan Miyagino, who swore to be faithful to him. This time he opens the tomb and finds his wife, dead for many years, as beautiful as the day he last saw her. Miyagino's ghost comes back to tell her bereaved husband this tale.

My curiosity was spurred by this story within the story of *Aura*, so I went back to Buñuel, who was now preparing the script for his film *The Milky Way*, reading through the 180 volumes of the Abbé Migne's treatise on patristics and medieval heresies at the National Library in Paris, and asked him to procure me right of entry into that bibliographical sanctuary, more difficult to penetrate, let me add, than the chastity of a fifteenth-century Japanese virgin or the cadaver of a courtesan of the same era and nationality.

Anglo-Saxon libraries, I note in passing, are open to all, and nothing is easier than finding a book on the shelves at Oxford or Harvard, at Princeton or Dartmouth, take it home, caress it, read it, take notes from it and return it. Nothing more difficult, on the contrary, than approaching a Latin library. The presumed reader is also a presumed kleptomaniac, a convicted firebug, and a certified vandal: he who pursues a book in Paris, Rome, Madrid, or Mexico City soon finds out that books are not to be read but to be locked up, become rare and perhaps serve as a feast for rats.

No wonder that Buñuel, in *The Exterminating Angel*, has an adulterous wife ask her lover, a dashing colonel, to meet her secretly in her library. What if the husband arrives? asks the cautious lover. And she answers: We'll tell him I was showing you my incunabula.

No wonder that Juan Goytisolo, when he invades a Spanish library in his *Count Julian*, fruitfully employs his time squashing fat green flies between the pages of Lope de Vega and Azorín.

But let me return to that bibliographical Leavenworth which is the Bibliothèque Nationale in Paris: Buñuel somehow smuggled me in and permitted me to grope in the dark, with fear of imminent discovery, for the ancestry of the Japanese tales of the *Togi Boko*, which in their turn were the forebears of Akinari's tales of the moon after the rain, which then inspired the film by Mizoguchi that I saw in Paris in the early days of September 1961, as I searched for the form and intention of *Aura*.

Is there a fatherless book, an orphan volume in this world? A book that is not the descendant of other books? A single leaf of a book that is not an offshoot of the great genealogical tree of mankind's literary imagination? Is there creation without tradition? But again, can tradition survive without renewal, a new creation, a new greening of the perennial tale?

I then discovered that the ultimate source of this story was the Chinese tale called the "Biography of Ai'King," part of the collection called the *Tsien teng sin hoa*.

Yet, could there conceivably be an "ultimate source" for the story that I saw in a Parisian movie house, thinking I had found in Mizoguchi's dead bride the sister of my Aura, whose mother, I deceived myself, was an image of youth defeated by a very ancient light in an apartment on the Boulevard Raspail and whose father, deceitful as well, was an act of imagination and desire on crossing the threshold between the lobby and the bar of a house in Mexico City's Colonia del Valle?

Could I, could anyone, go beyond the "Biography of Ai'King" to the multiple sources, the myriad, bubbling springs in which this final tale lost itself: the traditions of the oldest Chinese literature, that tide of narrative centuries that hardly begins to murmur the vastness of its constant themes: the supernatural virgin, the fatal woman, the spectral bride, the couple reunited?

I then knew that my answer would have to be negative but that, simultaneously, what had happened did but confirm my original intention: Aura came into this world to increase the secular descent of witches.

FIVE, at least five, were the witches who consciously mothered Aura during those days of my initial draft in a café near the rue de Berri through which passed, more or less hurried and/or worried by the urgent, immediate events of this world, K. S. Karol the skeptical reporter, Jean Daniel the questioning journalist, and Françoise Giroud the vibrant First Lady of the French press, all of them heading toward the pressroom of *L'Express*, the then great weekly that they had created to fight against bombs and censorship and with the close cooperation—it is hallucinatory to imagine it today—of Sartre and Camus, Mendès-France and Mauriac.

These five bearers of consolation and desire, I believe today, were the greedy Miss Bordereau of Henry James's *Aspern Papers*, who in her turn descends from the cruelly mad Miss Havisham of Charles Dickens's *Great Expectations*, who is herself the English daughter of the ancient countess of Pushkin's *Queen of Spades*, she who jealously keeps the secret of winning at cards.

The similar structure of all three stories only proves that they belong to the same mythical family. You invariably have three figures: the old woman, the young woman, and the young man. In Pushkin, the old woman is the Countess Anna Fedorovna, the young woman her ward Lisaveta Ivanovna, the young man Hermann, an officer of the engineering corps. In Dickens, the old woman is Miss Havisham, the girl Estella, the hero Pip. In Henry James, the old woman is Miss Juliana Bordereau, the younger woman her niece Miss Tina, the intruding young man the nameless narrator H.J.—"Henry James" in Michael Redgrave's staging of the story.

In all three works the intruding young man wishes to know the old lady's secret: the secret of fortune in Pushkin, the secret of love in Dickens, the secret of poetry in James. The young girl is the deceiver—innocent or not—who must wrest the secret from the old woman before she takes it to the grave.

La señora Consuelo, Aura, and Felipe Montero joined this illustrious company, but with a twist: Aura and Consuelo are *one*, and it is *they* who tear the secret of desire from Felipe's breast. The male is now the deceived. This is in itself a twist on machismo.

And do not all three ladies descend from Michelet's medieval sorceress who reserves for herself, be it at the price of death by fire, the secrets of a knowledge forbidden by modern reason, the damned papers, the letters stained by the wax of candles long since gone dead, the cards wasted by the fingers of avarice and fear, but also the secrets of an antiquity projecting itself with greater strength than the future?

For is there a secret more secret, a scandal more ancient, than that of the sinless woman, the woman who does not incite toward sin—Eve—and does not open the box of disgrace—Pandora? The woman who is not what the Father of the Church, Tertullian, would have her be, "a temple built on top of a sewer," not the woman who must save herself by banging a door like Nora in Ibsen's *Doll's House*, but the woman who, before all of them, is the owner of her time because she is the owner of her will and of her body; because she does not admit any division between time, body, and will, and this mortally wounds the man who would like to divide his mind from his flesh in order to resemble, through his mind, his God, and through his flesh, his Devil?

In John Milton's *Paradise Lost*, Adam rebukes the Creator, challenges him, asks him:

> Did I request thee, Maker, from my Clay
> To mould me Man, did I sollicitte thee
> From darkness to promote me, or here place
> In this delicious Garden?

Adam asks his God, and even worse,

> . . . to reduce me to my dust,
> Desirous to resigne, and render back
> All I receav'd, unable to performe
> The terms too hard, by which I was to hold
> The good I sought not.

This man divided between his divine thought and his carnal pain is the author of his own unbearable conflict when he demands, not death, but at least, because she is worse than death, life without Eve—that is, life without Evil, life among men only, a wise creation peopled by exclusively masculine spirits, without this fair defect of nature: woman.

But this life among masculine angels shall be a life alienated, mind and flesh separated. Seen as Eve or Pandora, woman answers from the other shore of this division, saying that she is one, body inseparable from soul, with no complaints against Creation, conceived without sin because the apple of Paradise does not kill: it nurtures and it saves us from the schizoid Eden subverted by the difference between what is to be found in my divine head and what is to be found between my human legs.

The secret woman of James, Dickens, Pushkin, and Michelet who finds her young granddaughter in Aura has, I said, a fifth forebear. Her name is Circe. She is the Goddess of Metamorphosis and for her there are no extremes, no divorces between flesh and mind, because everything is transforming itself constantly, everything is becoming other without losing its anteriority and announcing a promise that does not sacrifice anything of what we are because we have been and we shall be: "Ayer se fue, mañana no ha llegado, / Hoy se está yendo sin parar un punto; / Soy un fue, y un seré, y un es cansado" (Yesterday is gone, tomorrow has not come, / Today is endlessly fleeing; / I am an I was, an I shall be, an I am tired).

Imitating old Quevedo, I asked the *Aura* papers, feverishly written as the summer of '61 came to an end: "Listen, life, will no one answer?" And the answer came in the night which accompanied the words written in the midst of the bustle of commerce and journalism and catering on a grand Parisian avenue: Felipe Montero, the false protagonist of *Aura*, answered me, addressing me familiarly:

You read the advertisement. Only your name is missing. You think you are Felipe Montero. You lie to yourself. You are You: You are Another. You are the Reader. You are what you Read. You shall be Aura. You were Consuelo.

"I'm Felipe Montero. I read your advertisement."

"Yes, I know . . . Good. Please let me see your profile . . . No, I can't see it well enough. Turn toward the light. That's right . . ."

You shall move aside so that the light from the candles and the reflections from the silver and crystal reveal the silk coif that must cover a head of very white hair and frame a face so old it must be almost childlike . . .

"I told you she'd come back."

"Who?"

"Aura. My companion. My niece."

"Good afternoon."

The girl will nod and at the same instant the old lady will imitate her gesture.

"This is Señor Montero. He's going to live with us."

SIX, only six days before her death, I met La Traviata. My wife, Sylvia, and I had been invited in September of 1976 to have dinner at the house of our old and dear friends Gabriella and Teddy van Zuylen, who have four daughters with the green eyes of Aura who spy on the guests near four paintings by Roberto Matta, Wifredo Lam, Alberto Gironella, and Pierre Alechinsky, without anyone being able to tell whether the girls are coming in or out of the paintings.

"I have a surprise for you," said our hostess, and she sat me next to Maria Callas.

This woman made me shake violently, for no reason I could immediately discern. While we dined, I tried to speak to her at the same time that I spoke to myself. From the balcony of the Theater of Fine Arts in Mexico City I had heard her sing *La Traviata* in 1951, when she was Maria Meneghini Callas and appeared as a robust young woman with the freshest, most glorious voice that I had ever heard: Callas sang an aria the same way that Manolete fought a bull: incomparably. She was already a young myth.

I told her so that night in Paris. She interrupted me with a velocity at once velvet-smooth and razor-sharp in its intention: "What do you think of the myth now that you've met her?" she asked me.

"I think she has lost some weight," I dared to answer.

She laughed with a tone different from that of her speaking voice. I imagined that, for Maria Callas, crying and singing were acts nearer to song than to speech, because I must admit that her everyday voice was that of a girl from the less fashionable neighborhoods of New York City. Maria Callas had the speaking voice of a girl selling Maria Callas records at Sam Goody's on Sixth Avenue.

This was not the voice of Medea, the voice of Norma, the voice of the Lady of the Camellias. Yes, she had slimmed down, we all knew it, without losing her glorious and warm voice, the voice of the supreme diva. No: no one was a more beautiful woman, a better actress, or a greater singer on an opera stage in the twentieth century.

Callas's seduction, let me add, was not only in the memory of her stage glory: this woman I now saw, thinned down not by her will but by her sickness and her time, nearer every minute to her bone, every second more transparent and tenuously allied to life, possessed a hypnotic secret that revealed itself as *attention*. I really think I have never met a woman who lent more attention to the man she was listening to than Maria Callas.

Her attention was a manner of dialogue. Through her eyes (two black lighthouses in a storm of white petals and moist olives) passed images in surprising mutation: her thoughts changed, the thoughts became images, yes, but only because she was transforming cease-lessly, as if her eyes were the balcony of an unfinished and endless opera that, in everyday life, prolonged in silence the suffused rumor, barely the echo, of the nights which had belonged to Lucia di Lammermoor and Violetta Valéry.

In that instant I discovered the true origin of *Aura*: its anecdotal origin, if you will, but also its origin in desire, since desire is the port of embarkation as well as the final destiny of this novella. I had heard Maria Callas sing *La Traviata* in Mexico City when she and I were more or less the same age, twenty years old perhaps, and now we were meeting almost thirty years later and I was looking at a woman I had known before, but she saw in me a man she had just met that evening. She could not compare me to myself. I could: myself and her.

And in this comparison I discovered yet another voice, not the slightly vulgar voice of the highly intelligent woman seated at my right; not the voice of the singer who gave back to bel canto a life torn from the dead embrace of the museum; no, but the voice of old age and madness which, I then remembered (and confirmed it in the Angel record I went out hurriedly to buy the next morning), is the unbelievable, unfathomable, profoundly disturbing voice of Maria Callas in the death scene of *La Traviata*.

Whereas the sopranos who sing Verdi's opera usually search for a supreme pathos achieved thanks to agonizing tremors and an attempt to approach death with sobs, screams, and shudders, Maria Callas does something unusual: she transforms her voice into that of *an old woman* and gives that ancient voice the inflection of madness.

I remember it so well that I can almost imitate the final lines: "E strano! / Cessarono / Gli spasmi del dolore."

But if this be the voice of a hypochondriac old lady complaining of the inconveniences of advanced age, immediately Callas injects a mood of madness into the words of resurgent hope in the midst of a hopeless malady: "In mi rinasce—m'agita / Insolito vigore / Ah! Ma io rittorno a viver'." Only then does death, and nothing but death, defeat old age and madness with the exclamation of youth: "Oh gioia!"

Maria Callas invited Sylvia and me to see her again a few weeks later. But before that, one afternoon, La Traviata died forever. But before, also, she had given me my secret: Aura was born in that instant when Maria Callas identified, in the voice of one woman, youth as well as old age, life along with death, inseparable, convoking one another, the four, finally, youth, old age, life, death, women's names: "*la* juventud," "*la* vejez," "*la* vida," "*la* muerte."

SEVEN, yes, seven days were needed for divine creation: on the eighth day the human creature was born and her name was desire. After the death of Maria Callas, I reread *The Lady of the Camellias* by Alexandre Dumas *fils*. The novel is far superior to Verdi's opera or to the numerous stage and film adaptations because it contains an element of delirious necrophilia absent from all the descendants.

The novel begins with the return to Paris of Armand Duval—A.D., certainly the double of Alexandre Dumas—who then finds out that Marguerite Gautier had died. Marguerite Gautier, his lover lost through the suspicious will of Duval *père*, who says he is defending the family integrity by demanding that Marguerite abandon Armand, but who is probably envious of his son and would like Marguerite all for himself. Anyway, Duval *fils* hurries desperately to the woman's tomb in Père Lachaise. The scene that follows is surely the most delirious in narrative necrophilia.

Armand obtains permission to exhume the body of Marguerite. The graveyard keeper tells Armand that it will not be difficult to find Marguerite's tomb. As soon as the relatives of the persons buried in the neighboring graves found out who she was, they protested and said there should be special real estate set apart for women such as she: a whorehouse for the dead. Besides, every day someone sends her a bouquet of camellias. He is unknown. Armand is jealous of his dead lover: he does not know who sends her the flowers. Ah, if only sin saved us from boredom, in life or in death! This is the first thing that Marguerite told Armand when she met him: "The companion of sick souls is called boredom." Armand is going to save Marguerite from the infinite boredom of being dead.

The gravediggers start working. A pickax strikes the crucifix on the coffin. The casket is slowly pulled out; the loose earth falls away.

The boards groan frightfully. The gravediggers open the coffin with difficulty. The earth's humidity has made the hinges rusty.

At long last, they manage to raise the lid. They all cover their noses. All, save Armand, fall back.

A white shroud covers the body, revealing some sinuosities. One end of the shroud is eaten up and the dead woman's foot sticks out through a hole. Armand orders that the shroud be ripped apart. One of the gravediggers brusquely uncovers Marguerite's face.

. The eyes are no more than two holes. The lips have vanished. The teeth remain white, bare, clenched. The long black tresses, dry, smeared onto the temples, cover up part of the green cavities on the cheeks.

Armand kneels down, takes the bony hand of Marguerite, and kisses it.

Only then does the novel begin: a novel that, inaugurated by death, can only culminate in death. The novel is the act of Armand Duval's desire to find the object of desire: Marguerite's body. But since no desire is innocent—because we not only desire, we also desire to change what we desire once we obtain it—Armand Duval obtains the cadaver of Marguerite Gautier in order to transform it into literature, into *book*, into that second-person singular, the You that structures desire in *Aura*.

You: that word which is mine as it moves, ghostlike, in all the dimensions of space and time, even beyond death.

"You shall plunge your face, your open eyes, into Consuelo's silver-white hair, and she'll embrace you again when the clouds cover the moon, when you're both hidden again, when the memory of youth, of youth reembodied, rules the darkness and disappears for some time.

"She'll come back, Felipe. We'll bring her back together. Let me recover my strength and I'll bring her back."

Felipe Montero, of course, is not You. You are *You*. Felipe Montero is only the author of *Terra Nostra*.

Aura was published in Spanish in 1962. The girl I had met as a child in Mexico and seen re-created by the light of Paris in 1961, when she was twenty, died by her own hand, a few years ago, in Mexico, at age forty.

PART TWO
OTHERS

Cervantes, or The Critique of Reading

When I was a young student in Latin American schools, we were
constantly being asked to define the boundary between the Middle
Ages and the Modern Age. I always remembered a grotesquely
famous Spanish play in which a knight in armour unsheaths his
sword and exclaims to his astonished family: "I'm off to the Thirty
Years' War!"

Did the modern age begin with the fall of Constantinople to the
Turks in 1453, the discovery of the New World in 1492, or the
publication by Copernicus of his *Revolutions of the Spheres* in 1543?
To give only one answer is akin to exclaiming that we are off to
the Thirty Years' War. At least since Vico, we know that the past
is present in us because we are the bearers of the culture we
ourselves have made.

Nevertheless, given a choice in the matter, I have always answered that, for me, the modern world begins when Don Quixote
de la Mancha, in 1605, leaves his village, goes out into the world,
and discovers that the world does not resemble what he has read
about it.

Many things are changing in the world; many others are sur-
viving. *Don Quixote* tells us just this: this is why he is so modern,
but also so ancient, eternal. He illustrates the rupture of a world
based on analogy and thrust into differentiation. He makes evident
a challenge that we consider peculiarly ours: how to accept the

diversity and mutation of the world, while retaining the mind's power for analogy and unity, so that this changing world shall not become meaningless.

Don Quixote tells us that being modern is not a question of sacrificing the past in favor of the new, but of maintaining, comparing, and remembering values we have created, making them modern so as not to lose the value of the modern.

This is our challenge as contemporary individuals and, indeed, as present-day writers. For if *Don Quixote*, by its very nature, does not define the modern world but only an aspect of it, it does, I believe, at least define the central problems of the modern novel. I remember discussing the matter over luncheon one cold day in 1975 with André Malraux: he chose Madame de Lafayette's *La Princesse de Clèves* as the first modern novel because, he said, it was the first psychological, interior novel, constructed around the reasons of the heart. Anglo-Saxon criticism would perhaps prefer, along with Ian Watt, to establish "the rise of the novel" in connection with the appearance of a middle class of affluent readers in England, politically emancipated and psychologically demanding of novelty in theme and characterization: Richardson, Fielding, Smollett.

Yet I shall not travel the road of Quixote's modernity alone. After all, as Lionel Trilling once wrote, "All prose fiction is a variation of the theme of *Don Quixote*: . . . the problem of appearance and reality." This all-encompassing fictitiousness in Cervantes is not at odds with Harry Levin's vision of its modernity: *Don Quixote* is seen by Levin as "the prototype of all realistic novels" . . . for it deals with "the literary technique of systematic disillusionment." And its universality is not in contradiction to Alejo Carpentier's discovery in Cervantes of the imaginary dimension within the individual: Cervantes invents a new I, says the Cuban novelist, much as Malraux said of Mme de Lafayette.

Wayne Booth's self-conscious narrator in *Don Quixote*; Marthe Robert's conception of *Don Quixote* as a novel in search of itself; Robert Coover's vision of *Don Quixote* in a world divided between reality and illusion, sanity and madness, the erotic and the ludicrous, the visionary and the eschatological; all of these highly articulate and penetrating discussions on the modernity and relevance of Cervantes accompany me in my own search for *Don*

Quixote. But it is, perhaps, Michel Foucault who has best described the displacement that occurs in the dynamic world of Cervantes: *Don Quixote*, writes Foucault in *The Order of Things*, is the sign of a modern divorce between words and things. *Don Quixote* is desperately searching for a new coincidence, for a new similitude in a world where nothing seems to resemble what it once resembled.

This same dynamic displacement, this sense of search and pilgrimage, is what Claudio Guillén calls the "active dialogue" in *Don Quixote*. A dialogue of genres, in the first place: the picaresque, the pastoral, the chivalric, the byzantine, all the established genres stake their presence and have their say in *Don Quixote*. But the past and the present are also actively fused and the novel becomes a critical project as it shifts from the spoken tale to the written narrative, from verse to prose and from the tavern to the printing shop.

Don Quixote, it is true, bears all the marks of what it leaves behind. If it is the first modern novel, its debt to tradition is enormous, since its very inception, as we all know, is the satire of the epic of chivalry. But if it is the last medieval romance, then it also celebrates its own death: it becomes its own requiem. If it is a work of the Renaissance, it also maintains a lively medieval carnival of games, puns, and references not far from Bakhtin's definition of festive humor in the novel, breaking down the frontiers between actors and audience. And finally, if it opens for all the adventure of modern reading, it remains a book deeply immersed in the society and the history of Spain.

Miguel de Cervantes was born in 1547 and died in 1616. He published the first part of *Don Quixote* in 1605, and the second part in 1615. So that everything I have said up till now happens historically within a contradiction. Cervantes's work is one of the great examples of Renaissance liberation. But his life occurs within the supreme example of the negation of that same liberation: the Spanish Counter-Reformation. We must judge Cervantes and *Don Quixote* against this background if we are to understand his achievement fully.

II

Caught between the flood tide of the Renaissance and the ebb tide of the Counter-Reformation, Cervantes clings to the one plank that can keep him afloat: Erasmus of Rotterdam. The vast influence of Erasmus in Spain is hardly fortuitous. He was correctly seen to be *the* Renaissance man struggling to conciliate the verities of faith and reason, and the reasons of the old and the new. Spanish Erasmism is the subject of Marcel Bataillon's monumental work *Erasme et l'Espagne*. The origins, influence, and eventual persecution of Erasmism in Spain are too important and lengthy a subject for this essay. Suffice it to remember that, as far as the formal education of Cervantes went, it was totally steeped in Erasmus, through the agency of his Spanish disciple, Juan López de Hoyos, the early and ascertained tutor of the author of *Don Quixote*.

The influence of Erasmian thought on Cervantes can be clearly perceived in three themes common to the philosopher and the novelist: the duality of truth, the illusion of appearances, and the praise of folly. Erasmus reflects the Renaissance dualism: *understanding* may be different from *believing*. But reason must be wary of judging from external appearances: "All things human have two aspects, much as the Silenes of Alcibiades, who had two utterly opposed faces; and thus, what at first sight looked like death was, when closely observed, life" *(In Praise of Folly)*. And he goes on to say: "The reality of things . . . depends solely on opinion. Everything in life is so diverse, so opposed, so obscure, that we cannot be assured of any truth."

Erasmus promptly gives his reasoning a comic inflection, when he smilingly points out that Jupiter must disguise himself as a "poor little man" in order to procreate little Jupiters.

Comic debunking thus serves the unorthodox vision of double truth, and it is evident that Cervantes opts for this Aesopian short-cut in creating the figures of Don Quixote and Sancho Panza, for the former speaks the language of universals, and the latter that of particulars; the knight believes, the esquire doubts; and each man's appearance is diversified, obscured, and opposed by the other's reality: if Sancho is the real man, then he is, nevertheless, a participant in Don Quixote's world of pure illusion; but if Don

Quixote is the illusory man, then he is, nevertheless, a participant in Sancho's world of pure reality.

It is one of the most brilliant paradoxes in the history of thought that Erasmus, in an age enamored of divine reason, should write, of all things, a praise of folly. There was, however, method in this madness. It is as though Erasmus had received an urgent warning from reason itself: Let me not become another absolute, such as faith was in the past, for I will then lose the reason of my reason. The Erasmian folly is a doubly ironical operation: it detaches the fool, simultaneously, from the false absolutes and the imposed verities of the medieval order; yet it casts an immense doubt on reason itself. Pascal would one day write: "Les hommes sont si nécessairement fous que ce serait être fou par un autre tour de folie de n'être pas fou."

This Pascalian turn of the screw of reason is precisely what Erasmus is driving at: if reason is to be reasonable, it must see itself through the eyes of an ironical madness, not its opposite but its critical complement; if the individual is to assert himself, then he must do so with an ironical conscience of his own ego, or he will flounder in solipsism and pride. The Erasmian folly, set at the crossroads of two cultures, relativizes the absolutes of both: this is a madness critically set in the very heart of Faith, but also in the very heart of Reason. The madness of Erasmus is a questioning of man by man himself, of reason by reason itself, and no longer by God, sin, or the Devil. Thus relativized by critical and ironical folly, Man is no longer subjected to Fate or Faith; but neither is he the absolute master of Reason.

How do the spiritual realities reflected on by Erasmus translate into the realm of literature? Perhaps Hamlet is the first character to stop in his tracks and mutter three minuscule and infinite words that suddenly open a void between the certain truths of the Middle Ages and the uncertain reasoning of the brave new world of modernity. These words are simply that: "Words, words, words . . ." and they both shake and spear us because they are the words of a fictional character reflecting on the very substance of his being. Hamlet knows he is *written*, represented, and represented on a stage, whereas old Polonius comes and goes in agitation, intrigues, counsels, and deports himself as if the world of the theater truly were the real world. Words become acts, the verb becomes a sword, and Polonius is pierced by Hamlet's sword: the sword of literature. Words, words, words, mutters Hamlet, and he does not say it pejoratively: he is simply indicating, without too many illusions, the existence of a thing called literature: a new literature that has ceased to be a transparent reading of the divine Verb or the established social order, but has been unable to become a sign reflecting a new human order as coherent or indubitable as the religious and social orders of the past.

Perhaps it is not fortuitous that *Don Quixote, King Lear,* and *Macbeth* should all bear the same date of birth, 1605: two old fools and a young assassin appear simultaneously on the stage of the world to dramatize this transition of two ages of the world. *Macbeth,* as G. Wilson Knight has observed, is a drama written with question marks, from the moment the Witches ask themselves, "When shall we three meet again?" to the moment when Macbeth prepares to die, "Why should I . . . die on mine own sword?", passing through the central questions of the play, "Is this a dagger which I see before me?" and "Will all great Neptune's ocean wash this blood / Clean from my hand?" And *Lear* is a drama of magnificent metaphors derived from a tumultuous universe, where stars and eclipses, planetary influences and the government of our state by the heavenly bodies mix with the images of the dislocated terrestrial elements: drama of rain and fire, of fog and thunder. And in the center of this tempest of heaven and earth, accompanied only by a Fool, struts an abandoned old man, incapable of learning more than he knows already, assimilated to a sorrowful and solitary world of nature.

All the world's a stage, and the words spoken from it are, indeed, full of sound and fury; the state of the world is undone and the actor who struts his hour upon the stage speaks wandering, orphaned words: we have lost our father, but we have not found ourselves. Words become the vehicle of ambiguity and paradox. "All is possible," says Marsilio Ficino. "All is in doubt," says John Donne. Between these two sentences, pronounced more than a century apart, the new literature appears as an opaque circle where Hamlet can represent his methodic madness, Robinson Crusoe his optimistic rationalism, Don Juan of Seville his secular sexuality, and St. John of the Cross his celestial eroticism: in literature, all things become possible. In the medieval cosmos, each reality manifested another reality, in accordance with symbols that were homologated in an unequivocal manner. But in the highly unstable and equivocal world that Copernicus leaves in his wake, these central criteria are forever lost.

All is possible, but all is in doubt. All things have lost their concert. In the very dawn of his humanist affirmation, the individual is assailed by the very doubts, the very criticisms, the very questioning with which Copernicus and Galileo have set free the dormant forces of the universe, expanding it to a degree such that the dwarfed individual, in response, must gigantically display his unleashed passions, his unbridled pride, the cruel uses of his political power, the utopian dream of a new city of the sun, the hunger for a new human space with which to confront the new, mute space of the universe: the spatial appetite that is evident both in the discovery of the New World and in the frescoes of Piero della Francesca.

Nothing should be refused, writes Ficino; human nature contains all and every one of the levels of creation, from the horrendous forms of the powers of the deep to the hierarchies of divine intelligence described by the mystics; nothing is incredible, nothing is impossible; the possibilities we deny are but the possibilities we ignore. The libertine and the ascetic, Don Juan and Savonarola, Cesare Borgia and Hernán Cortés, the tyrant and the adventurer, Marlowe's Faust and Ford's incestuous lovers, Machiavelli's Prince and Thomas More's Utopian traveller, rebellious intelligence and rebellious flesh, a chronophagic and omni-inclusive imagination: human faults no longer reestablish an ancestral order. They consume themselves in the self-sufficient fires of pride, passion, reason, pleasure, and power. But, even as they are won, these new realities are doubted by the critical spirit, since the critical spirit founded them.

III

All is possible. All is in doubt. Only an old hidalgo from the barren plain of La Mancha in the central plateau of Castile continues to adhere to the codes of certainty. For him, nothing is in doubt and all is possible. In the new world of criticism, Don Quixote is a knight of the faith. This faith comes from his reading, and his reading is a madness. (The Spanish words for *reading* and *madness* convey this association much more strongly: reading is *lectura*; madness is *locura*.)

Like Philip II, the necrophiliac monarch secluded at El Escorial, Don Quixote both pawns and pledges his life to the restoration of the world of unified certainty. He pawns and pledges himself, both physically and symbolically, to the univocal reading of the texts and attempts to translate this reading into a reality that has become multiple, equivocal, ambiguous. But because he possesses his readings, Don Quixote possesses his identity: that of the knight-errant, that of the ancient epic hero.

So, at the immediate level of reading, Don Quixote is the master of the previous readings that withered his brain. But at a second level of reading, he becomes the master of the words contained in the verbal universe of the book titled *Don Quixote*. He ceases to be a reader of the novels of chivalry and becomes the actor of his own epic adventures. As there was no rupture between his reading of the books and his faith in what they said, so now there is no divorce between the acts and the words of his adventures. Because, assimilated to Don Quixote, we read it but do not see it, we shall never know what it is that the goodly gentleman puts on his head: the fabled helm of Mambrino, or a vulgar barber's basin. The first doubt assails us: is Quixote right, has he discovered the legendary helmet where everyone else, blind and ignorant, sees only the basin?

Within this verbal sphere, Don Quixote is at first invincible. Sancho's empiricism, from this verbal point of view, is useless, because Don Quixote, each time he fails, immediately reestablishes his literary discourse, undiscouraged, the words always identical to the reality, the reality but a prolongation of the words he has read before and now enacts. He explains away his disasters with the words of his previous, epic readings, and resumes his career within the world of the words that belong to him.

Harry Levin compares the famous "play within the play" scene in *Hamlet* with the chapter on the puppet theater of Master Pedro in *Don Quixote*. In Shakespeare's drama, King Claudius interrupts the mummery because imagination starts to resemble reality too dangerously. In Cervantes's novel, Don Quixote assaults Master

Pedro's "Moorish puppetry" because representation starts to resemble imagination too closely. Claudius desires that reality were a lie: the killing of Hamlet's father, the King. Don Quixote desires that fantasy were a truth: the imprisonment of the Princess Melisendra by the Moors.

The identification of the imaginary with the real remits Hamlet to reality, and from reality, naturally, it yields him to death: Hamlet is the envoy of death, he comes from death and goes toward death. But the identification of the imaginary with the imaginary remits Don Quixote to his books. Don Quixote comes from his readings and goes toward them: Don Quixote is the ambassador of readings. In his mind, it is not reality at all that interposes itself between his enterprises and reality: it is the magicians he knows through his readings.

We know this is not so; we know that only reality confronts the mad readings of Don Quixote. But he does not know it, and this ignorance (or this faith) establishes a third level of reading in the novel. "*Look* your mercy," Sancho constantly says, "*Look* you that what we see there are not giants, but only windmills." But Don Quixote does not *see*: Don Quixote *reads* and his reading says that those *are* giants.

Don Quixote wants to introduce the whole world within his readings, as long as these are the readings of a unique and consecrated code: the code that, since the action at Roncesvalles, identifies the exemplary act of history with the exemplary act of books. Roland's sacrifice defended the heroic ideal of chivalry and the political integrity of Christendom. His gest shall become ideal norm and ideal form of all the heroes of the fictions of chivalry. Don Quixote counts himself among their number. He, too, believes that between the exemplary gestures of history and exemplary gestures of books there can be no cracks, for above them all stands the consecrated code that rules both, and above the code rises the univocal vision of a world structured by God. Issued from these readings, Don Quixote, each time he fails, finds refuge in his readings. And sheltered by his books, he will go on seeing armies where there are only sheep, without losing the reason of his readings: he will be faithful unto them, because he does not conceive any other licit way of reading. The synonymity of reading, madness, truth, and life in Don Quixote becomes strikingly apparent when he demands of the merchants he meets on the road that they confess the beauty of Dulcinea without ever having seen her, for "the important thing is that without having seen her you should believe, confess, swear, and defend it." This *it* is an act of faith. Don Quixote's fabulous adventures are ignited by an overwhelming purpose: what is read and what is lived must coincide anew, without the doubts and oscillations between faith and reason introduced by the Renaissance.

But the very next level of reading in the novel *Don Quixote* starts to undermine this illusion. In his third outing, Don Quixote finds out, through news that the Bachelor Sansón Carrasco has transmitted to Sancho, that there exists a book called *The Most Ingenious Hidalgo Don Quixote de la Mancha*. "They mention me," Sancho says in marvelment, "along with our lady Dulcinea del Toboso, and many other things that happened to us alone, so that I crossed myself in fright trying to imagine how the historian who wrote them came to know them." Things that happened to us alone. Before, only God could know them; only God was the final knower and judge of what went on in the recesses of our conscience. Now, any reader who can pay the cover price for a copy of *Don Quixote* can also find out: the reader thus becomes akin to God. Now the Dukes can prepare their cruel farces because they have read the first part of the novel *Don Quixote*. Now Don Quixote, the reader, *is read*.

On entering the second part of the novel, Don Quixote also finds out that he has been the subject of an apocryphal novel written by one Avellaneda to cash in on the popularity of Cervantes's book. The signs of Don Quixote's singular identity suddenly seem to multiply. Don Quixote criticizes Avellaneda's version. But the existence of *another* book about himself makes him change his route and go to Barcelona so as to "bring out into the public light the lies of this modern historian so that people will see that I am not the Don Quixote he says I am."

This is surely the first time in literature that a character knows that he is being written about at the same time that he lives his fictional adventures. This new level of reading is crucial to determine those which follow. Don Quixote ceases to support himself on previous epics and starts to support himself on his own epic. But his epic is no epic, and it is at this point that Cervantes invents the modern novel. Don Quixote, the reader, knows he is read, something that Achilles surely never knew. And he knows that the destiny of Don Quixote the man has become inseparable from the destiny of *Don Quixote* the book, something that Ulysses never knew in relation to the *Odyssey*. His integrity as a hero of old, safely niched in a previous, univocal and denotative epic reading, is shattered, not by the galley slaves or the scullery maids who laugh at him, not by the sticks and stones he must weather in the inns he takes to be castles or the grazing fields he takes to be battlegrounds. His faith in his epical readings enables him to bear all the batterings of reality. But now his integrity is annulled by the readings he is submitted to.

It is these readings that transform Don Quixote, the caricature of the ancient hero, into the first modern hero, observed from multiple angles, scrutinized by multiple eyes that do not share his faith in the codes of chivalry, assimilated to the very readers who read him, and, like them, forced to re-create "Don Quixote" in his own imagination. A double victim of the act of reading, Don Quixote loses his senses twice. First, when he reads. Then, when he is read. Because now, instead of having to prove the existence of the heroes of old, he is up to a much, much tougher challenge: he must prove his own existence.

And this leads us to a further level of reading. A voracious, insomniac reader of epics he obsessively wants to carry over to reality, Don Quixote fails miserably in this, his original purpose. But as soon as he becomes an object of reading, he begins to vanquish reality, to contaminate it with his mad reading: not the reading of the novels of chivalry, but the actual reading of the new novel, *Don Quixote*. And this new reading transforms the world, for the world, more and more, begins to resemble the world contained in the pages of the novel *Don Quixote*.

In order to mock Don Quixote, the world disguises itself with the masks of Don Quixote's obsessions. Yet, can anyone disguise himself as something worse than his own self? Do not our disguises reveal our reality with greater truth than our everyday appearance? The disguised world of those who have read Don Quixote within the pages of *Don Quixote* reveals the undisguised reality of the world: its cruelty, its ignorance, its injustice, its stupidity. So Cervantes need not write a political manifesto to denounce the evils of his age and of all ages; he need not recur to Aesopian language;

he need not radically break with the strictures of the traditional epic in order to surpass it: he dialectically merges the epic thesis and the realistic antithesis to achieve, within the very life and logic and necessity of his own book, the novelistic synthesis. No one had conceived this polyvalent creation within a book before him; not Tasso's mock heroics, not the picaresque's stark documentary, not Rabelais's gargantuan, insatiable, terrifying affirmation of the surfeit energy of the world pitted against the vacuum of heaven.

Don Quixote, the knight of the faith, meets a faithless world: both no longer know where the *truth* really *lies*. Is Don Quixote really mocked by Dorotea when she disguises herself as the Princess Micomicona, or by the Bachelor Carrasco when he defies Don Quixote disguised as the Knight of the Mirrors? Is Don Quixote really fooled by the Dukes when they stage the farces of the wooden horse Clavileño, the Sorrowful Lady with her twelve bearded duennas or the government of Sancho in the Island Barataria? Or is it really Don Quixote who has mocked them all, forcing them to enter, disguised as themselves, the immense universe of the reading of *Don Quixote*? Perhaps this is disputable matter for psychoanalysis. What is indisputable is that Don Quixote, the bewitched, ends by bewitching the world. While he read, he imitated the epic hero. When he is read, the world imitates him.

But the price he must pay is the loss of his own enchantment.

Prodigal writer that he is, Cervantes now leads us to a further level of reading. As the world comes to resemble him more and more, Don Quixote, more and more, loses the illusion of his own being. He has been the cipher of the act of reading: a black ink question mark, much as Picasso was to draw him. But by the time he reaches the castle of the Dukes, Don Quixote sees that the castle is actually a castle, whereas, before, he could *imagine* he saw a castle in the humblest inn of the Castilian wayside.

The incarnation of his dreams in reality robs Don Quixote of his imagination. In the world of the Dukes, it will no longer be necessary for him to imagine an unreal world: the Dukes offer him what he has imagined in all its reality. What, then, is the sense of reading? What is the sense of books? What is their use? From then on, all is sadness and disillusionment. Paradoxically, Don Quixote is bereft of his faith at the very moment when the world of his readings is offered to him in the world of reality. His crucial passage through the castle of the Dukes permits Cervantes to introduce a triple wedge in his critique of reading. One, he is stating, is Don Quixote's idea of an epic coincidence between his readings and his life. It is a faith born from books and totally defined by the way Don Quixote has read those books. As long as this mental coincidence is supreme, Don Quixote has no trouble coexisting with what is outside his own universe: the very fact that reality does not coincide with his readings permits him, again and again, to impose the vision of his readings on reality. But when what only pertains to his univocal readings finds an equivalent in reality, the illusion is shattered. The coherence of epic reading is defeated by the incoherence of historical facts. Don Quixote must live through this historical reality before he reaches the third and definitive level proposed by Cervantes: the level of the novel itself, the synthesis between the past Don Quixote loses and the present that annuls him.

Thrust into history, Don Quixote is deprived of all opportunity for his imaginative action. He meets one Roque Guinart, an authentic robber, alive in the time of Cervantes. This Guinart, totally inscribed in history, was thief and contrabandist of the silver cargoes from the Indies and a secret agent of the French Huguenots at the time of the St. Bartholomew's night massacre. Next to him and his tangible historicity, as when he sees (but does not partake in) a naval battle off Barcelona, Don Quixote has become a simple witness to real events and real characters. Cervantes gives these chapters a strange aura of sadness and disillusionment. The old hidalgo, forever deprived of his epic reading of the world, must face his final option: to be in the sadness of reality or to be in the reality of literature: this literature, the one Cervantes has invented, not the old literature of univocal coincidence that Don Quixote sprang from.

Dostoevsky calls Cervantes's novel "the saddest book of them all"; in it, the Russian novelist found the inspiration for the figure of the "good man," the idiot prince, Myshkin. As the novel ends, the knight of the faith has truly earned his sorrowful countenance. For, as Dostoevsky adds, Don Quixote suffers from a disease, "the nostalgia of realism."

This phrase must give us pause. What realism are we talking

about? The realism of impossible adventures with magicians, chivalrous knight-errants, and frightful giants? Exactly so. Before, everything that was written was true . . . even if it was a fantasy. There were no cracks between what was said and what was done in the epic. "For Aristotle and the Middle Ages," explains Ortega y Gasset, "all things are possible that do not contain an inner contradiction. For Aristotle, the centaur is a possibility; not so for us, since biology will not tolerate it."

And this is what Don Quixote feels such intense nostalgia for: this realism without inner contradictions. The new science, the new doubts, all the skepticisms that anachronize the faith of the knight of the unique reading, of the ambassador of the licit reading, cross Don Quixote's path and undermine his illusions. But above all, what shatters the monolith of the old realism Don Quixote yearns for are the plural readings, the illicit readings to which he is subjected.

Don Quixote recovers his reason. And this, for a man of his ilk, is the supreme folly: it is suicide. When he accepts conventional "reality," Don Quixote, like Hamlet, is condemned to death. But Don Quixote, thanks to the critical reading invented by Cervantes in the act of founding the modern novel, shall go on living another life: he is left with no resource but to prove his own existence, not in the univocal reading that gave him his original being, but in the multiple readings that deprived him of it. Don Quixote loses the life of his nostalgic, coincidental reality but goes on living, forever, in his book and only in his book.

This is why *Don Quixote* is the most Spanish of all novels. Its very essence is defined by loss, impossibility, a burning quest for identity, a sad conscience of all that could have been and never was, and, in reaction to this deprivation, an assertion of total existence in a realm of the imagination, where all that cannot be in reality finds, precisely because of this factual negation, the most intense level of truth. Because the history of Spain has been what it has been, its art has been what history has denied Spain. This is equally true of the mystic poetry of San Juan de la Cruz, the baroque poetry of Luis de Góngora, Velázquez's *Meninas*, Goya's *Caprichos*, and the films of Luis Buñuel. Art gives life to what history killed. Art gives voice to what history denied, silenced, or persecuted. Art brings truth to the lies of history.

This is what Dostoevsky meant when he called *Don Quixote* a
novel where truth is saved by a lie. The Russian author's profound
observation goes well beyond the relationship of a nation's art to
its history. Dostoevsky is speaking of the broader relationship between reality and imagination. There is a fascinating moment in
Don Quixote when the Knight of the Sorrowful Countenance arrives
in Barcelona and forever breaks the bindings of the illusion of
reality. He does what Achilles, Aeneas, or Sir Lancelot could never
do: he visits a printing shop, he enters the very place where his
adventures become an object, a legible product. Don Quixote is
thus sent by Cervantes to his only reality: the reality of fiction.

The act of reading, in this manner, is both the starting point
and the last stop on Don Quixote's route. Neither the reality of
what he read nor the reality of what he lived were such, but merely
paper ghosts. Only freed from his readings but captured by the
readings that multiply the levels of the novel on an infinite scale;
only alone in the very center of his authentic, fictional reality, Don
Quixote can exclaim:

> Believe in me! My feats are true, the windmills are giants, the
> herds of sheep are armies, the inns are castles and there is in the
> world no lady more beautiful than the Empress of La Mancha,
> the unrivaled Dulcinea del Toboso! Believe in me!

Reality may laugh or weep on hearing such words. But reality
is invaded by them, loses its own defined frontiers, feels itself
displaced, transfigured by *another* reality made of words and paper.
Where are the limits between Dunsinane Castle and Birnham Wood?
Where the frontiers that might bind the moor where Lear and his
Fool live the cold night of madness? Where, in fact, does Don
Quixote's fantastic Cave of Montesinos end and reality begin?

Never again shall we be able to know, because there will never
again be a unique reading of reality. Cervantes has vanquished
the epic on which he fed. He has established the dialogue between
the epic hero, Achilles, Lancelot, Amadis, and the *pícaro*, the
rogue, the blind man's guide, Lazarillo. And in doing so, he has
dissolved the severe normativity of scholastic thought and its univocal reading of the world.

Of course, Cervantes is not alone in this task of demolition; he
is, legitimately, a Renaissance man in this and many other aspects.

But he is also a Spaniard caught between the flux of renewal and the stagnant waters of reaction. Where others can go perilously forward to instate reason, hedonism, capitalism, the unbounded optimism of faith in unlimited progress inscribed in lineal time and a future-oriented history, Cervantes must wrestle between the old and the new with far greater intensity than, say, Descartes. And he certainly cannot face the world with the pragmatic assurance of Defoe. Robinson Crusoe, the first capitalist hero, is a self-made man who accepts objective reality and then fashions it to his needs through the work ethic, common sense, resilience, technology, and, if need be, racism and imperialism.

Don Quixote is the polar opposite of Robinson. His failure in practical matters is the most gloriously ludicrous in recorded history (perhaps it is only paralleled by the great clowns of the silent screen: Chaplin, Keaton, Laurel and Hardy . . .). Robinson and Quixote are the antithetical symbols of the Anglo-Saxon and Hispanic worlds.

Américo Castro, the greatest modern interpreter of Spanish history, has defined it as "the story of an insecurity." France, he goes on to say, has assimilated its past, at the price of maximal sacrifices, through the categories of rationalism and clarity; England, through those of empiricism and pragmatism. The past is not a problem for the Frenchman or the Englishman. For the Spaniard, it is nothing *but* a problem; the latent strains of its multiple heritages—Christian, Muslim, and Jewish—throb unresolved in the heart and mind of Spain. The Spanish ethos oscillates violently between exaltation and passivity, but always in relation to a transcendental mission which divorces and opposes the absolute values of life or death, the temporal or the eternal, honor or dishonor. Spain has been unable to participate in modern European values, defined by a rational articulation between the objective world and the subjective being. Her capacities for political and economic efficiency have been nil; her scientific and technical prowess, scarce; but her capacity for art has been absolute.

It is no wonder, then, that the greatest works of Spanish genius have coincided with the periods of crisis and decadence of Spanish society. The Arcipreste de Hita's *Libro de Buen Amor* saves and translates into Spanish the literary influences of the Caliphate of Cordoba after the brilliant world of the Omeya dynasty in Al Andalus has been destroyed by the Almoravide and Almohad invasions. Fernando de Rojas's *La Celestina* is the masterpiece of Jewish Spain: it coincides with the expulsion and persecution of the Spanish Hebrews and of the *conversos*. The whole Golden Age of Spanish literature—Cervantes, Lope de Vega, Quevedo, Góngora, Calderón—flowers as the power of Spain withers. Velázquez is the painter of the crepuscular court of Philip IV, and Goya the contemporary of the blind and venal Bourbons, Charles IV and Fernando VII, who lose their crown to Joseph Bonaparte and their American empire to the rebellious creoles. And only when Spain lost the remnants of empire in the Spanish-American War did the dearth of her nineteenth-century culture give way to an extraordinary assertion of thought, science, and art: Unamuno, Valle Inclán, Ramón y Cajal, Ortega y Gasset, Buñuel, Miró, and the poetic generation of García Lorca. The absolute value of art has always shone in Spain at its brightest when its political, economic, and technical fortunes have been at their lowest.

So Cervantes is no exception to a general rule. But what are the particular values he instates in the heart of reality, he, the orphan child of both the Renaissance and the Counter-Reformation; he who cannot proceed to the rational clarity and self-contention of a Madame de Lafayette or the pragmatic efficiency of a Defoe? I have recalled the influence of Erasmus on Cervantes. *Don Quixote*, a Spanish extension of the Praise of Folly identical to the praise of Utopia, contains an ethic of Love and Justice. A moral reality occupies the center of Cervantes's imagination, since it cannot occupy the center of the society he lives in.

Love and Justice. Don Quixote, the madman, is mad not only because he has believed all he has read. He is also mad because he believes, as a knight-errant, that justice is his duty and that justice is possible. Again and again, he proclaims his credo: "I am the valiant Don Quixote de la Mancha, undoer of wrongs and torts": "The duty of my office is to correct injustices and fly to help the needy." We know the sort of gratitude Don Quixote receives from those he succors: he is beaten and mocked by them. Cervantes's social irony reaches a high pitch indeed in these scenes. The poor and miserable and wronged ones Don Quixote aids do not want to be saved by him. Perhaps they want to save themselves. This is an open question. In any case, there is not a shred of a

Polyanna in Cervantes: he sees the common people capable of being every bit as cruel as their oppressors. But then, does this not pose the implicit commentary that an unjust society perverts all of its members, the mighty and the weak, the high and the lowly?

Don Quixote, in spite of his recurrent disasters as a do-gooder, never fails in his faith in the ideal of justice. He is a Spanish hero: the transcendent idea cannot be wounded by the accidents of ordinary reality. And what is the ideology that sustains Don Quixote's search for Justice? It is the utopia of the Golden Age:

> A happy age, and happy centuries, those that the ancients called golden, and not because gold, so esteemed in our iron age, was to be found without any hardship in that felicitous age, but because those who then lived knew not these two words *yours* and *mine*. All things, in that holy age, were common . . . The clear fountain and the flowing rivers offered men, in magnificent abundance, their tasty and transparent waters . . . All was peace then, all friendship, all concord . . . Then were the loving concepts of the soul dressed in simplicity, as the loving soul conceived them . . . Fraud and mendacity were unknown, malice did not then parade as truth and sincerity. Justice was faithful to its name, and men of favor and interest did not dare perturb what today they so discredit, disturb and persecute . . .

None of this, Don Quixote ends by saying, is true "in our detestable times," and so he has become a knight-errant in order to "defend young women, protect widows, and bring help to the orphaned and the needy." Don Quixote's concept of Justice is thus a Concept of Love. And through Love, Don Quixote's abstract Justice achieves its full realization.

The power of Don Quixote's image as a madman who constantly confuses reality with imagination has made many a reader and commentator forget what I consider an essential passage of the book. In Chapter XXV of the first part of the novel, Don Quixote decides to do penance, dressed only in his nightshirt, in the craggy cliffs of the Sierra Morena. He asks Sancho to go off to the village of El Toboso and inform the knight's lady Dulcinea of the great deeds and sufferings with which he honors her. Since Sancho knows of no highly placed lady called Dulcinea in the miserable hamlet of El Toboso, he inquires further. Don Quixote, at this extraordinary moment, reveals that he knows the truth: Dulcinea, he says, is none other than the peasant girl Aldonza Lorenzo; it is she Sancho must look for. This provokes gales of laughter in the roguish squire: he knows Aldonza well: she is common, strong as a bull, dirty, can bellow to the peasants from the church tower and be heard a league away; she's a good one at exchanging pleasantries and, in fact, is a bit of a whore.

Don Quixote's response is one of the most moving declarations of love ever written. He knows who and what Dulcinea really is; yet he loves her, and because he loves her, she is worth as much as "the most noble princess in all the world." He admits that his imagination has transformed the peasant girl Aldonza into the noble lady Dulcinea: but is not this the essence of love, to transform the loved one into something incomparable, unique, set above all considerations of wealth or poverty, distinction or commonness? "Thus, it is enough that I think and believe that Aldonza Lorenzo is beautiful and honest; the question of class is of no consequence . . . I paint her in my imagination as I desire her . . . And let the world think what it wants."

The social, ethical, and political content of *Don Quixote* is obvious in this reunion of Love and Justice. The myth of the Golden Age is its ideological core: a utopia of brotherhood, equality, and pleasure. Utopia is to be achieved not in a nihilistic sweeping away of the past and starting from scratch to build a brave new world, but in a fusion of the values that come to us from the past and those we are capable of creating in the present. Justice, Don Quixote insists, is absent from the present times; only Love can give Justice actuality, and the Love Don Quixote speaks of is a democratic act, an act surpassing class distinctions, a truth to be found in the lowliest of peasant girls. But to this love must be brought the constant, aristocratic values of chivalry, personal risk in the quest for justice, integrity, and heroism. In Don Quixote, the values of the age of chivalry acquire, through Love, a democratic resonance; and the values of the democratic life acquire the resonance of nobility. Don Quixote refuses both the cruel power of the mighty and the herd instinct of the lowly: his vision of humanity is based not on the lowest common denominator but on the highest achievement possible. His conception of Love and Justice saves both the oppressors and the oppressed from an oppression that perverts both.

It is through this ethical stance that Cervantes struggles to bridge the old and new worlds. If his critique of reading is a negation of the rigid and oppressive features of the Middle Ages, it is also an affirmation of ancient values that must not be lost in the transition to the modern world. But if Don Quixote is also an affirmation of the modern values of the pluralistic point of view, Cervantes does not surrender to modernity either. It is at this juncture that his moral and literary vision fuses into a whole. For if reality has become plurivocal, literature will reflect it only in the measure to which it forces reality to submit itself to plural readings and in multiple visions from variable perspectives. Precisely in the name of the polyvalence of the real, literature creates reality, adds to reality, ceases to be a verbal correspondence to verities unmovable, or anterior to reality. Literature, this new printed reality, speaks of the things of the world; but literature, in itself, is a new thing in the world.

As if he foresaw all the dirty tricks of servile literary naturalism, Cervantes destroys the illusion of literature as a mere copy of reality and creates a literary reality far more powerful and difficult to grapple with: the reality of a novel is its existence at all levels of the critique of reading. The moral message of *Don Quixote*, instead of being imposed from above by the author, thus passes through the sieve of the multiple readings of multiple readers who are reading a work that is criticizing its own artistic and moral propositions. By rooting the critique of creation in the creation itself, Cervantes lays claim to being one of the founders of the modern imagination. Poetry, painting, and music will later demand an equal right to be themselves and not docile imitators of a reality that they ill serve by reproducing it. Art will not reflect *more* reality unless it creates *another* reality.

Through his paper character Don Quixote, who integrates the values of the past with those of the present, Cervantes translates the great themes of the centerless universe and of individualism triumphant, yet awed and orphaned, to the plane of literature as the axis of a new reality. There will be no more tragedy and no more epic, because there is no longer a restorable ancestral order or a universe univocal in its normativity. There will be multiple levels of reading, capable of testing the multiple layers of reality.

IV

It so happens that this rogue, convicted galley slave, and false puppeteer, Ginés de Pasamonte, alias Ginesillo de Parapilla, alias Master Pedro, is writing a book about his own life. "Is the book finished?" asks Don Quixote. And Ginés answers him: "How can it be, if my life isn't over yet?"

This is Cervantes's last question: Who writes books and who reads them? Who is the author of *Don Quixote*? A certain Cervantes, more versed in grief than in verse, whose *Galatea* has been read by the priest who scrutinizes Don Quixote's library, burns the books he dislikes in an immediate auto-da-fé, and then seals off the hidalgo's library with brick and mortar, making him believe it is the work of magicians? A certain de Saavedra, mentioned by the Captive with admiration because of the acts he accomplished, "and all of them for the purpose of achieving freedom"?

Cervantes, like the character Don Quixote, is read by other characters of the novel *Don Quixote*, a book without an original author and, almost, a book without a destiny, a book that agonizes in the act of being born, reanimated by the papers of the Arab historian Cide Hamete Benengeli, which are then translated into Spanish by an anonymous Moorish translator and which will be the object of the abject apocryphal version of Avellaneda . . . The endless circle of reading and writings winds itself anew: Cervantes, author of Borges; Borges, author of Pierre Ménard; Pierre Ménard, author of Don Quixote; Don Quixote, author of Miguel de Cervantes Saavedra.

Cervantes leaves open the pages of a book where the reader knows himself to be read and the author knows himself to be written and it is said that he dies on the same date, though not on the same day, as William Shakespeare. It is further stated that perhaps both were the same man. Cervantes's debts and battles and prisons were fictions that permitted him to disguise himself as Shakespeare and write his plays in England, while the comedian Will Shaksper, the man with a thousand faces, the Elizabethan Lon Chaney, wrote

Don Quixote in Spain. This disparity between the real days and the fictitious date of a common death spared world enough and time for Cervantes's ghost to fly to London in time to die once more in Shakespeare's body. But perhaps they are not really the same person, since the calendars in England and Spain have never been the same, in 1616 or in 1987.

But then again, if not the same *person*, maybe they are the same writer, the same author of all the books, a wandering polyglot polygraphist named, according to the whims of the times, Homer, Vergil, Dante, Cide Hamete Benengeli, Cervantes, Shakespeare, Sterne, Defoe, Goethe, Poe, Dickens, Balzac, Lewis Carroll, Proust, Kafka, Borges, Pierre Ménard, James Joyce . . . He is the author of the same *open book* which, like the autobiography of Ginés de Pasamonte, is not yet finished because our lives are not yet over. With other words, Mallarmé will one day say the same thought as the rogue of Parapilla: "A book neither begins nor ends; at the most, it feigns to . . ."

Cervantes wrote the first open novel as if he had read Mallarmé. He proposes, through the critique of reading that seems to start with the hidalgo's reading of the epics of chivalry and seems to end with the reader's realization that all reality is multi-leveled, the critique of creation within creation. *Don Quixote*'s intemporal and, at the same time, immediate quality derives from the nature of its internal poetics: it is a split poem that converts its own genesis into an act of fiction: it is the poetry of poetry (or the fiction of fiction), singing the birth of the poem, narrating the origin of the very fiction we are reading.

Gaston Bachelard has written that all great writers know that the world wants literature to be everything and to be something else: philosophy, politics, science, ethics. Why this demand, asks the French thinker. Because literature is always in direct communication with the origins of the spoken being, at that very core of speech where philosophy, politics, ethics, and science themselves become possible.

But when science, ethics, politics, and philosophy discover their own limitations they appeal to the grace and disgrace of literature to go beyond their insufficiencies. Yet they only discover, along with literature itself, the permanent divorce between words and things: the separation between the representative uses of language and the experience of the being of language.

Literature is the utopian operation that would like to reduce that distance. When it simply disguises the divorce, it is called epic. When it reveals it, it is called novel or poetry. Such is the novel and the poem of the Knight of the Sorrowful Countenance in his struggle to make words and things coincide. Don Quixote finds out, as we all do in our lives, that things do not belong to all; but words do. Words are like air: they belong to all or to no one. Language is the first and most natural instance of common property. If this is so, then Miguel de Cervantes is only the owner of his words in the same measure that he is not Miguel de Cervantes but all men: like Joyce's Dedalus, he is the poet, singing the uncreated conscience of his race, mankind. The poet is born after his act, the poem. The poem creates its author, much as it creates its readers. The final description of Cervantes's critique of reading is this simple, lapidary statement: *Don Quixote*, written by everybody, read by everybody.

Two Centuries of Diderot

I

When Milan Kundera hears the well-worn critical question "Is the novel dead?" he brings out his literary pistol and shoots out five syllables: De-nis Di-de-rot.

Diderot, born in 1713 and dead in 1784, did many things and did them all well. Editor of the Encyclopedia, theoretician of the theater, founder of modern literary and art criticism, materialist philosopher, and, if that were not enough, mentor to Catherine of Russia, Diderot is, as the Mexican writer José Emilio Pacheco has said, unembraceable.

Unembraceable Diderot was (besides? above all?) a novelist and, according to Kundera, the greatest example we have that, far from exhausting its possibilities, the novel has yet to saunter down unexplored or forgotten paths, listen to muffled calls, and fully accomplish its possibilities in the realms of playfulness and criticism, fabulation, humor, creative novelty, and the endless potentialities of the *ars combinatoria*. This call to novelistic arms—risk, discovery, a growing perception of an endless reality—is there, if one wants to hear it, in the fictions of Denis Diderot.

Kundera's critical concept of the potential novels contained in the inexhausted novels of the past is part of an aesthetics of reception. How to make the past present? Diderot wrote in the eighteenth century. Why are we capable of reading and understanding him more and more with the passage of time? Why does a writer such as Diderot become more and more present instead of more and more absent? What is the secret of artistic presence? This is my question from and for Diderot on the bicentennial of his death: my question homage.

Boileau, in his *Poetics*, excludes the novel from his system of genres, and in order to make themselves look respectable, the novelists of the seventeenth and eighteenth centuries swear eternal fealty to the classics in their prefaces. The novel is born without parents because it makes its debut as a potential fact, unforeseeable and unclassifiable in a world which only wants to recognize itself in the classical, since the classical is, by definition, the recognizable, or, as Hegel put it, classical is that which signifies itself and interprets itself, with no need for mediation.

Given this orphaned background, Diderot sets out, precisely, to write a novel that is nothing but an act of perpetual mediation between the author and the reader, an exchange of insecure signs, a constant rupture of the dramatic unities and of linear narrative. Diderot's fiction is an emission of uncertain questions: Is this a novel? Are you a reader? Am I a writer?

Jacques le Fataliste, Diderot's great novel, was published between 1796 and 1798, more than two centuries ago, and posthumously. Yet it is not only one of the great novels of the eighteenth century; it is one of the great novels of the twentieth century: it is vibrantly contemporary. The novel begins as a dialogue between Jacques the servant and his master; but it finally becomes a vast debate between the author and the time of his readers. But the premise of what I am saying is this: Diderot the philosopher is acutely conscious of the demands of classical poetics; the narrative must respect the unities of time, place, and action. Diderot the sociologist is equally aware of the traditional expectations of the reading public of his own time. But Diderot the artist swiftly proceeds to break the unities and to frustrate the expectations. The artist finally triumphs over the rationalist and the statistician.

This does not mean, of course, that Diderot's art is deprived of either philosophical reason or social content. Diderot the materialist philosopher, a profound reader of Lucretius, wishes to think and write in the same fashion that nature produces: indifferently, in perpetual clash, and open to the accidents of chance. Akin to nature, the narrative text in Diderot never rests. Comparable to matter, it mixes, assimilates, digests, and expels everything (this was the principal romantic criticism—Schlegel's—against Diderot): but, once more like matter and like nature, Diderot's narrative performance is constantly rehearsing new forms. The reader of Lucretius is also a reader of Heraclitus, and one of the most beautiful definitions of the philosophy of movement comes from the pen of Diderot:

> All is perpetual flux. The spectacle of the universe offers but a passing geometry, a momentary order.

Instead of "the spectacle of the universe," Diderot could have said the presence of the world, or the presence in the world of human beings, the societies they inhabit, and the cultures they generate.

II

Diderot has ceased to be, strictly, a novelist of the eighteenth century. He is a contemporary novelist and he shows us that art does not progress: art is and makes itself present.

Presence, points out Roger Kempf in his admirable study *Diderot and the Novel*, is the passion which rules Diderot's relationship to the novel. The passion for presence is, likewise, the technique that the French writer employs to give life to his fictions. "Sensation," states Diderot, "does not possess the successive development of speech; and if sensation could speak through twenty mouths, each mouth saying its own word, all that I have said could have been said at the same time."

Diderot is fascinated by the possibility of identifying the intensity of presence and the simultaneity of expression. On another occasion, he declares: "Everything has been written at the same time." Borges would analyze the anguish of the literary mind, capable of seeing the simultaneity of things, as in a painting, but only capable of writing those same things down successively, because language is successive. In Borges's story *The Aleph*, everything can be seen at once, and each and every one of the actions of this world, "pleasurable or atrocious," can occupy the same point in space, without superimposition or transparency.

Before Borges, but after Diderot, Balzac in his novel *Louis Lambert* had given the most desperate literary form to a desperate endeavor: how to give verbal expression to thought processes far swifter than words. Lambert is the most intelligent man in the world, yet his verbal impotence transforms him into the world's most stupid man. His thoughts are far too quick, and rich, and immediate, to achieve verbal expression. So he sits in a darkened room, unfurnished save for the chair (Van Gogh's chair?) occupied by this forecast of the man Nietzsche, Louis Lambert, whose thoughts take place in the order of the simultaneous while his words occur in the order of the successive. He can no longer communicate. The poignancy of this novel is all the greater since Balzac presents Lambert as his alter ego: they share the same biographical origins (in this novel, Balzac describes his life as a schoolboy) but not the same biographical destiny. Balzac writes a vast constellation of novels before his death at age fifty. Lambert cannot write, or even say, anything. He cannot communicate. In *Louis Lambert*, Balzac powerfully foresees not only the Nietzchean figure of intelligence and stupidity hand in hand but also Mann's Adrian Leverkühn in his Faustian exchange of creativity for illness and of genius for death. He poses all these literary and philosophical possibilities within the boundary of the relationship between time and the manifestation of time.

This is a subject that affects us directly in Latin America, and is central to our literature. We were born into modernity (after being excluded from it by the Spanish Counter-Reformation) during the Enlightenment. The eighteenth century offered us a linear conception of time; there was no other way of being modern. We were told to forget the instantaneous, circular, and mythical times of our origins in favor of a progressive, irreversible time, destined to an infinitely perfectible future. We traveled from the time of otherworldly Christianity to the time of secular Christianity, a time without a final judgment but, again like Christian time, a future-oriented temporality. Christianity leaves behind the paradise of the origin, the place of the fall and the corruption of nature, and addresses itself to redemption in a future, otherworldly paradise. The creso-hedonist societies of modern industrialism rush from the past, the cavern of the barbarian in Voltaire's eyes, in order to conquer an admirable future of infinite wealth and pleasure: progress is the name of secular eternity.

When this dream proved to be vain, and the brutal experience of our own time, from the war of the trenches to the concentration camps, demonstrated that progressive linearity offered too many exceptions for us to put our wholehearted, innocent faith in it, the critique of linear time became, positively, a way of recovering other times: the times of others, including our own, Latin American, time. The final judgment did take place, between the Marne and Dachau, between the Gulag and Hiroshima, and the creation of new times by Proust and Kafka, Woolf, Joyce, and Faulkner was a way of offering alternative temporalities to the exhausted linearity of eighteenth-century time. All of the rediscovered times of the West further coincided with the recovery of the true times of Latin American culture by Borges, Asturias, and Carpentier; by Neruda, Vallejo, and Paz; by Rulfo, Cortázar, and García Márquez: times in which the present contains past and future, because the present is the place of both memory and desire.

We shall not sacrifice anew what we are. We shall let them all speak: the twenty voices offered to us as a gift, from the heart of eighteenth-century France, by our friend Diderot.

III

Elisabeth de Fontenay has written that Diderot is the avant-garde which we lack today. He is, I repeat, our contemporary. During the ceremonies in Mexico City celebrating the seventy years of the poet Octavio Paz, the Brazilian poet Haroldo de Campos was telling me that the best Latin American novelist of the nineteenth century was the Brazilian Machado de Assis. I certainly agreed with him, but was ignorant of the reason Campos gave me: Machado had carefully read *Jacques Le Fataliste*, and by reading the European writer of the eighteenth-century avant-garde, he had become the writer of Latin America's nineteenth-century avant-garde, which, needless to say, became our own twentieth-century reality: both Diderot and Machado were, thus, our contemporaries.

Fontenay and Campos are warning us, besides, against the dangers of generalizing too much (as I, a confirmed reader of Vico, sometimes tend to do), against certain evils that, joyfully and guiltily, our own century hangs around the neck of the eighteenth century. If the Enlightenment consecrates a linear and progressive notion of human time, it is also true that, in the novels of Laurence

Sterne and Denis Diderot, it discovers all the intelligent exceptions to the futurizing ideology of Condorcet and the French Revolution.

A Latin American can be irritated by the Eurocentrist arrogance of the Enlightenment; but we must also recognize that the century of revolutions denied would-be social inferiorities, dissolved entrenched hierarchies, and granted to all human beings (while confusing Europeans with humankind and human nature) maximum potentialities. All this demanded an intensity of presence (Danton on the grandstand, Sade in the bedchamber) which, in the case of Diderot the novelist, is accompanied by a critical concept of time which he shares, as if it were the mission of the novel to save and project the best of the eighteenth century for our own times, with Sterne and *Tristram Shandy*. This critical concept can be presented, almost, as an equation: the greater the intensity of presence, the greater the intensity of time and the greater the sensation of the simultaneous.

Diderot chooses the form of the novel (the genre without genre, or the genre of all genres) to say that the sense of presence in a narrative text is what can transform the successive into the instantaneous and, in this way, identify desire and its object. For, after all, Diderot's problem is our problem: How to obtain what we desire? How to overcome the social, political, psychological, and purely material obstacles—time and space—which constantly rise between ourselves and the object of our desires? His answer is, typically, both direct and sinuous: Let us make ourselves present. Where? In a book. With whom? With the author and with the readers.

But it is the answer to the *How?* that is most important in Diderot. Yet it is a simple response: We make ourselves present through movement. We overcome obstacles and we obtain what we want because we move. It moves, therefore it desires.

Diderot employs an abbreviated time which hastens, stylizes, and finally makes visible a vivid sensation of the passage of time. Instead of describing, Diderot produces movement with the purpose of diminishing or accelerating the march of time. The production of movement as abbreviation, as velocity, occupies the place of the descriptive. Diderot sees description as an obstacle to presence. Do not describe, he pleads in *Jacques le Fataliste*:

Do me this favor, I beg of you, spare us the description of the
house and the doctor's character . . . and the progress of the cure;
jump, jump over all of that. Fact! To the fact! [*Au fait! Allons au
fait!*] Your knee is almost mended . . . and you have fallen in love.

Like most novelists past or present, Diderot has his own problem
with time. Perhaps there have been times without novels, but there
has never been a novel without time: *how* to present the temporal
fact is a fundamental narrative decision, for Scheherazade as well
as for Dumas, for Proust and for Agatha Christie. Scheherazade
narrates in order to gain time; Dumas, perhaps and deservedly so,
to lose it; Proust to recover it; and Christie to kill it. (There is thus
a double murder in her novels: both Roger Ackroyd and Time are
killed. Why not? comments Ezra Pound: Kill time, if you like your
time dead.)

Diderot's modernity is designed by the way he gains, loses,
kills, and recovers time. He does so because he has a quarrel with
the march of time. And he has this quarrel because the human
time known by the writer does not satisfy his immediate desires;
it postpones or cancels them. Diderot responds to this insufficiency
by creating a narrative time: he invents a time for his desire.

IV

Ever since the eighteenth century, Diderot knew that only a perfect
memory is chronological. No one has it. And who wants it?

Diderot tells us that true time is created by desire. But if desire
and time are to coincide, duration must be saved from the demands
of chronology. Rabelais achieved this through the verbal carnival
(as Mikhail Bakhtin has brilliantly defined it) which abolishes all
barriers between classes and between bodies. Cervantes achieved
it thanks to the multiplication of the levels of reading and of the
points of view of his character, Don Quixote. And Sterne, in
Tristram Shandy, obtained it through the mediation of paradox:
the constant digression in the mind of the narrator.

Diderot saves time from the tyranny of the calendar by producing
movement. He writes novels with the purpose of uniting movement,
time, and desire, which in reality are separated. He writes to clear

the obstacles erected by chronology on the way to the fulfillment of our desires. How does he do this? His works abound in dazzling suppressions of mediate time in benefit of immediate time, a time in which duration, movement, and desire identify one another instantly.

In *Le Salon*, for example, the author encounters "a woman as beautiful as an angel . . . I want to go to bed with her; I go: I have four children."

Diderot's novels do not depend on the verisimilitude or psychological autonomy of the characters. They depend on the author's capacity to draft (the expression is Kempf's) the reader as co-creator of the work.

The author (and how!) is already present in the book. Diderot is not coy about it; he does not disguise his author-ity; he makes it evident. He demands that the writer—Diderot—be recognized as the *creator* and not as the *mediator* of the narration. The conventional narrator supplies facts for the narration. But the iconoclastic narrator, such as Diderot, supplies the narrative itself. He refuses to answer the reader's questions about the characters. "What are they called, how did they meet?" asks the reader. And the author, because he is such, answers: "By chance"; or: "None of your business."

Yet this authorial presence, fulsome as it may seem, will need another presence: that of the reader. Diderot introduces the reader into the narrative with as much brio as he introduced the author, transforming the reader into the interlocutor of the author. In *Jacques le Fataliste*, the servant and his master travel the length of the roads of France, from inn to inn. This is the classical form of the pilgrimage, and literature has not been able to exhaust it: from the *Odyssey* to *Lolita*, passing through Cervantes and Lesage. It has also become one of the preferred formulas of the movies, from Chaplin's *Pilgrim* to Buñuel's *Milky Way*, with a stop at the lunch counters, motels, and highways of Capra's *It Happened One Night*. Histories of the road, marching histories, they are full of a sort of kinetic felicity. I underline the traditional character of the situation in Diderot so as to see clearly the novelty of the movement he then impresses on the form of movement itself: the ludicrous odyssey of Jacques and his master.

It so happens that this master has lost his watch, his tobacco pouch, and his horse, the three things that keep him going in life and, of course, on this trip. He is thus obliged, along with his servant, to occupy the time of the trip looking for what he lost during the trip itself, so that the loss of the objects becomes the object of the trip. But the interesting fact is that to this search for things Jacques and his master add, as a way of passing their time, a search for the narration. The master, who, in the narrator's words, is an obsessive and boring man, wants to hear the story of "The Loves of Jacques."

The search for the lost object thus becomes the search for the lost narrative. Over this double operation, yet another one hovers: the search for an abbreviated time so that desires can be fulfilled.

"What about your loves, Jacques?"

This question becomes the novel's *ritornello*: "Let us go back to your loves, Jacques." [*Revenons à tes amours.*]

Certainly this, the announced theme of the novel, is evaded, postponed, and constantly disguised, because, in the first place, the theme of Jacques's loves cannot be separated from the author's whim; second, it cannot be separated from the author's will as it confronts the reader's presence; and, finally, it cannot be separated from the variety and energy of movement which determine the duration that both author and reader are a part of.

The extraordinary thing about this situation is that Diderot should raise such obstacles with the purpose of hastening the meeting of desire and its object. The irony of the "Loves of Jacques" theme, of course, is that it is not the real theme or the real object of the narrative, but only the pretext for the author and the reader to show themselves naked, radically an *Author* and radically a *Reader*, bereft of the realistic, psychological, or melodramatic disguises that they should wear if the subject of *Jacques le Fataliste* truly were the "Loves of Jacques."

The author, then, presents himself as such and validates his most authoritarian rights. "It would depend only on me to make you wait for a year, or two or three, before you hear the story of the loves of Jacques," the author warns the reader, adding: "What would prevent me?" "I could send Jacques off to the islands," he concludes, only to exclaim later on: "Ah, imagine what this story could become in my hands, if only I felt like exasperating you, reader!"

The author's gleeful, playful, mocking exclamation would push us to ask him, wielding the sword of the reader's defense: Yes, tell us, what would you transform this story into, dear writer?

For this author who would have the reader wait three years while he sends Jacques off to the islands; this author who would drive the reader crazy out of sheer whim; this author, finally, can only exercise his irritating caprice by addressing himself to you: to the reader, the interlocutor. Indeed, Diderot constantly instates the reader within the book and finds in the book the common ground (the common-place) between author and reader. Baudelaire's hypocritical reader, brother, and fellow creature is in Diderot

> A passionate man such as you, reader
> A curious man such as you, reader
> A man as indiscreet as you are, reader
> A questioning man like you, reader

Diderot is telling us that the author's freedom is inseparable from the freedom of a reader recruited so as to give relief (relieve-relive), with his presence, to the presence of the writing: to its immediacy. This is the boundary of the author's whim: the reader's co-creation of the narrative, the engagement of another presence so that the author's presence may not vanish and become a whimsical redundancy: a false freedom. Without the reader, the author would speak to Nothing. Yet this does not mean (far from it; he is stubborn, indeed) that the author renounces his capriciousness. The reader is bound to win his own rights, fighting the author, not receive them as a gracious concession from him. Diderot establishes an agreement between the arbitrary possibilities of the writer and the narrative expectations of the reader. At a given moment, the narrator offers the following self-criticism of his authorial freedom as it meets the requirements of the reader.

Author addresses reader: "You are going to believe that now a bloody battle will ensue, with many wounded, etc."

The author proceeds to describe the battle. Then he adds: "And it would depend only on me for this to really occur; but if I did so, we would have to bid farewell to this story, which is the story of the loves of Jacques."

In this manner, Diderot confronts his right as an author with the reader's rights, but he also introduces the story of the battle and minutely relates it, while promising that he will do no such thing so as not to frustrate what he has in fact constantly frustrated: the continuation of a story that has yet to begin: "The Loves of Jacques." He proposes, by the way, the profoundest theme posed by the author's freedom: the author has to choose among several themes, and in so doing he is free, but he sacrifices the freedom to follow the other roads. We can only be free by constantly sacrificing other possibilities of freedom; freedom is made of the choices we do not or cannot make, as much as of those we do make.

The contract between the author and the reader is a game. And this game, Milan Kundera warns us in his theatrical adaptation of Diderot's novel *Jacques et Son Maître*, is one of the greatest inventions of Western civilization: the game of telling stories, inventing characters, and creating the imaginary paradise of the individual, from whence no one can be expelled because, in a novel, no one owns the truth and everyone has the right to be heard and understood.

I believe that Diderot understood this dimension of the novelist's work perfectly. His author, so sovereignly capricious, knows nevertheless that he owns only a small parcel of truth and is fully conscious that his rights, whatever these may be, would not exist without the reader (you). That is why the author, in the middle of the adventures of Jacques le Fataliste, can say to the reader:

> Reader, you treat me like an automat, and that is not correct . . . Enough! . . . Doubtlessly, it is sometimes necessary that I address your fancy, but it is also necessary that, at times, I address my own fancy.

Diderot's game is extremely serious. He wants to offer us our time as a synonym of our freedom. Jacques, the fatalist, constantly informs us that, when all is said and done, nothing is of any importance whatsoever, because "everything is written up there." But precisely because there are far too many things already written "up there," Jacques and his author, far from resigning themselves, multiply what is written "down here." Their writing is unforeseen, capricious, demanding, playful, free. This freedom becomes real in literature because Diderot presents it with a literary technique which is a technique of freedom: we are all in time, but we all have or should obtain the right to choose our time. This is an obligation, but also a right. It is a fatality, but also the freedom which transcends it. We choose to tell a story by sacrificing all the other stories we might tell. We do not have twenty mouths. We have only the comical, the humble, the superb possibilities of the mouth of fiction. These are its limits, but also its potentialities.

The impetus of movement in *Jacques le Fataliste* breaks through all expectations. If ever there was a revolutionary work of fiction, it is this: Diderot's novel offers the servant a fabulating gift which frees him from mental servitude, while obligating the master to yield authority as he loses himself in the interminable web of Jacques's stories. The author displays in all this an extraordinary freedom, but the reader, constantly, must exercise his own liberty vis-à-vis the author and decide, among the several versions proposed by the latter, "that one which suits you best, reader" [*celle qui vous conviendra la mieux*]. The reader, on receiving the work, shall be faced with the same dilemma that the author faced when writing it: he must choose.

V

Perhaps this is the very center of Diderot's narrative challenge: he writes the novel as a repertory of possibilities for the reader's freedom. The reader thus becomes the elector. (Again, the Spanish pun is clearer: the Reader, El Lector, is also Elector, the person who elects).

These possibilities are inscribed in time. Diderot's time is a repertory of possibilities: time is duration plus its possibilities. Time is movement, it is rhythm, it is an interrupted story, it is a postponed story; it is even, at times, a repeated story.

An example:

(First) We hear a story about what happened to a comrade of Jacques's captain when the servant served in the armies of France.

(Second) This story is interrupted and repeated exactly as it occurred to another person, a French officer called de Guerchy.

(Third) Both stories are postponed and the speakers (Jacques and his master) go back to the story of the loves of Jacques, in itself an eternally interrupted and postponed story.

But then (four) Diderot gives us an immediate synthesis of all three previous narrative moments, asking us: "But why could not the story of the loves of Jacques have happened to his captain, since it actually occurred to the French officer de Guerchy?"

Diderot's narrative syllogism presents us with a series of different events that sometimes coincide and sometimes do not, so that

(A) The interrupted stories
(B) The repeated stories and
(C) The stories postponed
become all together
(E) The simultaneous stories

The perimeter of our freedom, like these stories themselves, is both the reduced space of a cell and the highest heaven. Diderot tells us that the texts of his stories were written one alongside the other: these are contiguous stories. Let me offer two examples of Diderot's technique of narrative simultaneity.

The first consists of the use of narrative within narrative, a technique invented by the first novelist, Scheherazade, in *The Thousand and One Nights*. Diderot sees to it that this interpretation takes place physically:

Jacques tells us that three thugs threw themselves at him, struck him down, and robbed him . . .

The servant then interrupts his own narration of the mugging— he looks at his master and asks him, "But, my Master, what is the matter with you? Why do you clench your teeth, why do you tremble so . . . as if you faced an enemy?"

To which the master responds that he does in effect confront an enemy. "My sword is in my hand; I attack the villains (who have attacked you) and revenge you," the master tells Jacques, physically participating in the action set off by Jacques, with as much conviction as Don Quixote when he attacks the Moorish puppets in Master Pedro's theater. Their motivations are similar: they make the narrative present, they make us believe in it, they liberate the past (what is evoked) by making it present. Or perhaps they are only approaching an abyss imagined by Coleridge, like Diderot a disciple of Sterne, the great juggler of the Enlightenment. Coleridge proposes an essay on "someone who lived, not in time, past, present or future, but alongside time; collaterally to time" (*Table Talk*, 1833).

In a way, Diderot invites us into this contiguity when he employs the techniques of montage to narrate the most celebrated novel within a novel in *Jacques le Fataliste*: the story of Madame de la Pommeraye.

Jacques and his master find themselves in an inn, where they listen to the innkeeper as she tells the story of Mme de la Pommeraye and her vengeance on the Marquis des Arcis, while, throughout, she copes with administrative details: she is interrupted, she gives orders, she looks after other guests, she takes care of food and drink. She may ask, "What will you have for dessert?" but she never skips a beat in her narration of Mme de la Pommeraye's story.

The narrator, with a wink, gives a realistic tinge to this comedy. It is not uncommon, he says, that "when we tell a tale . . . brief as it may be . . . the narrator may be interrupted at times by his listener." In truth, Diderot is creating a new poetics of time and space in which narrator and listener are obligated to relate, to act in front of each other, to recognize that their text is not a definitive text but only a potential text.

Diderot creates a space-time continuum in which space-time A (the innkeeper's) fuses with space-time B (Mme de la Pommeraye's). He achieves this through successive cuts, overlaps, voices-off, flashbacks, and flashforwards. We read a flux of signs and feel as if Diderot, in the eighteenth century, had invented the cinema. It is not strange, indeed, that Robert Bresson should have filmed an adaptation of this section of *Jacques le Fataliste*. The film, called *Les Dames du Bois de Boulogne*, found in Maria Casares the perfect actress to play Mme de la Pommeraye, the passionate lady who, abandoned by her lover the Marquis des Arcis, drafts two lowly con women, mother and daughter, prostitutes and gamblers, and introduces them to the Marquis as examples, among other virtues, of piety and chastity. When the deluded Marquis marries the young woman (who won't accede to his advances otherwise), Mme de la Pommeraye reveals the truth and wreaks revenge on the dissolute though enlightened *macho*.

Kundera's theatrical adaptation, as staged by Susan Sontag at the American Repertory Theater in Cambridge, underlines the simultaneity achieved through narrative and filmic montage. The actress who plays the innkeeper and who tells the story becomes physically and seamlessly Mme de la Pommeraye: narrator and narrated are, materially, visually, temporally, the same. Kundera and Sontag both make us feel that Diderot's will to simultaneity is at the service of constant rupture. The object of this rupture is customary duration: the aim is to transform our habits of duration into a repertory of possibilities. And the purpose of this transformation, in its turn, is to quicken our sense of the presence of time. The film and the play are extremely acute ways of keeping alive Diderot's sense of freedom toward time, and they universalize his proposition of the interaction between reader and author in a book. We now have spectator and author, spectator and narrator, actors and audience, teller and listener, proving the validity of Diderot's premise.

There is a moment in the pilgrimage when Diderot offers us the following set of possibilities:

Jacques and his master—the author imagines—separate, "and I do not know, for the life of me, which of the two I should follow." What the author does advertise (to remind us that there *is* an author and *who* he is) is that if the reader decides to follow Jacques, he will have to deal with a long and complicated story; but if he follows the master, he will surely die of tedium.

This is a simple, binary choice. Later on, Jacques and his master approach a castle. But this is not true. They are simply approaching the place where they spent the past night. But where did they spend the past night?

1) In a great city, in a whorehouse.
2) With an old friend who offered them a splendid feast.
3) With some mendicant monks, who mistreated them in the name of God.
4) In an immense hostelry where they were overcharged for a meal served in silver trays.
5) In the house of a French peer, where they lacked all the necessities in the midst of all the superfluities.
6) With a country priest.
7) Drinking excellent wines in a Benedictine abbey.

All these options are narratively possible, but they do not interest the master. Obsessed, he only wishes to return to the story of the loves of Jacques.

"What about your loves, Jacques?"

The servant has said a hundred times that "up there it was written that he would never end his story," and "now I see—says the author as he concludes the novel—that he was right." Yet he adds: "I see, reader, that this irritates you. Very well. You can then take up the story where we left it and continue it as you feel fit. Or if you prefer . . . discover the name of the prison where Jacques is serving time" (purging a crime he did not commit, the murder of the Chevalier de St. Ouin, a crime committed by the master, which the fatalist accepts as his own since "it was written up above") and, concludes the Narrator, "search him out; question him."

In the meantime, adds Diderot, the reader can always reread the conversations between Jacques and his master, "the most important work to have appeared since the *Pantagruel* of Master François Rabelais." After this advertisement for himself, Diderot lets the reader, if he so wishes, become the new author or continue to be the reader—or rather—the rereader.

VI

Diderot culminates his narrative discourse with a reference to Rabelais. It is not an isolated allusion. Sterne and *Tristram Shandy*, Cervantes and *Don Quixote*, are the other two Musketeers, along with Rabelais, of the potential novel, the incomplete novel, as Bakhtin calls it. Diderot is the d'Artagnan of this story. Deriving the lessons from Rabelais, Cervantes, and Sterne, his narrative radicalism contemporaneously informs us that the novel, far from dying, has hardly scratched the surface of its possibilities. The novelty and freedom of Kundera's *Book of Laughing and Forgetting*, Calvino's *If on a winter's night a traveler* . . . , Grass's *The Flounder*, Goytisolo's *Count Julian*, Roth's *The Counterlife*, Saramago's *The last year in the life of Ricardo Reis*, Rushdie's *Shame*, and Ackroyd's *Hawksmoor* are the best proof that the great lessons of Rabelais, Cervantes, Sterne, and Diderot have not been lost, and that the post-Joycean death of the novel of realism, psychology, and linear unities in fact secretly heralded the birth of the potential novels of a Bakhtinian stripe. These are the novels that, without

thematically needing to espouse them, truly address the alterity of
life in the post-industrial world, the uncertainties of life under the
nuclear threat, the multiplication of communications, and the swamps
of information competing for our attention today.

One of the proofs of Diderot's genius is that he transformed the
heritage of potentiality in the novel into the very subject matter of
his open narrative: the novel as an inexhaustible repertory of possibilities. We will be satisfied with nothing less in the present time.
Rabelais, Sterne, Cervantes, and Diderot remind us of the forgotten
possibilities hidden in the origin of the novel. But they also remind
us that a novel is a permanently open and unfinished work. All
great novels, in this sense, are potential novels.

First, they are not exhausted by the politics practiced when the
novel was written, or by the society in which the novel appeared.
These may disappear or change, but the work of art remains.

Second, the novel does not limit itself to the social, political,
psychological, and philosophical contexts that inevitably accompany it; rather, it remains permeable to new meanings, new inter-
pretations, and new manners of reception by readers unforeseen
by the author. These readers, on reading the novel, approach an
unread work: they read it for the first time. And no matter, as
Borges says in *Pierre Menard, Author of Don Quixote*, how much
prestige, criticism, or simple enjoyment has accreted to the work.
Hearsay will never substitute the experience of reading *Don Quixote*, for the first time, in the year 2000.

Third, the novel is able to be or do all this because its formal
definition is uncertainty and this lack of certainty leads it to look
for openings. The novel, if it is a genre at all, is an open genre,
and openness means, again in Bakhtinian terms, dialogue, but not
only dialogue of characters; it also means dialogue of genres, of
languages, of historical times, of civilizations, of unpublished possibilities.

The novel both reflects and creates an unfinished world made
by men and women who are also unfinished. Neither the world nor
its inhabitants have said their last word. The potential novel is
thus the announcement and perhaps even the guaranty of a potential
history. Of a potential life. We hope that we are part of an unfinished human presence expressing itself through narrative language.
All great novels, of course, say this, but Diderot makes it evident.

Gogol

Great minute, solemn minute. At my feet burns my past; above
me, through the fog, shines the indecipherable future. Life of my
soul, of my genius, I implore thee: Do not hide! Watch over me at
this minute and do not abandon me throughout this year that so
seductively announces itself. Be brilliant, full of activity, and totally
dedicated to work and tranquillity . . . Mysterious, impenetrable
year of 1834! Look at me. Here I am, kneeling at your feet.

Nikolai Gogol wrote this letter during a night of passage: between
December 31, 1833, and January 1, 1834. Its tone indicates a
certain pathos whose very invocation of tranquillity for creation
disguises its turbulent complexity. We suspect that behind the
New Year's resolution there stands a restless imagination, however
simple daily life may be. And it isn't, in spite of appearances. To
be sure, this life lacks sensational incidents: it is memorable only
because it is the life of Nikolai Gogol. Little happens in it, especially those things that thicken the plot of human existence;
there are no passions, no erotic intimacy with men or with women,
no political convictions.

There is family and fatherland, but for Gogol the question is
how to leave them behind as soon as possible. There is an admiring
friendship for one man only, and he is a generous genius: Alexander
Pushkin, founder of modern Russian literature, the incomparable
Pushkin, equal only to Dante and Shakespeare. But a Dante and
a Shakespeare eccentrically set in the vast, powerful, enigmatic

country that "does not give answers" about its future, as Gogol puts it in the famous final passage of *Dead Souls*:

> And where do you fly to, Russia? Answer me! . . . She doesn't answer. The carriage bells break into an enchanted tinkling, the air is torn to shreds and turns into wind; everything on earth flashes past, and, casting worried, sidelong glances, other peoples and nations step out of her way.

If we compare this passage with the less celebrated epistolary excerpt that I quoted earlier, we come (in the letter) upon several constants of the Gogolian imagination and (in the novel) upon the way the writer transcends his own obsessions. In the letter, there is movement up and down, down and up, as in a column of words: "At my feet burns my past; above me . . . shines the . . . future . . . Here I am, kneeling at your feet." But this movement is also horizontal, as in a fugue: time cannot be deciphered; it develops through time, a hidden time: a succession of masked days: "I implore thee: Do not hide!" Time, almost by definition, flees, disguises itself, shrouds itself in fog; time is an impostor, a disguised being who always refuses to show us its true face.

The response to time conceived in this way can only be that of a pathetic imagination: kneeling, but without giving up the aspiration toward higher things: going from low to high, from the contemplation of the past that burns "at my feet" to the future that shines "above me." Time is a constant postponement: a perpetually deferred identity. Poised on the threshold of a year that will be decisive for him, Gogol implores the fruits of an enigmatic, displaced time, vertically conceived, and confronts it with the romantic forms of time and literature: flight, displacement, voyage.

In the landscape of the novel, Gogol draws a vast horizon perpendicular to an erect time. This horizontality has a name: Russia. This name has an object that incarnates it: the troika. And this thing, the troika, moves quickly, aiming for the future, the goal, destiny, sowing admiration and terror among all "other peoples and nations." But this noisy and swift contraption has two characteristics of its own. The first is that it is driven by a crook, an adventurer, and a rogue (*picaro*), a disguised man whose identity is unknown to anyone: a man, in this sense, whose identity depends on who others decide him to be. His name is Chichikov, an em-

bezzler of uncertain identity who deals in identities far more uncertain than his own, those of dead serfs, which the great Russian
con man tries to buy from landowners, to declare them to the
authorities as having perished in a catastrophe, and so pocket
40,000 rubles, a profit on an investment of 500 rubles, on the
basis of five to ten rubles per dead soul.

A deception; but, above all, a postponement of identity. Time
does not deliver us its destiny; neither does the character; and the
land certainly doesn't. Why, then, should the writer do so: deliver
unto us his destiny or that of his time, his space, his character?
The art of Nikolai Gogol swirls around the problem of identities
and identification which is postponed, or deceptive. Gogol raises
it to literary form with such force and imagination, with such irony
and sense of the fantastic, that he actually reaches but one identity,
and that is his own identification with the problem of existence.

Let us bear this final triumph of the writer in mind as we consider
the multiple formal aspects of his work. For, as Donald Fanger
indicates in his admirable book *The Creation of Nikolai Gogol*, the
Russian author exemplified more radically than anyone else in his
century the power of the literary medium, and he did so, precisely,
through a fusion of form and content. Both are form, and both are
content. To investigate where one ends and the other begins is to
discover the very nature of Gogol's art, an art in which Georg
Simmel's warning, quoted by Fanger, becomes the operating principle and evidence of composition: form and content are relative
and subjective areas of thought; what is form in one aspect is
content in another.

Let me return to the two texts, dissimilar but finally complementary to one another, that I have quoted here. How can we
separate in the letter, the vital statistics—the dates, the common-
place of good resolutions for the New Year, Gogol doing what we
all do on comparable anniversaries—from the writing; that is, from
imagination as applied to time, from the postponement of certitude,
from the pathos of a prostrate humiliation, from the evoked expression of desire, and from the expression of a certain unarmed (if
not disarming) frankness which, on reflection, we start to understand as false sincerity, a sincerity expressed only to justify sincerity, and thus an insincere sincerity?

What counts is the literary reality of the letter, not the toast to the New Year, and this reality is dynamic, imaginary, and ironic. It responds to the enigma of time with the enigma of man, in the same manner that the invocation of the Russian troika responds to the enigma of a national destiny with one answer only. That answer consists of the irony of the writer who postpones his own destiny and his own identity, in the same way that time and space (the year 1834 and the Russian land) do so, so that all these elements are transformed into the only reality that is truthful, worthy of our attention, or, at the very least, handy: the reality of literature. A fragile reality. Was Gogol's life less so?

II

Gogol affirms repeatedly that "I have no life outside of literature." In this, as in so many other things, he is the elder brother to Franz Kafka, who said, "All that is not literature bores me, including conversations about literature." Kafka writes in his diary: "I hate everything that is not literature." Gogol foreshadows him: "I have no life outside of literature."

This attitude, explains Fanger, goes against the grain of the romantic expectation: the creation of a superior art "confers meaning on the person of the creator, confers upon him an exemplary quality," in relation both to his vision and to his thought, and "stimulates curiosity" about a double transmutation. Conscience and the experience of life become art, and art becomes conscience and experience. Finally, it is the person's identity that achieves primacy, even if to do so, it must become an artistic identity.

This romantic alchemy is not possible in the case of Gogol. Gogol is the Russian anti-Byron, without Missolonghis or incest, scandal, or duels, or lovers of either sex: no wife, no children. No profound relations with politics, with sex, with society, family, or nation, unless they all serve to reflect an absence and a lie: an exaggeration which in its absence, falsity, or disproportion can evoke the verbal ghosts capable of approximating us to their only reality and their only identity, which is that of a text by Nikolai Gogol.

This radical poetics is essential to understand the artistic and human achievement of Gogol. "We all came out of Gogol's 'Overcoat,' " Dostoevsky said, famously though apocryphally. I always wondered how another writer of such extraordinary magnitude could have said this and why we should believe him. Why does *The Idiot* come out of "The Overcoat"? Why, as Wordsworth said, is the child the father of the man?

Gogol lives his short life—barely forty-two years—as a long illness or, better still, as a fatigue.

In this, too, he resembles Kafka, who in his notes jots down a legend of Prometheus in which "all are finally fed up with this senseless legend. The Gods are tired, the eagles are tired, the wound heals painfully." This image of a tragic fatigue brings to mind Nietzsche's affirmation: "Whoever has built a new heaven has found the strength to do so only in his own hell." Camus sees in Prometheus the great myth of the rebellious intelligence: he is the father of messianism, fraternity, and the refusal of death.

But where Camus may see an intelligent rebellion and Kafka an equally lucid fatigue, Gogol would have found the intelligence of an absence. Camus describes a rebellious and melodramatic intelligence, not tragic, which can never decide that its enemy is right. Kafka embodies a tired intelligence as the root of his own lucidity. Gogol, finally, represents the lucidity of absence. His true biography, Donald Fanger implies, can only be expressed as art, as implication, as absence.

Fanger adds: "He did not come to define himself through being bound in some continuing experiential way to class or politics or place, and if he was a slave to his body, he contrived to be that in the way that could not further his self-knowledge through experience of another."

Gogol's reflection on and knowledge of the body is limited to the realms of hypochondria and the functioning (or nonfunctioning) of the digestive system. His sole personal erotic text is perhaps a letter of the year 1837, written as he watches the slow agony of a beautiful Russian youth, Joseph Vielgorsky, in Rome. To be sure, there is nothing to be gained by speculating on the probable impotence or homoeroticism of Gogol. The importance of the circumstance is that for Gogol the other's body is only attractive *in extremis*: the body is only desirable in death or the proximity of death.

But this fact, along with the rest of his short life, has no reality except insofar as it translates into literature, and one cannot say that necrophilia is a central erotic factor in Gogol: death, in his work, is also ironical. Akaky Akakyevich, the petty Petersburg bureaucrat, returns as a ghost to frighten and despoil the owners of elegant topcoats. Irony is always a displacement of identity (it is also, at all times, the only possible relation with the present): who are the dead, the list of serfs, or the landlords who sell them to Chichikov: Sobakevich, Plyushkin, Nozdryov?

The author's manifest intentions perhaps deserve more respect than any psychoconarion speculation: life is indistinguishable from literature: "I live and breathe through my works." That is why Fanger entitles his book *The Creation of Nikolai Gogol*. Not the art of Gogol separate from the life of Gogol, but the creation of the work as a reality inseparable from the creation of the man. The measure of Gogol the individual is that of his art. Gogol has no existence outside of his art, and his art is but the projection of the absence of his life. Like Akaky Akakyevich in "The Overcoat," like Khlestakov in *The Inspector*, and like Chichikov in *Dead Souls*, Nikolai Gogol is also a character in a text.

I do not think, therefore, that I betray Donald Fanger's intentions if I dare, in passing, to invert his definition in order to find in Nikolai Gogol the most Gogolian of characters: Gogol created his own life as if it occurred in a Gogol story.

Balzac said that "reality has taken great pains to imitate fiction." He meant by this something that people in Latin America understand fully: reality constantly surpasses the imagination of its inventors. The Mexican dictator Antonio López de Santa Anna has not yet found an imagination that encompasses his grotesque splendor; we have many other contemporary characters who equally surpass the imaginative fever of any contemporary Gogol. The autumns of our patriarchs are, naturally, also winters and springs, as well as dog days of a quietude akin to death.

In 1967, in London, Vargas Llosa and I invited a group of Latin American novelists to contribute to a book that would be titled *The Fathers of the Fatherlands*. Each of them—Gabriel García Márquez, Alejo Carpentier, Augusto Roa Bastos, José Donoso, Julio Cortázar, Miguel Otero Silva—would write fifty pages on his favorite national tyrant. But it turned out to be impossible to coordinate that many dissimilar wills. The book did not jell, but from this initiative were born *The Autumn of the Patriarch, Reasons of State,* and *I, the Supreme.* Surely, in this original idea as well as in its rich, although unforeseen, results, it was not only the model of past reality—Juan Vicente Gómez, Cipriano Castro, Doctor Francia—that permitted the creation of these works, but, perhaps above all, the quality of the imagination of García Márquez, Carpentier, and Roa Bastos. The dictators rest—in peace or in torture, who can know?—but securely in their graves. Their paper reality was not determined by any event in their lives. And yet: can we now imagine those lives without the refraction given us by those novels?

The life of Nikolai Gogol occupies this singular position in relation to his own work: it lacks any interest except if it is seen as the creation of Nikolai Gogol. The text presupposes the life in the sense that the latter has any sense (or is legible) as a text by Gogol. Retrospectively, although simultaneously, that life is part of a Gogolian universe which transcends the author and his works in order to create a Gogolian tradition. Its contemporary lineage is clear in such works as those by Franz Kafka and Milan Kundera. But Gogol himself is the heir to the carnival tradition of literature employed by Mikhail Bakhtin to describe the work of Rabelais, as he is the heir also of the tradition of Cervantes, whose grand themes coincide notoriously with those cited by Fanger to explain Gogol: metamorphosis, the road, displacement, identity, recognition.

Only within these bounds do I speak of a Gogolian life inseparable from a Gogolian work and a Gogolian tradition.

III

Gogolian Gogol:

Donald Fanger recalls two statues of the author. One, done in 1909, is by the sculptor Andreev. Seated wrapped in an overcoat, head hanging and shoulders drooping, Nikolai Gogol is a figure of perverse melancholy. The statue reflects a work that, according to Merezhkovsky, was "a long exercise in artistic deformation." The other statue, erected in Moscow on orders from Stalin on the occasion of the writer's one hundredth anniversary, presents a tall, erect, defiant man, his eyes blazing, his chin thrust forward: this is Gogol the realist, Gogol the progressive, Gogol the citizen about to jump onto his tractor. Useless to remember that the apparition of the second statue signified the disappearance of the first, which was restored only on the death of the dictator.

Between both statues—the tragic, the heroic—jumps a gnome. This is Gogol the character in Gogol, the "new" student who arrives from the Ukrainian countryside at the school of higher sciences at Nezhin, with a beaked profile and a little head bobbing out of his winter clothing as if out of a collar of feathers. A bird hermetically sealed, writes his fellow student Lubich-Romanovich, inside his excessive clothes, far too warm for the climate. He takes a long time to undress, adds the school companion. The clothing—the overcoat—is a carapace like Samsa's in *The Metamorphosis*: the body is absent, its presence and its pleasure postponed.

He is called "the mysterious dwarf." He must, his biographer Henri Troyat tells us, be secretive: secrecy is the spring of his life. He writes to his mother from school: "No one hears me complain . . . I praised those who were the cause of my disgrace. It is true that for all of them I am an enigma. No one guesses who I am . . ." This human enigma, beaked bird and mysterious gnome, appears in the academic, bureaucratic, editorial, and literary world of Russia. He is a reality that is also a deception: his mother believes that Gogol, like a character in Gogol, is the author of all the successful novels published in Russia. The son is responsible for sowing the seed of this new deception. He is what he is, but with a dimension that disguises him and deceives all others. The disguise can be quite delirious: his mother comes to believe, and says so to anyone wishing to listen to her, that her son Nikolai Gogol is the genius who has invented all the technological marvels appearing in Russia, one after the other, in those days. Mother attributes to son nothing less than the invention of the railroad engine and the steamship. Mother is son's accomplice, the ideal reader of Gogol the character in Gogol.

But, besides the mother-reader, the Gogolian Gogol has yet another accomplice for this displacement of identities: the brother-writer. The origin of *Dead Souls* is worthy of a novel in itself. It is the gift—the offering, rather—that Pushkin, one night, makes to Gogol. Gogol writes in his *An Author's Confession:* "For some time now, Pushkin has been inviting me to undertake a great work . . . He has told me: Why, having the power to divine man and to paint his full body with but a few strokes, as if he were alive, do you not undertake an important work? What a pity! He went on to talk about my weak complexion, the illnesses that could put an end to my days. He cited the example of Cervantes, who, though the author of a few admirable novellas, would never have occupied among writers the position he now holds if he had not sat down to write *Don Quixote.* In conclusion, Pushkin offered me his own theme, from which he wanted to extract a sort of poem. Listening to him, I believe that he never would have ceded this story to anyone else but me." Pushkin's gift was the story of an adventurer who bought, at a low price, the dead souls of the propertied estates, profiting from an anomaly in the law which permitted the owners to retain the names of dead serfs, deriving economic profit from the swindle.

In possession of his theme, which he conceived as a comic displacement within the width and breadth of Russia, Gogol the Gogolian must flee Russia so as to write secretly, from afar, disguised as a Russian in Paris and Rome, inventing deceits parallel to those of Chichikov and thus maintaining the Gogolian homonymy of life and work, the continuing creation of Nikolai Gogol. Is there anything more Gogolian, for example, than his return to Russia in 1839, when, already safely back in Moscow, he writes a letter to his mother from there but dated as if from Trieste, in which he tells her: "As regards my return to Russia. I have not yet made up my mind. I am in Trieste, where I have begun taking sea baths . . ."

Back in the Ukraine, Mrs. Gogol's white head nods. She deserves the lie: she is her son's original accomplice. As Troyat notes: "The same way that others feel relief in telling the truth, [Gogol] feels at ease only in imposture . . ."

He tries to heal his body; he tries to heal his fortunes. He seeks time for his imagination and his writing; he moves in official circles; he seeks patronage, praises the Tsar and authoritarianism. He maneuvers ceaselessly to survive as a creative enigma, as a disguised being, as a Gogolian character, offending in equal measure the Occidentalizing progressives gathered under the renovating banner of Belinsky and the traditionalist Slavophiles and officialists grouped under the reactionary aegis of Pogodin.

One must conclude that he preferred the former because he was more Gogolian with the latter. He asks Pogodin to lodge him in his house in Moscow in 1842, the year of the censorship first and the publication later of *Dead Souls*. In Pogodin's house, he then lives an unpublished chapter of Chichikov's comic epic. Gogol detests Pogodin, surely because of the Slavophile critic's weakness in giving him lodging, and ceases to speak to him. The host and his undesired guest communicate through letters sent from bedroom to bedroom, and in them they insult and mutually pity each other for having to live together under the same roof. Pogodin sends Gogol his food; he even sends him money. These are reasons for Gogol to hate him even more and to insist on overstaying his welcome. He is a haughty beggar indeed, worthy of a comedy from the pen of Plautus, Molière, or Sheridan: worthy, let us say it, of Gogol's *Inspector-General*. He deserves it all and is obliged to give nothing in return. He is Gogol, a character in Gogol.

Pogodin complains bitterly. He reproaches Gogol for his whims, his hypocrisy, his lies, his crude manners toward Pogodin, Pogodin's wife, and Pogodin's mother. But Gogol has established only one condition to accept the hospitality of the suffering literary critic: "No one should oppose me, ever."

When, a short time after the publication of the novel, Gogol at long last leaves the Pogodin place, each of the parties has his final say in letters that they send to other people. Pogodin writes: "I sigh with relief . . . A mountain has fallen from my shoulders . . . Gogol is an abominable being . . ." And Gogol writes: "Pogodin is vile, dishonest, and lacking in delicacy . . . It is a vile thing to remind the man you are lodging that he must be grateful . . . Pogodin deserves nothing but my scorn . . ."

There is no difference between daily life and the literary work: both are the object of constant deformation. Gogol leaves the stage shared with the Pogodins and displaces himself anew, flees Russia, the popular success of *Dead Souls*, and the stupid critical reaction the novel receives: "A superficial work, a potboiler, a caricature of real Russian life," writes Bulgarin in *The Northern Bee*. "A gross cartoon . . . Unbelievable characters, exaggerated, repulsive rotters, imbeciles" opposed to the patriotic conception of literature, says Polevoi in *The Russian Messenger*. "A vulgar story. Gogol is a poor writer who thinks that Chichikov exists in real life . . . Bad grammar, solecisms, pleonasms," exclaims Senkovksy in *Library for Reading*. And all together now: Gogol is worse than Paul de Kock.

Belinsky, the great Belinsky, takes up the burden of the defense. But Gogol goes off to take the waters in Germany, and from Gastein he demands, as if his health depended on it, to know the adverse criticism he is fleeing from. "My sins, show me my sins, my soul thirsts to know them," he writes in 1842.

He has given his body to no one. So the doctors take it over. That same year, everyone can see a character by Gogol taking cold baths at the beach at Ostende in Belgium: a trembling, wet bird surrounded by Gogolian medics. Dr. Krikkenberg in Halle orders him to go live on a cold island to cure his nerves. Dr. Carus in Dresden orders him to take the waters at Carlsbad until he swells and cures his liver. Dr. Preissnitz in Gralfenburg orders him to immerse himself once again in cold waters.

From a wintry beach, Gogol writes in 1845: "I live as in a dream, at times draped in wet sheets, at times sunk in a tub, at times frictioned, at times sprinkled, at times running convulsively until I heat up. All I feel is cold water; I neither feel nor know anything else."

"My God!" Balzac wrote from his deathbed. "Twenty thousand cups of coffee have killed me!" Oh, my demons, Gogol could have echoed him, I have been killed by twenty thousand immersions in freezing water: I prefer the heat of hell!

He returns to Russia in 1848, emaciated and bent, his body a perpetual question mark. The character now comes to bid farewell to the land without answers and to indecipherable time. He goes to parties, he gives them. Sometimes he appears disguised as a charming rogue, a mime, a seducer, a perfect host who prepares punch and reads aloud; other times, he is the miserable and uncouth landlord, the provincial sleaze who knows it all and yawns in his guests' faces: he is Khlestakov, he is Sobakevich, he is Nozdryov, all at once.

In agony, he receives a certain Father Mathias, a priest with a red beard (again stepping out of a work by Gogol) who assails him on his deathbed: "The debility of your body is no excuse for avoiding the fast!" "Denounce Pushkin, he is a sinner and a pagan!" "Think about saving your soul, not about stringing phrases together on a piece of paper!"

He does not write. He does not eat. He does not sleep. He dreams: diabolical temptations. He prepares for death by wrapping himself in a cold sheet. The final physician, a Dr. Klimmentov, arrives and sprays his head with a mouthful of vodka. Cold water; hot water. Gogol, delirious, exclaims—his last words: "Forward! Charge, charge the windmill!"

The step toward death is the step toward the written page: Gogol the character in Gogol dies invoking Don Quixote and enters the living tomb of the book, the source of modern narrative: the Cervantean universe. What matter if his funerals are Gogolian unto death? Slavophiles and Occidentalists fight for the privilege of burying the tiny body crowned in laurels and seemingly made of wax. The earthly struggle resolves itself in final chaos: the mob invades the church, everyone wishes to kiss the writer's dead hand, pluck a leaf from the wreath, ascertain if the cadaver laughs still; they overturn the bier; they flee.

Gogolian Gogol is dead. He leaves as inheritance only a golden watch that almost certainly belonged to Alexander Pushkin, and an overcoat with a velour collar that perhaps belonged to Akaky Akakyevich.

IV

Gogol's complete works were in the process of being printed when the writer died in 1852. Censorship immediately suppressed them. Gogol, who in life wanted only to be a man of order, respectful of constituted authority, was feared, says Troyat, in death. Did he become a revolutionary when he died?

Rather, Gogol's ghost, a character in Gogol, continued to refuse all forms of facile characterization: he was neither Andreev's tragic Gogol nor the heroic Gogol of Stalin. He was only a writer whose life and death confuse and construe themselves (or reconstruct themselves, since life and work are also constantly annihilating each other in the act of creation/re-creation) in a pulverized encounter of minimal humors and spectral anti-matter: life and work, work and life.

Gogol's life and work germinate from a microscopic reality which breeds thanks to an anomalous vision of things: deformed, eccentric, grotesque. Traditional criticism has lent minute attention to Gogol's perverse inclination to give human faces and bodies the form of grotesque and banal objects. In *Dead Souls*, for example, there are characters whose faces are like elongated cucumbers, or like the gourds from which balalaikas are made. Plyushkin the landlord has eyes that spring like swift little mice from under his high, bushy eyebrows. And in "Nevsky Prospekt," the ladies' sleeves would allow them to rise suddenly in the air "if their escorts did not hold them back." "To lift a lady in the air"—concludes the Gogolian sentence—"is as easy and enjoyable . . . as taking a glass of champagne to one's lips."

Gogol's fiction is dominated by sudden change, says Fanger. But the point is not to evoke the several metamorphoses, descendants of Ovid and forerunners of Kafka, that illustrate many of Gogol's tales: the transformations of women and witches in the Mirgorod tales; the transformation of a man into his own nose in the tale of that name. Rather, the point is to understand that the theme of transformation—of change—is deeply important; it is, in a way, the root of all things: the reality of reality, so to speak.

Gogol puts it beautifully in "Nevsky Prospekt." The symbol of romantic purity, the painter Piskaryov, for whom the loss of purity is identical to the loss of intelligence, has followed a strikingly beautiful girl down the principal avenue in Petersburg, the Nevsky Prospekt. The girl, as you may recall, leads the painter to the castle of impurity. On entering the bordello, Piskaryov discovers that his sweetheart is a courtesan, as foolish as she is vulgar. He loses his ideal but he gains his dream. And yet, between both—ideal and dream—a sensation of intense restlessness permits the author to understand that "a demon had broken the whole world into pieces, immediately mixing them up without any order."

Metamorphosis, which is one of Gogol's great themes, means something that goes beyond sudden change, and this something is the reconstitution of our original unity, broken and tossed to the winds by diabolical forces: we do not know who we are; what we take to be real is a deceit; the task of men and women, especially of the artist, above all of the artist, is to struggle, with no hope of victory, but without losing heart, to discover the hidden reality, the reality one can reconstitute behind the appearance of dispersion. There is a true reality behind the screen of social position, bureaucratic function, the false identity that others give us, and, above all, behind a falsifying use of language.

I shall say of the art of Luis Buñuel that rupture is the price of experience. But it is also the condition of poetry, nurtured by the plurality of the senses. This acceptance of the diverse permits art to truly aspire to and perhaps to actually reconquer the unifying vision. The paradox of the poetic is that it feeds on this rupture while at the same time trying to heal it and build a new unity on the synthesis of lost originality and concrete experience.

One could say something similar about the art of Nikolai Gogol. The Gogolian metamorphosis is not gratuitous. It is no mere spectacular effect. And it is no simple diversion (which it could, legitimately, be). In Gogol, it is not, because metamorphosis does not stop at its own game but, rather, insistently presents itself as the basis for a whole formal and thematic construction, without which it would be difficult to conceive modern fiction.

V

"Nevsky Prospekt lies at each hour of the day and night," writes Gogol as he concludes his first tale of St. Petersburg. It is the devil himself who there lights the street lamps and sheds light on men and things, but only so as to "show them under an illusory and untruthful aspect."

In order to see reality once more, transcend lies, and clarify deceit, Gogol sets up quite a literary strategy. He asks us, first of all, to confide in perspective, but also in proximity. The lenses we need to see the sun are as necessary as those we require to see insects.

Yet we shall see nothing at all unless we bathe the whole world in the light of strangeness. Reality will always deceive us if we complacently accept it as such. Gogol—this is his second weapon, following that of metamorphosis—invites us to conceive reality as a deception and violently wake up through the sensation of strangeness that the writer, with quite extraordinary results, employs throughout his work. Donald Fanger has remarked that it is almost impossible to render outside of the Russian language this Gogolian strangeness, what he calls this rendering strange, or *ostranenie*, which first expresses itself through the communication of language. But if Gogol's language does not carry over in translation, the style does: in Gogol, it is the style of a strangeness which orchestrates the multiple voices of the narrative and of the dialogue. Gogol creates a new literary discourse based on synecdoche, in which a detail reveals the totality—the Latin formula of the *pars pro toto*—and so integrates a mosaic style, or an orchestra style, in which disparate and discrete elements unite to create the illusion of totality.

This illusion depends on a certain use of language, and it is at this level, immediately, that stylistic totality starts conspiring against itself: we must not believe even in this unity; it is yet another deception, and Gogol's language, "exotic," "strange," "unfamiliar," is a forecast of Bertolt Brecht's alienation of the spectator.

I am incapable of citing the examples of Gogol's verbal strangeness. But I can evoke the strangeness of actions which could not sustain themselves without a comparable strangeness of language. Such as this: The landowner Sobakevich, who looks like a crow and whose possessions—tables, chairs, sofas—proclaim, "I, too, resemble Sobakevich!", offers Chichikov an epic meal—mutton, cream tarts, turkey stuffed with eggs, rice, and liver—served by a woman who resembles a goose. Sobakevich's speech is as copious as the meal, and his powers of persuasion and haggling are extravagant as he negotiates the sale of the dead souls. Yet all this wealth of characterization does not attain its Gogolian pinnacle until the moment when Chichikov offers his hand in farewell to the headstrong Sobakevich and the landlord does not let go but, rather, steps on Chichikov's foot and holds him there with a mad, comic violence which we will recognize, to a different purpose but with the same Gogolian strangeness, in Stavrogin in *The Possessed* and in Buñuel's *L'Age d'Or*. Stavrogin pulls the nose (that most Gogolian of appendages) of a guest at a party. Buñuel's actor (Gaston Modot) pulls the beard (the most Castilian of offenses) of an orchestra director while he is conducting Wagner. Their acts are the offspring of a Gogolian-style provocation, as are the cel-

ebrated pranks of the Surrealists in the Paris of the twenties: Peret
& Breton's invitation to slap the faces of the dead; the public
slapping of a society lady (like Margaret Dumont?) by Louis Aragon
during a banquet at the Closerie des Lilas.

Keep your hands to yourself: Chichikov refuses to play cards
with the cheat Nozdryov; this gambler, who calls his own hands
tenderly, in French, *les superflues*, attempts to strike his guest's
cheek with an arm as uncontrollable as Richard Nixon's, but Chichikov locks Nozdryov's arms together and holds on while his host
calls his servants to save him from the unwanted embrace.

This same phenomenon takes over other scenes in *Dead Souls*,
notably in Chapter 8, when in Chichikov's bedroom, "a room well
known by the reader, with the door blocked by a wardrobe and
the corners swarming with cockroaches," the protagonist looks at
his face in a mirror, admiring himself for one whole hour, until
he gives himself a gentle punch on the chin and says to himself:
"Come on, handsome!" This is neither strange nor exceptional;
one could write another novel concerning what people do in front
of mirrors when mirrors are looking back at us. What is exceptional
is that Chichikov should top his self-celebration by executing a
cartwheel. The effects of such an exercise, adds Gogol, were not
harmful: the night table trembled and the clothes brush fell on the
floor.

Gogolian strangeness, in its minute but insinuating aspects, is
characterized at times by an overriding sense of metamorphosis.
There are women with red shawls but *sans* stockings, crossing the
streets like bats at dusk; there is the superior use of the verbal
non sequitur, almost an intimation of Lewis Carroll: "The patients
. . . are recuperating like flies," the major is optimistically told,
and he is, indeed, a poet of the absurd: "Alexander the Great is
a hero, but why destroy the furniture?" he says.

There is, finally, a strange gaze, unusual in narrative before
Gogol, but to which movies have accustomed us: Chichikov falls
asleep surrounded by the feathered snowfall of his down blanket,
curls up like a pretzel, and wakes up the following morning to see
a fly looking at him from the ceiling while two others have come
to rest, one on his eye and the other on his nose; the latter is
sucked in by the tunnel of breath and Chichikov is fully awake,
sneezing.

It should be pointed out that the most remarkable thing about Gogol's strangeness is that it envelops a theme that in its time was received with scandalized criticism for its "vulgarity." Gogol is, indeed, the novelist who introduces the despicable into Russian literature; that is, precisely, the vulgar, the insignificant, the banal theme. His forerunner, certainly, is Pushkin, but the great poet has this to say about Gogol: "No other writer has had the gift of exhibiting so clearly the *poshlost* of life."

The Russian word *poshlost*—so similar to the Amerindian word potlatch—signals something of little worth, a lowly thing, as ordinary as trash. The American potlatch is an escalation of values by which each gift from the individual or the tribe must be matched, and topped, by another one. The tribe or the individual whose potlatch can no longer be equaled is the victor: You're the top. I have written of James Joyce as the master of ceremonies of a contemporary verbal potlatch which transforms the trash of language into the gold of literature. Gogol's *poshlost* plays a comparable role: "The more ordinary the object," he writes, "the greater the poet must be to extract the extraordinary from it."

For Gogol there are no vulgar themes. "Blessed be the creator for whom there are no lowly themes in nature," we read in "The Portrait." "In banality, the artist-creator is as great as in the great; in the contemptible, he finds nothing contemptible . . ."

We have seen that thematic vulgarity was one of the sins Gogol was charged with by many critics when *Dead Souls* appeared. This kind of finger-wagging accompanied Gogol throughout his career. Starting with the publication of his first book, *Evenings on a Farm*, Pushkin addresses his friends, pleading with them, "for the love of heaven, to come to Gogol's defense if journalists, as is their wont, reproach him for inconvenience of expression, bad taste, etc. The time has arrived to confound the precious ridicules of our Russian literature."

Indeed, Gogol, from his very first book, was classified by a certain (universally unavoidable) type of book reviewer as inferior to Paul de Kock, possessed of a vulgar and incorrect language destined to be read only by an inferior sort of audience. Yet Gogol never renounced his belief, proclaimed yet again in a letter addressed to the critic and future memoirist Sergei Aksakov in 1840:

"Few undoubtedly know to what vigorous ideas and profound images an insignificant theme can lead . . ."

Gogol's so-called poor theme was indispensable to his literary strategy, which attempted to call attention both to the false reality we take to be true and to another reality, less fragmented and decomposed than "everyday reality," which hides behind it. How to achieve this without establishing, first of all, a point of tension in banality itself, within the "realistic" comedy of bureaucrats, landowners, rogues, misers, provincial governors, eligible young women, and gossipy matrons? What Gogol had achieved wasn't lost on Aksakov, and in a letter the critic wrote to his son Ivan in 1850, two years before Gogol's death, he initiates a just evaluation when he states: "An art as lofty, consisting in showing a sublime aspect in the most vulgar individual: this one can only find in Homer. Today, only Gogol can do it."

The metamorphosis, the strangeness of language and action in tension with its lowly theme, supposedly vulgar and despicable, place Gogol's thematic world, as it serves his strategy of indirect restructuring of an atomized reality. But immediately the Gogolian universe, thus established, is blown apart by the motion of displacement.

VI

Metamorphosis is Gogol's first avenue (or perspective) toward the reconstitution of reality. From it we look out on the parks, buildings, and sewers of a language, a style, a set of situations that pull us out of our own complacency through successive thrusts of strangeness. This grand avenue flows into a circular plaza: the circle of identity. But hardly have we gazed upon this central place of Gogol's thematics when we are tempted by the openings toward other avenues (or perspectives) which distract us, remove us from the rotunda of identity, and postpone the possibility of certifying it.

These tempting perspectives are called displacement, trip, fugue, and they constitute the second grand Gogolian theme, after that of metamorphosis, which Donald Fanger has proposed. Displacement provides the dynamism for all the elements we have been considering until now: metamorphosis, estrangement, the poor theme, life in the work.

If metamorphosis is the (initial) process of fiction in Gogol, the road, writes Fanger, is its central image. When we sketched the life of the Gogolian character we call Gogol, we could already perceive that the voyage is seen as an absolute necessity, salvation and medicine not only for his hypochondriac body but for his creation. The displaced one, in this sense, is not only Gogol the biographical man but, above all, Gogol the textual man. Displacement achieves all of its meanings in Gogol.

First, it means flight from Russia. There is a troika on permanent call in Gogol's soul, and its purpose is to carry him away from Russia. Perhaps the most Russian of all literary works is *Dead Souls*. It was written in Rome because, as Gogol says, "the contemporary author, the comic author, the portrayer of mores, must be as far as possible from his country. The prophet finds no honor in his homeland."

When he quits Russia in June 1836, he insists that his thoughts, his name, and his works "shall belong to Russia," but he, his perishable part, "shall be far away." After all, he adds, "I really do have a Russian heart." He would like to travel again in a Russian train and listen to the "Babylonic speech" of the passengers; he even feels nostalgia for the humidity, the fog, the chill of St. Petersburg. But his nostalgia, after all, depends on his absence, and from afar he also fears that returning to Russia would mean a renewal of his anger toward his beloved fatherland. The complexity of Gogol's feelings toward Russia is transparent in a letter written from Lake Geneva in 1836. To all the previous reasons, he adds this one: abroad, he feels that his "indignation" toward all things Russian weakens; he then fears he shall lose his anger, "the anger without which . . . little can be said; only in anger can one say the truth."

Gogol has implicitly explained that he would give his kingdom for a troika that would keep him perpetually poised, rhythmically, between farness and nearness. This horizontal, lyrical space— space proper to Russia—is imagined only through displacement. The author accompanies this statement with a spectacular use of modifying clauses: space in Russia disappears from sight, but Gogol's prose qualifies it and limits its very boundlessness with a necklace of reticence, of "inclusive" and "it would seem," "sort of," "somehow." For Andrei Bely these limiting expressions "throw a veil of immovable spots" on the narrative. Suffice it to remember the first chapter of *Dead Souls*, where the governor is described: "like Chichikov, neither fat nor thin; he was, nevertheless, a man of good disposition and even knitted silk stockings."

Here the verbal qualification of what might be an extensive character limits Gogol's comedy, places him within a finite space, and displaces him within the Russian immensity. I reflect that the Latin American novel, from Rivera's *La Vorágine* and Gallegos's *Canaima* to Carpentier's *Los Pasos Perdidos* and Guimarães Rosa's *Gran Sertão: Veredas*, has walked a (tropical) path as hazardous as this Russian steppe, in order to limit the extension of a nature that had already seemed superhuman to the discoverers of the sixteenth century. "They were swallowed by the jungle," José Eustasio Rivera dramatically declares at the end of *La Vorágine*. "Don't let them be swallowed by the steppe," Nikolai Gogol comically says throughout *Dead Souls*.

Yet this struggle against pure extension, qualified and modified rather than denied, constitutes another form of displacement, and this is the up/down and down/up movement which forms an (orthodox) cross with space and confers its ironic dynamism (and, perhaps, its internal thickness) upon Gogol's narrative.

An example comes to mind: the structure of that short-story masterpiece "The Overcoat," where all things are distributed according to displacements of the vertical kind—floor and heaven; inferior and superior ranks; darkness below and clarity above. The story of Akaky Akakyevich Bashmachkin first names itself through its protagonist: *bashmak* means shoe and Akaky Akakyevich is presented as a man who always "looks downward." He has a low rank in the bureaucracy, he walks staring at his shoes, and he works looking down at official documents.

Night falls over the Russian capital. Akaky is the scion of a family obsessed with shoes and determined to change their soles several times a year. When Akaky's fellow workers mock him, they shower him over the head with small pieces of paper like snowflakes. Akaky "possessed the knack of being under a window at the precise moment when all kinds of trash was being thrown out"; his hat, therefore (the top of him, in other words), is always decorated with melon and watermelon rinds. Akaky Akakyevich is always rained down upon, from above: he is a shoeman, a humiliated man.

The upward movement in "The Overcoat" begins when the poor clerk decides to exchange his old, useless overcoat, which one can almost see through, for a new one, in the same way that his family used to change the soles of their shoes. He goes up the stairs to the tailor Petrovich, thinking of the high price of a brand-new coat. He finds the tailor in bare feet; the tailor recommends that Akaky use his old coat to warm his own feet. Akaky saves: he walks on the points of his shoes so as not to wear out the soles.

He buys the overcoat and has only one night to show it off; a gang of muggers steal it from him as he returns home. He appeals to the higher authorities; he demands justice from an exalted personage in the bureaucracy, a man who is quite courteous to his peers but behaves insufferably toward his inferiors in rank. Justice comes to Akaky from above; but death comes to him from below. He dies of a fever and then returns, as a ghost, neither high nor low, but implacable, to despoil thieves and functionaries of their coats, without ever implying that one and the other are synonymous.

The dynamic displacement of the splendid narrative structure in "The Overcoat" is heightened by the space in which it takes place. This is the space of the city, a Petersburg of infinite labyrinths. This is a city lit by the central problem of Gogolism: the postponement of identity. Action and language displace themselves so that identity can be deferred. In the labyrinth of Petersburg, "streets and buildings . . . confuse themselves . . . in the head." It is impossible to orient oneself: to identify. The displacement of place (*Dead Souls*, like *Don Quixote*, begins: "In a certain" place in the provinces, which the author does not wish to remember) resembles displacement in time: "The Overcoat" occurs during a day . . . a day . . . a . . . a . . . No, says Gogol, "truthfully I am not able to state with precision the day on which Petrovich finally delivered the overcoat."

There is, finally, displacement in the Freudian sense: as omission, modification, or regrouping of the material of dreams; a work of oneiric censorship which displaces the character, distancing him from the thoughts that do not really interest him and thrusting him toward impulses that at first might seem alien to his actions but which in the end the character cannot resist because they are truly his own. He does not know it: displacement leaves him exhausted (like Kafka's Prometheus), and his will voluntarily surrenders to a speculation, at times silly but sometimes frightening, which forces the character to flee, to displace himself, and, finally, slowly to change his strategies in dealing with reality: he has learned that he can displace his compulsions infinitely, but he cannot dissipate them.

Gogol does not sublimate this psychological picture. He transforms it into a symmetrical literary art of constantly postponed identities. Displacement serves to pluralize identification, which becomes social (Akaky is the urban victim of official indifference), which becomes religious (Akaky's soul is invincible, even if his body is fragile and ephemeral), which is ethical (Akaky personifies a longing for fraternity, which is denied him), which is political (Akaky belongs to a group that is defenseless for the very reason that should strengthen him: his individual freedom), and which is, finally, aesthetic: the form of the story, as Boris Eikhenbaum said, "is the focus of its value."

Such plurality of meanings (of identities) is the work of displacement and it transforms "The Overcoat" into a perpetual "hermeneutical challenge" where the possibility of evocation, which is infinite, does not diminish the pleasure of comprehension. Being all that it is and can be, "The Overcoat," as we know, is a story about significance and insignificance in life and literature. It is, as Fanger remarks, a "monument to the capacity of art—not to 'reflect' the great realities of life but to join them."

VII

I think that, by the very methods proposed by Gogol, we are nearing the center of his work: identity. We are coming to it as Gogol desired us to, through a displacement which is also a postponement. The Russian formula for this rhythm, Fanger tells us, is called *ne to*: things are not what they seem, they are not where they should be, and they are not what they could be; the surest expectations are frustrated and give way to astonishment. Displacement does reveal an identity, but it is an astonished identity: postponed: finally, comic.

This procedure is something that Hispano-speakers (perhaps even better: Hispano-thinkers) can understand with special ease and interest. Along with Russia, Spain and Hispano-America have been eccentric communities and, perhaps for this reason, dogmatic ones. When he questions himself on the role peculiar to the writer in Eastern Europe, Vissarion Belinksy noted, in the time of Gogol, Pushkin, and Dostoevsky, that "the public sees in Russian writers its only readers, defenders, and saviors." This is an undesirable burden. In a sane civil society, such an obligation should be shared by diverse sectors of the society. We live the extremes defined by Philip Roth: in the East, everything matters and nothing goes; in the West, nothing matters and everything goes.

This "Rothian" humor is not peculiar to the West. Speaking about the importance of literature in Russia, the critic Kireyevsky has this to say: ". . . The indefatigable solicitude of a far-seeing government frees private individuals from the necessity of concerning themselves with politics, and thus the sole index of our intellectual development remains literature." This critique of critical criticism contains a great dose of irony: the privilege of literature here becomes the burden of literature. True, the Slavic world has been particularly demanding of its writers in the performance of these "social" duties. The reason is ancient and has to do with the position of the elder, the narrator, the starets, the holder of the word: in the world of the villages, the holder of the word and of memory is the center of truth: its bequeather.

The great Russian critics of the nineteenth century—Belinsky, Chernyshevsky, Mikhailovsky—ask that literature speak for the village-nation and be the bearer of institutional change. From Gogol to Chekhov, by way of Dostoevsky, Goncharov, and Tolstoy, literature is seen as "a psychological and moral agency"—as Fanger puts it, "an essentially personalistic instrument of what might legitimately be called consciousness-raising, in the belief that a better society" would at length come into being.

Fanger's suggestion is that Gogol only possesses an identity as a writer at the price of not having any personal identity. When, in his "Four Letters to Various Persons," he decides to explain himself to his readers, he becomes vague, hyperbolical, and arbitrary; he falls into solipsism and personal pathology. When Gogol ceases to be Gogol, he makes a call to engagement: "The writer— he proclaims—shall be strictly called to account if his works do not generate some benefits for the soul." Once this is said, Gogol ceases to write literature and sinks into the metaphysical, moralizing, preachy, and jingoistic swamp of his *Selected Passages from Correspondence with Friends*.

Let us come back to the creation of Nikolai Gogol, not to his destruction. It is a creation based on a search for identity which constantly postpones such identification. From these presuppositions arises what Fanger calls "the Gogolian universe," both "wider" and "more primitive" than what could be termed a Gogolian world. This universe has its sources in Gogol's text and only incidentally, or reflectively, in "reality." "Five years were needed," states the French critic Gustave Aucouturier, "to bring the first part of *Dead Souls* into a safe harbor; ten years were needed to pilot the second part into shipwreck."

Gogolian satire, for example, offers us a picture of "radical cretinism" fed by an obstinate fidelity to the values of complacency, vanity, rank, and gossip. But the source of this stupidity, no matter how true and extended it is, both in society and in nature, is to be found for Gogol in neither, but rather in the Gogolian text itself, without which these realities would certainly have a social but not an artistic existence.

The condition for such an art, an art that does not reflect reality but becomes one with reality, completes it, or constitutes a counterpart of the real, is a peculiar form of irony. In Gogol, irony is more radical than in other post-Cervantes authors (the English novelists from Defoe to Thackeray, or the first French realists) because it is an irony that, far from hastening the identification of reality, as in Fielding or Balzac, postpones it, as if the author feared being discovered or placed biographically, and thereby being ironically discovered in the midst of nothing. But there is more: Gogol proceeds by postponing the very things he is searching for (identity) because he believes that the existence of his text depends on the postponement of that identity.

If it is true that all irony is dissimulation, Gogol employs it to reveal something more important than his personal identity or the immediate, realistic identification of his ideological intentions.

Identification in the case of Gogol is, first of all, identification of the literary creation. By deferring the question of the meaning of the text, Gogol brings to the forefront the question of the creation of the text: A text offered as a reality synonymous with possibility—the possibility of art.

Gogol's is an art that speaks of the possibility of art. The condition for this is that nothing should possess a stable identity in his text, not the author or his characters, not the literary meaning, not the political, social, or psychological message.

To identify a person or group immediately is the province of propaganda: "lackey of imperialism," "red stooge," lynchable black, exterminable Jew, displaceable Palestinian. In this, its most strident manifestation, instant identification has its place (that is, in the political pamphlet, the crusading journal, the bureaucratic ukase). But Gogol's work is art precisely because it radicalizes the question of identification, deferring it throughout a text which only becomes identifiable thanks to a paradox: its identity is being questioned.

But this, as we shall now see, hastens another, far more critical identity: the literary and moral identity of the novel as the form of an unfinished speech, as work which is perpetually open. That is why the novel is the privileged vehicle of two ways of being: narrative and freedom: to be new (novel) in a speech open to all, and to be free in a speech that never concludes.

VIII

The comic genius of Gogol brings all this into proper focus. There are the masterpieces, *Dead Souls* and *The Inspector-General*, and the characters Chichikov and Khlestakov.

Both works are a gift from the generous genius of Pushkin. The story of the wild entrepreneur in *Dead Souls* was given to Gogol by Pushkin. So was *The Inspector-General*: "Do me a favor," Gogol writes to Pushkin, "give me a subject, even an anecdote, funny or not, but purely Russian. My hand trembles to write a comedy."

Pushkin's second gift to Gogol is the most extraordinary comic play of nineteenth-century theater. I believe that Gogol owes Pushkin something more than the theme, and this something is the narrative velocity, comparable to that of an opera buffa by Rossini, but comparable, most of all, to the splendid lesson on velocity to be found in another masterwork of rhythm, Pushkin's *Eugene Onegin*.

In Gogol's play, a poor drifter called Khlestakov arrives in a provincial town, where he is mistaken for the feared inspector-general that the central government periodically sends to the provinces, like the *missi dominici* of the Carolingian empire or the judges of residence of the Spanish colony, to see that things are proceeding properly in the domains of our Lord the King.

Donald Fanger has noted that Gogol's genius consists of presenting the false inspector as a naïf and not, as demanded by tradition, as a rogue. This innocent man finds a perfect partner in stupidity in the town mayor; both embark on a *folie à deux*, a shared madness. This is Gogol at his greatest: his comedy is based on the absence of a deliberate deceit: the false identities of Khlestakov and even of Chichikov are the creation of others. Khlestakov never pretends that he is the inspector; he is not, as the author indicates, "a habitual liar; sometimes he even forgets that he is lying . . . He feels expansive, he feels well, he sees that everything is going well, he is listened to . . . He lies with sentiment . . . This is the best and most poetic moment of his existence, almost an inspiration." Chichikov, too, is the proprietor of all the hypothetical identities assigned to him by the townsfolk.

The problem of lie is here intimately related to the problem of identity. Curiously, Gogol's two great liars are not liars at all: their false identities are the creation of others. This is certainly not the case of the classical liar of the Gogolian universe, the landowner Nozdryov, a man who lies constantly, without any need to do so. Nozdryov is a master of euphemism—he calls his lies "a rich invention"—and it is he who unleashes the finale of the novel when he appears at the governor's ball and tells the truth about Chichikov: the stranger is a vulgar merchant in dead souls.

Now, everyone knows that Nozdryov is a liar. But it suffices to launch a lie, as long as it is also news, to ensure that it will be passed on to other mortals, even if only for the pleasure of saying: "Look what whoppers they are telling these days!" The new persona attributed by Nozdryov the liar to Chichikov is in fact the real one, but it is one which has accreted on top of all the identities that the impressionable ladies of the town have already conferred upon him. Yet, because this is the true identity, it dissolves Chichikov's deceit and forces him to flee. This is not the result of the community's moral values but rather the work of poetic chance and truth in a world where language is inauthentic and the sense of original unity between truth and objects has been lost.

Language: Chichikov speaks to a servant woman in the first stop of his picaresque tour:

"Who are you?" asked the old woman.
"A gentleman, good woman."
The word gentleman seemed to impress the old woman.
"One moment, I will go and tell my lady," she said.

This same linguistic deceit affects Chichikov's false public position; the ladies of the town are impressed by him and decide that he is a millionaire. But it is the word, its sound, not what the word means, which dazzles them. And it is not a sentiment of greed that makes them call him a millionaire. They do it to honor him, laugh with him, and bow before him—all this stemming from the name they themselves invent.

But appearance is a deceit as well, and language then appears to support a truth which, otherwise, no one would perceive: Chichikov arrives at the house of the miser Plyushkin and asks a man who looks like a majordomo:

"Is the master at home?"
"The master is here," says the man.
"Where?" asks Chichikov.
"Are you blind?" comes the reply. "I am the master."

As in Dracula's castle, the servant is the master. In this roundelay of mistaken identities in which appearance does not support words and language does not support perception, there is a final point, and it is called old age and death. "Today's young man would recoil in horror if he saw the old man he will one day become," Gogol comments in *Dead Souls*. But, between life and death, what insinuates itself is a profound indifference toward the other: the other is forgotten, and this turns out to mean we have forgotten ourselves.

Alongside Balzac's *Colonel Chabert*, Gogol initiates one of the tragicomic traditions of modernity: that of a man forgotten by his fellow men. Kafka will give it its fullest expression. But if K the land surveyor in *The Castle* has been radically forgotten by everyone, the false inspector of Gogol's comedy has been remembered by all. Khlestakov has been given an identity, even if a false identity. K is deprived of an identity, even if a true identity. Such is the distance between the nineteenth and the twentieth century.

Another great writer in the tradition of Gogol and Kafka, Milan Kundera, entitles one of his works *The Book of Laughter and Forgetting*. In *Dead Souls*, the city fathers ask themselves, about Chichikov: "Who is he, truly?" And they answer: "Although they did not know for sure who Chichikov was, undoubtedly Chichikov was something." Even as perception displaces itself, a being true to Gogolian form affirms itself: Chichikov is, but who is he?—although he undoubtedly *is*. Kafka's land surveyor does not enjoy the benefit of this doubt: K is not the land surveyor engaged by the Castle; therefore, he is not.

Kundera opens and closes anew this painful modern question. His book does not propose the binary opposition memory–forgetting. It says something far graver: "Those who remember me, forget me." The deceit has become transparent: to forget is the memory of all those we do not wish to identify.

These are some of the fruits of Gogol's vast narrative, moral, and political influence, as he displaces and postpones our knowledge of self. His question is: Who are you? But he refuses to answer it in a facile way. As in the alleys and byways of the modern city to which he gives a charter of literary citizenship, unity is shattered and "it would seem that a demon had broken up the totality of the universe into pieces and then mixed them up without any order."

I constantly return to this quote from the "Nevsky Prospekt." Is it one of the keys to Gogol? Of his cities and his nation, Gogol said: "Moscow is necessary to Russia, but Russia is necessary to Petersburg." This formula was completed by Dostoevsky when he referred to Petrograd as "the most abstract and intentional of cities." In these definitions, a labyrinth and its fiction come together: the city on the Neva, invented by Peter the Great so that it could be inhabited by Akaky Akakyevich the melancholy and Rodion Raskolnikov the terrible, is a mystery, but its enigma is fictitious, intentional, and at war with its own abstraction.

In another of his exemplary books of criticism, *Dostoevsky and Romantic Realism*, Donald Fanger tells us that the appearance of romantic realism and the appearance of the city as the preferred theme and space of that literary and human posture (or imposture) are inseparable. The character of the new urban life, the fate of human traditions set in anti-natural spaces create a world of strangeness, of crime (and punishment), of expectations (great), and of illusions (lost), as well as of bureaucrats (petty) who are killed by the indifference of others and return to unmask their torturers. The romantic novelists of the city—Gogol and Dickens, Balzac and Dostoevsky—need a common technical inventory, says Fanger: the sense of mystery and of atmosphere, the sentiment of the grotesque, of contrast, of the improbable, the sensational, and the dramatic.

I emphasize the masked character of the city, its roulette of identities, as a theme common to the metropolitan novelists. Expatriates of romanticism, the heroes of the city are satanic beings who find, in the urban labyrinth, their privileged abode. For these new protagonists, the city is a human gift which compensates for the expulsion from Paradise. *Terra incognita*, place of exile, the city "possesses all the astonishment of what is strange in what is familiar." It receives the devil in exile: the urban demons called Vautrin, in Balzac; Fagin, in Dickens; and Raskolnikov, in Dostoevsky. All of them live most fully in the masked mystery of cities; theirs is the identity of a somber carnival in which we can again hear Balzac's words: "Humanity has but two forms, the deceiver and the deceived . . ."

Gogol, who in the city finds perfectly identifiable victims and victimizers—Akaky and the bureaucrats—needs the vast Russian hinterland, the non-city, the village, the imaginary countryside, in order to project onto this economic and political backwardness the urban experience of masked identities. But it is precisely this miserable, provincial, eccentric world that confers its false identity on the displaced city-zens, Khlestakov and Chichikov.

Gogol thus wins two prizes, as it were. For, without sacrificing one bit of his artistic genius, he gives presence to a kind of Russian national cry: Let me recognize myself in my literature. The Russian public awaited Gogol so that Gogol would identify the strangeness of Russia. Or, as Andrei Bely (himself the author of the most extraordinary modern novel of Petersburg) put it, "Gogol opens up the literary techniques that no one had discovered before him, saturating the verbal texture with a shower of popular, colloquial, occupational words which he polishes until they become pearls of language. Here and there, people had spoken like this, but no one had written like this."

Pushkin complained: research, politics, and philosophy lack a language in Russia; the cosmopolitanism of the upper classes has exhausted itself; one cannot accept, as a substitute, the repressive triad of autocracy, orthodoxy, and nationality as specifically Russian entities. Then Gogol appears and Belinsky proclaims: "You are unique among all." He was not unfaithful to the truth: Gogol emerges without any competition and fills a capital need. His historical fortune consisted in writing in an era when absence and immobility could be read as a necessary and profound social and cultural commentary. How many novelists of the Hispanic world have not said or thought the same in one moment or another of our lives, when our literary snail's pace has been quicker than that of our societies: José Revueltas in Mexico was faster than the pace of the deadened Mexican Revolution in the forties; Juan Goytisolo was swifter than Francoism in Spain. But how many, as well, have been able to reestablish the perspective when the velocity of the historical Achilles demonstrated that, notwithstanding, there was a vulnerable heel and the novelist could point to it, as Azuela did in *The Underdogs*, as Carpentier did in *Explosion in a Cathedral*, as Cortázar did in *Hopscotch*—rowdy critiques of the Latin American project of modernity.

IX

I was saying that we Spanish Americans can understand Gogol's ironic proceedings better than most, because the great Russian writer uses deferral and irony to tell us that nothing is what it seems, and the culture of Hispanic origin is, likewise, permeated by the skeptical irony of Erasmus and his mistrust of appearances, of dogmas, and of physical and moral strictures. Precisely because the Counter-Reformation, in its virulent Spanish version, imposed on us a highly rigid ethical and religious order, our culture recalls Erasmism as a vital lesson. From the beginnings of the sixteenth century to the Council of Trent, Spanish Erasmism promoted the hope of reform within the Roman Catholic Church and of Spanish adaptation to the dynamics of European modernity. These were the three rules offered by the sage of Rotterdam: all truth is double and perhaps multiple; absolute reason is as dangerous as absolute faith; reason also has its madness.

Spanish Erasmism was condemned and banished from the peninsula; yet its subterranean lesson flowered, magnificently, in Cervantes's *Quixote*, which is the meeting point of all modern literatures. In it Gogol, Dostoevsky, and Flaubert recognize themselves, but also Borges, Cortázar, and García Márquez.

In an extraordinary paper presented in the summer of 1983 to the first conference on comparative literature celebrated in post-Maoist Beijing, Donald Fanger calls upon three figures—Rabelais, Cervantes, and Dostoevsky—to explain the theory of the novel of the great Soviet critic Mikhail Bakhtin. Bakhtin's lesson is Gogol's: it is the lesson of the novel, of its openness, its novelty, and its freedom. Or rather, of its novelty and its freedom as a result of its openness.

Bakhtin discovers in Dostoevsky the principles of the polyphonic novel, in which the primacy of explicating the modern world is banished, in favor of the text's orientation toward the world of the other, toward the word rival to the novel under scrutiny. "In Dostoevsky," Bakhtin explains, "there is almost no word that does not direct a tense glance at another word." The critic opposes this form to what he calls the monological or univocal novel dominated by the "voice" of an author or a protagonist. In the polyphonic novel, words are a crack, a window, an opening to a possible alternate meaning, which accompanies each word like a shadow.

Literally, each word should be final. But this is only its (Erasmian) appearance. In fact, there is never a final word; the polyphonic novel exists thanks to a plurality of truths. The novel (again, in the Erasmian manner) is always relative. Its home is the individual conscience, which by definition is partial. Bakhtin states: "It is possible to conceive that truth, in order to be unique, requires a multitude of consciences; that, in principle, truth cannot be contained within the limits of only one conscience; that truth is naturally social and is born at the point where several consciences meet."

Bakhtin distinguishes between epic and novel. Epic, he says in his *Epic Narrative and Novel* (1941), is based on "a unique and unified vision of the world, obligatory and undoubtedly true for its heroes, as well as for its authors and its audience." Epic deals in categories and implications proper to a completed world, past, understood (or, at least, understandable) once and for all. The novel, in contrast, reflects better than any other discourse the tendencies of a new world in the process of making itself. Whereas the epic is a world whose hierarchical unity has not yet been pulverized by history, the novel is a world where every discourse lives on the frontier between its own context and another, alien context.

From this plurality of contexts proper to the novel, or neighboring it, or even rivaling it, the narrative text extracts and orchestrates a series of dialogical confrontations between languages which permit the novelist to use words that others have used before him, in order to generate new and, above all, problematic meanings. The novel is an instrument of dialogue in this deeper sense: of a dialogue not only between characters but between languages, between genres, between social forces, between contiguous or distant historical times.

The novel, says Bakhtin, is the expression of a Galilean perception of language. Far from being one more genre among others, the novel uses other genres and places authors and readers within an era of competitive languages.

This is the conclusion: the dynamic notion of the novel is equal to its incomplete nature. "As long as man is alive," Bakhtin concludes without concluding, reinitiating his own critical discourse, "he lives by virtue of being incomplete, of not having said his final word."

Rabelais, Cervantes, Dostoevsky: in them it is specially true that the novel is, in Bakhtin's words, a "radical revolution in the destinies of human discourse," a "liberation of semantic-cultural and emotional intentions," and a liberation, as well, "from the hegemony of a unique and unitarian language": a "simultaneous loss of the sense of language as myth, that is, as an absolute form of thought."

Gogol is not Rabelais, Cervantes, or Dostoevsky, the great constructors of the polyphonic universe of the novel. Gogol is closer to the hero and the victim of the novel, rather than its architect. He knows everything about the worlds of fiction, like Rabelais, Cervantes, and Dostoevsky in their respective times. But he also forgets everything about them—he is Gogol, a character in Gogol, finally disguised, deferred, displaced: a gigantic dwarf, a very small giant: David and Goliath in one single slingshot; Perseus first, then Medusa. Gogol murders Gogol.

X

He writes in *Dead Souls*: "Fear my gaze when it is penetrating; you yourselves fear to gaze penetratingly at anything; you like to slide down things with eyes that think not." In these few words is contained the literary drama of Gogol: the drama of his postponed perception, his identity and his conscience postponed so that the novel, as indicated by Bakhtin, may maintain its vitality: that being an unfinished discourse.

Gogol is a Perseus who cuts off the heads of the Medusas of certainty. Everything in him is deformed, refracted, postponed. We must not end: the gaze of certainty will transform us into stone. But to be seen authentically (writes Fanger) is to be known. It is to acquire a certain rank in a world of values. For the majority of Gogol's characters, this is a negative rank: to look is to judge; the gaze petrifies or annihilates. The recognition of the gaze that identifies us is the recognition of the gaze that places us, radicalizes us (as in *radix*, root), terrifies us (as in *terra*, land): paralyzes us.

This is the terrible gaze of the other—*le regard d'autrui*—to which Sartre dedicates some of his most brilliant pages. Donald Fanger recapitulates Sartre's arguments with special intensity in *The Creation of Nikolai Gogol*: To know that we are seen is to know ourselves seen in the world and from the point of view of the world. I am my possibilities: I am what I am not and I am not what I am, but always in the measure in which I am seen by the world. The eyes of the world transform me into someone. The other who perceives me represents "the death hidden in my possibilities." For the other, I am not a project but a fact; I shall not be, I am. I am finished. The gaze of the other has exhausted my fictional possibilities, my perpetually unfinished being is over.

Fanger says of Gogol that pride and faith were his possibilities, and fear both his premature identification and his premature judgment. The mysterious dwarf from the Nezhin Lyceum exclaims: Do not judge me yet! You do not know who I am yet, I myself do not know it, not yet, please!

He insists: To be a writer is a riddle whose solution is to be found in a perpetually unreachable future. The work joins this work of postponement; it is intrinsic to it because the work is a verbal counterreality that can be rooted only in the feeling that "each man, at least once in his lifetime, has an encounter that induces in him sentiments that were until then unknown" *(Dead Souls)*.

Gogol can express this same idea with comic verve. "There are faces that nature has not wished to finish," he says while observing the landlord Sobakevich. But the comic phrase is the perfect indication of Gogol's artistic adherence to the novel as the art of novelty, of the unfinished, of the free. The order of these factors does not alter the product.

But the product is sumptuous: it is a novel pregnant with itself, giving birth to true narrative constellations, unexpected and autonomous. For example, all those imaginary biographies of the dead serfs that Chichikov must invent. They are a marvelous foretaste of Marcel Schwob, Max Beerbohm, and Jorge Luis Borges. The art of these imaginary lives is that they are born of the paucity of hearsay, not of academic solemnity. They are part of an art of the unfinished and the potential, and its seeds are malicious tongues, old wives' tales, opinion, rumor: maybe Chichikov is Napoleon, his profile resembles Napoleon's. Chichikov *is* Napoleon scooting about Russia under the name Chichikov. Chichikov invents fictions, orchestrates them, and inspires others to join in his creation. We read in *Dead Souls*:

> Penetrating into the most far-flung byways, this novel was subjected to numerous versions . . . Since ordinary people are most interested in the gossip of the upper classes, this adventure was discussed,

commented upon and beautified in homes where the existence of Chichikov, up till then, had been unknown . . .

Thus, in its very detail, the narrative art of Gogol explores the polyphony of what is pluralistically narrative. He embodies democratic truth in comic movement: the refusal of the final vision is the refusal of the final version. Identity is problematic because it is always becoming, on the road, in exchange, in doubt, in inspiration.

"There is more in those works than what they are." With these words, Sinyavsky defined not only the art of Gogol but perhaps all narrative art. "No one heard me complain," Gogol writes to his mother from school. "I praised those who were the cause of my disgrace. It is true that for all of them I am an enigma. No one guesses who I am." Fiction, says Donald Fanger, offers the absences that fiction itself has exhibited. And he adds: Gogol's task was to protect himself from the gaze of the Medusa.

But his death consisted, also, in succumbing to the Gorgon: he became his own Medusa; he finally identified himself. He ceased to be Perseus. But since Gogol is a textual character with a textual biography, this gaze could happen only within the creation of Nikolai Gogol. It occurs in 1846, when Gogol, subjected to the freezing rigors of the waters at Ostende, decides to tack on a new final act to that perfect work, *The Inspector*. In this act, an actor crowned with laurels (Gogol himself) explains to the audience that his play is not a vulgar satire but a work of profound mystical meaning. The actor/author even declares to the public: "The inspector is our conscience."

We gasp at this betrayed Kafka: now we know who is who in *The Castle*. Now Joseph K knows why he is on trial. Now Gregor Samsa declares from his hard bed that the world is cruel, ingratitude an everyday happening, and appearances decisive.

Gogol's final metamorphosis was as a failure. He was the author, as his biographer and critic Vladimir Nabokov says, of his own auto-da-fé. When he accepted that things have a final version, he imposed on them a unique vision. In *Selected Passages* and in the second part of *Dead Souls*, the fateful announcement contained in the phony final act of *The Inspector* comes true: Gogol wants to be taken seriously; he wants to be the conscience of Russia. He was precisely that, up until then, because he did not pretend to be that. He ceased to be that as soon as he took on this redeeming mission. He ceased to write; he ceased to live.

But from his death, and in his life, something arose, living: the heroic effort to reconstruct the world shattered into a thousand pieces by the demons of the Nevsky Prospekt: Gogol's world of transvestite narrators, disguised, filled to the brim with stories, both stories and author unfinished, partial, authors of a ruined but generous reality.

XI

Too often, between a writer and the reader of criticism on the writer, a wall of misunderstanding rises. The writer is sometimes reduced to fit a preformed ideologic or aesthetic shoe. Or he is accused by the critic of not writing what the critic wanted to read; he is asked, in other words, to write as the critic would like him to write and about what the critic would want him to write.

Donald Fanger does exactly the opposite: he creates a continuous critical transparency between Gogol's work and the critical correspondence that this work deserves. In Fanger, Gogol has found his critical correspondence, much as Balzac in Curtius, Kafka in Benjamin, Conrad in Leavis, Proust in Barthes, Neruda in Dámaso Alonso, Fernando de Rojas in Stephen Gilman, Cervantes in Claudio Guillén, Emily Brontë in Georges Bataille, Rabelais in Bakhtin, Faulkner in Cleanth Brooks, Sterne in Shklovsky, Rubén Darío in Paz, or, supremely, Homer in Simone Weil.

This correspondence supposes a reading equivalent, not more, not less, to the creative effort critically considered. It may be a full-length work, such as that devoted by Albert Béguin to the romantics; or an acute theoretical note, such as Bertrand Russell's on *Tristram Shandy*; or a few pages, as Lawrence's on Melville; or even a few sentences, as Borges on a thousand and one things. The work has been answered; it has found, like metaphor itself, the other shore of intelligence. It shall never again be an isolated fact, but a continuous event. Thanks to the true critic, the work starts to resemble its readers. This is the dimension of Donald Fanger's reading of Gogol.

Luis Buñuel and the Cinema of Freedom

In the first scene of *An Andalusian Dog* (1928), a young Spaniard called Luis Buñuel slowly puffs on a cigarette and sharpens a razor. He looks at the nocturnal sky. A passing cloud bisects the moon. Buñuel separates with his fingers the eyelids of a woman who looks at us and sees that we see her. Buñuel brings the razor close to the open eye and slits it with one swift slash. Vision overflows. Vision becomes contagious.

More than fifty years later, a Spaniard called Luis Buñuel—not an old man, simply a young man who now happened to be eighty-three—sat in the bare study of his house in Mexico City, surrounded by high monastery walls crowned with broken glass, and repeated his steadfast credo: "If only it were free, the cinema would be the eye of freedom. But for the time being, we can sleep in peace. The eye of the cinema is shackled by audience conformity and commercial interests. The day the eye of the cinema awakens, the world will catch fire!"

Ever since *An Andalusian Dog*, for Buñuel the screen was a sleeping eye that could only be awakened by a camera as sharp as a razor, a nail, an ice pick: the eye of the cinema would be a wound that never heals.

The unity of Buñuelian cinema is born of a conflict between the way you see and what you see. And this conflict is inseparable from a pilgrimage, a going from the security of the enclosed place to the risks of the shelterless outdoors. Milan Kundera has said that the world changes when Don Quixote leaves the enclosed universe of his God and his library and goes out of himself to meet a changing world. This is both the Hispanic and the modernist root of Buñuel's cinema: the Spanish hero is not Tom Jones or Robinson Crusoe, who are the product of the progressive peak attained by their society and are, in this sense, attuned to it. Nothing—the Inquisition, the Counter-Reformation, the Hapsburg monarchy—validates the creation of Don Quixote, whereas everything—the expansion of commerce, the rising middle class, Parliament, and political freedom—validates Robinson Crusoe. The English hero is invented thanks to society; the Spanish hero, in spite of society. The Spaniard is the hero of what is lacking, what is not there, what he hungers for, what he desires.

"Desire" is the key word for the understanding of the Buñuelian universe. But in him this most human, erotic, and earthbound of words achieves an almost mystical tone, as though desire were the sacrament that truly sends men and women on these daring pilgrimages of the psyche and soma where they confront both the dark night of the soul and the bondage of the flesh as though they were accomplishing some sort of priestly mission, a *sacerdocium*, a sacrifice through movement.

The erotic sacredness of the lovers in *L'Age d'Or* (1930) is inseparable from the sacrality of solitude, work, and fraternity in Buñuel's version of *Robinson Crusoe* (1952). And the paranoid, masochistic, necrophiliac, and fetishistic priesthoods of Séverine de Cérizy in *Belle de Jour* (1967) and of Heathcliff in *Abismos de Pasión* (Buñuel's Mexican version of *Wuthering Heights*, 1954) are as important and valuable as the mystical priesthood of the clergyman Nazarín and the novitiate Viridiana in films Buñuel made in 1959 and 1960. For all these contradictory characters have something in common: in one way or another, through eroticism or fraternity, through crime or perversion, they perceive a world beyond their skins, and this perception forces them to act, to connect with a world they must transform if their desires are to be actualized.

The cinema of Luis Buñuel describes a trajectory that abandons the original enclosed space, traverses the open fields of a Castile of the soul, and finally, depending on the nature of the pilgrimage, creates the bonds of a precarious community or simply returns to the sterility of a new and definitive isolation.

The cloister is the origin, the first place. You come out of the unity of the beginning—the childhoods of Archibaldo de la Cruz and Séverine de Cérizy; the convent of Viridiana and the garret of Nazarín, Robinson's hulk of a motherly English ship and the maternal womb-hut of the children in Los Olvidados (1950): all of them primordial forms of one big earth belly. You come out and follow a road that takes you to another cloister—the prison of Nazarín, the tomb of Heathcliff and Cathy, the abandoned house of Viridiana, the monastery in Él (1953), the besieged church in The Exterminating Angel (1962), the garbage dump in Los Olvidados, the castle of the 120 days of Sodom in L'Age d'Or.

During the pilgrimage, unity is dispersed. Opposites explode. Sense becomes fragmentary. Rupture is the price of experience; it is also the condition for poetry, nurtured by the plurality of sense if it is really to aspire to, and perhaps reattain, the unified vision. The paradox of the poetic is thus that it feeds on this rupture as it aspires to build a new unity drawn from the synthesis of lost originality and concrete experience.

Rich, even prodigious in instants of associative poetry, Buñuel's filmic dialectics are inseparable, of course, from a certain vision central to Surrealism: the reunion of opposites. In Buñuel, this takes place outside the ego: it is an acknowledgment of the world. But it depends, at the same time, on a personal vision of reality. So the cinema of Buñuel is always faithful to its root conflict: a struggle between two styles of looking, and, through either of them, a conflict between the decision to connect yourself to the world or to refuse that bond.

Now, Buñuel's cinematographic eye first of all depends on, catches sight of, the specific presence of the most banal objects. Generally, the director uses rather static medium or full shots that tend to collect, with no comment, the disordered proliferation of objects in the world. As leveled and unrelievedly prosaic as the novels of the Marquis de Sade, Buñuel's immobile camera pictures a life that flows without distinction—although with autonomy.

Then, with a velocity shared by no other film director of his time—and with a sudden tension also reminiscent of Sade's prose style—the unexpected movement of the camera first equals, then overtakes, and finally surpasses the parallel rhythm of photographed reality. Because neutrality is the norm, the close-up, the traveling, and the cut are more convulsive than usual. And the object, the face, the foot, or the gesture selected by Buñuel from the abundant disorder of the surrounding, immediate world acquires a breathless, at times unbearable heightening of its presence and reveals itself in a connection previously unthought of to the totality of the world. But Buñuel does not stop to celebrate the lyrical moment; he again submerges us in the grayness of normality.

An example. In *Él* (1953), the action takes place in the conventional milieu of the Catholic bourgeoisie of Mexico City. Everything, fashions, décors, characters, movements, is captured within the unrelieved flatness of melodrama. Francisco, a rich and devout man, fortyish and virginal, marries Gloria, a young woman of his class. Their meeting is one of the great Buñuelian moments. It is Good Thursday in the Cathedral of Mexico City. Francisco is piously performing the ritual of washing and kissing the feet of the poor. Suddenly, the succession of leathery, mud-caked extremities is interrupted by a close-up of a pair of well-shod feet, slim ankles, sheer-stockinged legs. Francisco's religious passion becomes an erotic passion; both are neatly encompassed in Freud's notion of fetishism: the objects—in this case, shoes and stockings—obviate the very body they are a part of: Francisco can desire purely because he desires things, and things are both available and secure, whereas bodies have to be wooed and are dangerous.

Gloria, of course, proves to be no object at all but an intelligent woman, and Francisco responds with an orgy of jealousy that only disguises the fact that he is jealous of Gloria's dangerous mind and body, a mind and body that will not gratify the husband by being only a pair of shoes and stockings. Be that as it may, up until this point the public thinks it is watching a soap opera with Hispanic overtones: a Palmolive tele-tamale. Francisco makes scenes, shadows his wife, and subjects her to mental torture.

But one night while his innocent Desdemona sleeps, Francisco selects, with a chilling sense of taxonomy, the following: rope, cotton, disinfectant, scissors, chloroform, needle and thread, and enters his wife's bedroom with these defined objects and a no less perfectly defined purpose: to sew up his virgin.

The melodrama then becomes a sort of dark encounter of Othello, the Marquis de Sade, and the illustrious restorer of maidenheads, the Spanish Celestina. The narrative takes a huge physical and qualitative leap: we are witnessing a ritual of possession through cruelty and, if need be, through death. Francisco, more than an Othello, turns out to be a latter-day Don Juan, nurturing a hidden grudge against the women who sent him to hell.

This misogyny is disguised by the deceptive virtues of virginity, honor, and faith. But little by little we realize that Francisco's marriage is one long vendetta against his wife, whom he would like to degrade, destroy, and condemn, in her turn, to hell. Francisco, too, appears accompanied by an ally, his butler. Both conspire against women as they spend late nights greasing bicycles. The masculine conspiracy against women is an inversion: Francisco and his butler (who plays Leporello to Francisco's Don Giovanni) behave in the way they imagine women do; they try to penetrate and forestall what they consider to be the irrationality, the wiles and tactics of women. We are both surprised and understanding when the film reaches its splendid finale: Francisco renounces the world and finds refuge in a monastery, the only place where, dressed in skirts, he can recover his communitarian bonds with other men who have transformed into a virtue what in Francisco was a crime: the impossibility of living with women.

In Buñuel, the camera drowns in the banality of everyday life as an act of faith in the marvelous: everyday ants jerkily travel over an everyday hand. The connection transports both elements to a new time and a new space—that is, to a new perception of things:

Milk spills over a woman's naked thighs.

Blood flows over a pair of black stockings.

A woman's pubic hair reappears, covering a man's mouth and chin.

A cow wakes up in the heroine's bed, portending her imminent rise to matriarchy.

You should caress your lover's back with pigeons.

Robinson salvages women's dresses from the shipwreck and wears them in front of a mirror. Does transvestism save him from solitude?

The doors of a Parisian apartment open onto the beaches of Normandy.

Crucifixes hide pointed knives—and novitiates travel with Gla
stone bags filled with the tools of their trade: nails, hammers, al
crowns of thorns.

A fat Korean client jingles a tiny golden bell and transforms a
elegant French bordello into a different place.

And Archibaldo de la Cruz (1955) treasures and caresses bra
and panties which he imagines have belonged to the women h
wishes to kill. But each of his criminal essays backfires because
in every case, the victims die accidentally, commit suicide, or ar
killed by others *before* Archibaldo can lay hands on them.

Again, the grand Spanish myth of Don Juan is traversed and
frustrated: in Buñuel, Don Juan's ladies are one step ahead of the
male conquistador—they destroy themselves before he can do it
for them; they rob Don Juan of the pleasure of exterminating them.

A lot of this has to do with Lautréamont's famous juxtaposition
of an umbrella and a sewing machine on an operating table. Objects
cease to behave normally and instead reveal their true beauty in
an unsuspected encounter; they cease to be invisible and inter-
changeable and become, instead, the dazzling trophies of the mas-
ochist, the fetishist, the sadist.

This is true and good. But Buñuel goes beyond this profanation-
revelation, and he also goes before it. Beyond it, he reaches for
a critique of society that owes a great deal to the director's Surrealist
education and to the handshake that was supposed to take place
over the bodies of the 12 million Europeans sacrificed in World
War I in the name of Fatherland and Property: the hand of Karl
Marx *(We Must Change the World)* shakes the hand of Arthur
Rimbaud *(We Must Change Our Lives)*. And before it, it goes to
the root of anarchy, revolt, and dream hidden deep in his Spanish
heritage and, I should add, present in his long Mexican exile.

Spain, Mexico, Surrealism: the firing line of black humor. But
Buñuel, in any case, comes more from the comic than from the
epic tradition of the cinema, less from Griffith and Eisenstein and
more from Buster Keaton, Chaplin, and Laurel and Hardy, all of
them men crushed by hierarchies, social dropouts because they
do not know how to amass wealth. Their failure is a sin in the
triumphant world of Calvinistic capitalism. And the targets of their
comic havoc are the rich and their property. Flooded hotels, fren-
zied vandalism in pastry shops, totally wrecked suburban homes,

disorder in public thoroughfares: the anarchist comedy of Hollywood parodies and uncloaks the true sense of the economy: the object of objects is not to be useful but to be frantically consumed. *What is conservative about this waste?*

Buñuel asks this question as if Freud had the frozen face of Buster Keaton, and Karl Marx the delirious gaze of Harpo Marx. Perhaps Buñuel, in *L'Age d'Or*, was the first film creator to deal critically with what came to be called the consumer society. The protagonist (Gaston Modot) walks the streets of Rome looking at ads for women's lingerie and perfume. This drives him to his fiancée's home, where, in order to assuage the sexual appetites aroused by the commercial invitation to seduce and be seduced, he must kick a dog, humiliate a blind man, fool a cop, condone the murder of a little boy by his father, crash through doors and windows, strike a wealthy dowager in the face, interrupt an entire orchestra playing Wagner, and drag his future father-in-law by the beard. When, having triumphed over all these obstacles, he finally reaches his beloved, they make love immediately on the mansion's gravel path.

Buñuel's characters understand that the economy invites them to make a simultaneous entity of the invitation to consume and the act of consuming. Like some of Dostoevsky's characters (notably Stavrogin in *The Possessed*), they are set in motion by social forces, but instead of accepting the limits of society, they transcend them to take the Faustian invitation to its extremes: nihilism, absurdity, and loneliness.

There is an economic arch in Buñuel that goes from this invitation to consume in *L'Age d'Or* to the consummation of everything in *The Exterminating Angel*. In this film, the guests at a high-society supper in a city that could be either Latin American or Italian (such is the insistence on forms and appearances: *la bella figura*) are stranded in their host's living room: none of the twenty persons present can leave the place, whether they want to or not. Trapped within this universal crisis of will and energy, they start by consuming a sumptuous banquet, follow up with bits of paper and water from the flower vases, and are on the verge of consuming one another when a truce of providence (what Henry James calls, in *The Beast in the Jungle*, "some accident of grouping") momentarily saves them from their confinement.

After their liberation, they reassemble, with their friends and kin, in a church to give thanks. But as the Te Deum ends, they once more realize that they cannot leave the place. We suspect that this time there will be no exit. The yellow flag that signals the plague goes up on the belfry. Civil disorder breaks out in the streets. A flock of sheep, baahing, enter the besieged church. The final custard pie thrown by Laurel and Hardy will blow us all up.

As in the poem by Pierre Reverdy, the twenty characters in *The Exterminating Angel* "promenade themselves elegantly on the edge of the abyss": their perception of things is reality, they are the twentieth-century descendants of Bishop Berkeley: *Esse est percipi.* Being is perceiving. What they see is the world; but they do not need what they do not see. Their enclosure (always this central image of claustrophobia in Buñuel) teaches them that, in the end, they do need one another in order to survive by devouring each other. They confuse need with extermination: extermination, the corollary of solidarity denied, is the final solution. Desire is as universal as the need that causes it. The characters in *The Exterminating Angel* cannot desire because they have never lacked.

"Esse non est percipi"—reality is not just what I perceive—replies Buñuel in a heretic, Surrealist, Marxist, anarchist epiphany: for he is all this, contradictorily, unrespectfully, generously, in the manner of a Spaniard; that is, of a European eccentric. Of an artist; that is, of an impotent liberator. And of a man of the Catholic and Mediterranean culture, fruitfully at odds with himself: a heretic because he would desire a higher spiritual good (Buñuel said: "Thank God I am an atheist"); a thinker capable of rebelling back into faith, as he states in *The Milky Way* (1969), because of his disgust with science and technology; a spiritual being, in the Pascalian sense, to whom God would speak thus: "You would not search for me if you had not already found me."

Yes: my generous, rich, contradictory friend Luis Buñuel, an artist who reached beyond causality (without totally spurning causality), back into that region where Nietzsche recalled "the tremendous awe which seizes man when he suddenly begins to doubt the cognitive modes of experience" and where the great wheel of fire of ancient wisdom, silence and word engendering the myth of the origin, human action engendering the epic voyage toward *the other*; historical violence revealing the tragic flaw of the hero who must then return to the land of origin; myth of death and renewal and silence from which new words and images will arise, keeps on turning in spite of the blindness of purely lineal thought. Reality has been broken up, much as the sculptured disk of Coyolxhuaqui the Goddess of the Moon, recently discovered in the historical center of Mexico City, dismembered and strewn about the lights and shadows of the universe.

Reality is more than any of us can see or hope to see; as intensely as I may see my parcel of reality, it is only that, a parcel, not the wholeness of reality: we cannot see reality without counting on what others see. And once you understand this, you will desire a vaster, more intense reality and you must act accordingly, for, as William Blake warns, he who desires and acts not, engenders the plague.

Freedom is the activation of desire. Buñuel's unsatisfied characters embody another perception, another way of seeing that is only achieved by slitting eyeballs, desiring the impossible, desiring all that for moral, political, or economic reasons has been hidden, mutilated, disfigured, or deprived of time, place, name, or reflection in our societies—he is a poet.

How to name the anonymous? How to see the invisible? Buñuel's oneiric insistence has this sense: to imagine an exacerbated desire. Through dreams, men and women (and children, of course: do animals dream?) attain the marvelous and terrible perception of what will never be. But the dream, if it becomes the reality of the dream, also becomes the being of an impossible reality, another, hidden, but no less true facet of reality, one of the most potent anchors of desire. Buñuel's films are an act of trust in the first and fragile encounter of desire and freedom in dream.

In *Wuthering Heights* (1954), Heathcliff descends into Cathy's tomb, beckoned by the dead woman's voice. The casket is before him. Behind him appears Cathy's brother armed with a shotgun. As he fires at Heathcliff, Heathcliff turns, mortally wounded, and imposes on the murderer the face of the lover, the woman, the sister.

In one dazzling image in this otherwise unsuccessful film, Buñuel makes us see how desire can assume and transfigure incest, sodomy, crime, and necrophilia so that the impossible love can take place, at least, in impossibility. And in *Nazarín* (1959), a girl dies

in a plague-ridden village but refuses the priest's spiritual consolation, with the words: *"Juan sí, cielo no"*: Give me Juan, not
heaven.

The contiguous nature of love and death makes Buñuel reflect
that in our world it is easier to die than to love; death, the realm
of the impossible, is much more possible than love, the very crux
of all possibility. Thus, the demonic characters in Buñuel take on
a cloak of evil, since death is the supreme expression of a supreme
absence, in order to attain love. Evil is forbidden yet it brings us
to the certainty of death. Good is endorsed yet it does not assure
the possibility of love.

Buñuel, who throughout his career constantly came under attack
by censors, clergymen, the police, housewives, and talk-show hosts
for fostering evil, and undermining morality, and defying conventional rationality, only indicates that good is not where society says
it is; and neither is evil. Buñuel's eternal question is in fact a
sadly severe one: You who judge as monstrous anomalies what you
yourselves are not—the fetishist, the necrophiliac, the rebel, the
lover, the dreamer—aren't you merely covering up your own repres-
sions and seeking to deny—to eradicate—the other's experience?
And if, physically and psychologically, the other is the strange
one—the madman, the homosexual, the dwarf—politically he is
the exterminable—the red, the Jew, the black, the rebel.

The first possibility (desire and freedom) of any human being is
to approach another human being. The cinema of Luis Buñuel is
one vast metaphor on the triumphs and defeats of being with others.
Hell is other people, said a character in Sartre. *But there is no other
heaven*, answers Buñuel.

Who fails? Perhaps Saint Simeon Stylites in *Simon of the Desert*
(1965), whipped by rain and wind high up on his splendid column
in the middle of the wilderness. I don't know. Is he not, useless
as it might seem, accomplishing his mad desire in pain, solitude,
and the turning away of temptation? Who shall judge him?

But Buñuel prefers the paradox of those who triumph through
failure: Nazarín and Viridiana. Perhaps the two most interesting
characters in the Buñuel canon are this complementary and very
Spanish pair: Viridiana, the young novice who seeks to save the
poor through prayer, cleanliness, and good manners; and Nazarín,

the priest who takes to the road in imitation of Christ. Both partake of the quintessential Spanish prototype: Don Quixote.

Don Quixote frees the galley slaves, who immediately stone their savior; Viridiana is mocked, dispossessed, and violated by the beggars she tries to save. Buñuel is faithful to the Surrealist slogan: Poetry shall be convulsive, or it shall not be. He extends this to the social and especially the religious realm: Fraternity shall be convulsive, or it shall not be; fraternity cannot be when it is but a disguise for our good conscience—repugnant, condescending, philanthropic.

Viridiana does not really wish to save the poor: she wishes to save her own bright image of sanctity. Viridiana/Quixote loves an abstract Christ/Dulcinea. The true Christ, in the parody of Leonardo's *Last Supper* (which happens to be the *First Supper* of the beggars), is a blind mendicant who cannot offer the novice (the bride of Christ) the erotic sustenance of her celestial vision.

Everyone, even a thief, a leper, or the physically handicapped, can be Christ. But Viridiana refuses the universality of redemption. Viridiana would not tolerate Christ incarnate, so she ends up accepting incarnation without Christ. Viridiana is initiated into the pot luck of sex by an elegant card shark, her cousin, and his lover, an erotic chambermaid. Viridiana, the female Don Quixote, has encountered the other two great Spanish archetypes, Don Juan and La Celestina, in a broken-down feudal manor where they form an unsanctified ménage à trois, playing cards and listening to records. Perhaps one day, having lived through the experiences of the flesh, Viridiana can return to the roads of La Mancha to redress torts, renounce the hell of innocence, and attain paradise.

Behind Buñuel, all of Spain. Kings and go-betweens, saints and lovers, monsters, madmen, and buffoons of the Spanish delirium ascend on the steps of Buñuel's films to the penthouses of Western progress. The figures of Western health, security, and optimism are lost in the baroque labyrinths of Spain.

A group of French gourmets can never sit together for a meal in *The Discreet Charm of the Bourgeoisie* (1972).

Two perfectly decent, rational pilgrims in *The Milky Way* would like to interpolate the experience of religion into the assimilated sequence of Western history; but faith proves to be a swirling, nonsequential reality of the imagination: if it is to be faith at all, it cannot be, by definition, proven: history is no history if it is not, in its turn, imagined: no one was present in the past, the past is an act of memory in the present: meet the ghosts, they are all here.

The linear progression of the narrative in *The Phantom of Liberty* (1974) is constantly violated by accident, non sequitur, tale-within-tale, dream, madness: time, culture, thought, have as many faces as there are different civilizations; the future has the name of a desire *now*.

Nazarín, saint, buffoon, and madman, decides to imitate Christ. And this decision, which at first glance would appear to be his greatest virtue, soon proves to be his supreme transgression. The imitation of Christ promptly leads the good Father Nazarín to brawls, scorn, superstition, mockery, jealousy, hate, injustice, and jail.

Before he sets his faith to the proof of experience, Nazarín believes that Christ individualizes redemption, makes it available to all. But, after the fact, he only knows that the imitation of Christ entails scandal, disorder, revolution. The Christian Way of Nazarín transforms him into an enemy of the established order.

He is accompanied in his pilgrimage by two women, two Sancho Panzas in skirts. The secret of this great film by Buñuel is its hidden eroticism. The two female squires of this holy Quixote do not allow Nazarín to idealize them: rather, they seduce and unsettle him as they substitute him for their lovers: a dwarf and a criminal. Don Quixote as witness to the monstrous and criminal loves of Dulcinea; Jesus, the voyeur before Mary Magdalene.

One of the possible ways of seeing the cinema of Buñuel, as I have indicated, is through this contemporary dilemma, adventure, or phenomenon: the religious temperament without religious conviction. Nazarín's solution seems at first rather obvious. The priest loses his faith in God but attains a faith in men. Only men shall redeem men. That is the important thing—whether they do it in the name of God or even against God.

The circle of Buñuel's themes thus closes in on itself, seemingly: saints and sinners meet and fuse and confuse themselves in the authentic experience of the world. All sense of scandal, violence, and critical humor in Buñuel consists, in the end, in this negation of negation, in this most fragile and most difficult act of love.

In an embrace but separate, forever united and forever alone:

Nazarín and the female camp followers; Robinson and Friday; Viridiana, the gambler, and the serving woman; Heathcliff and Cathy's ghost; Séverine and her invalid husband; the fetishist Archibaldo de la Cruz and his wax image of the woman he desires; a Jesuit and a Jansenist forever dueling in the ruins of a church designed by Piranesi; Tristana, mutilated of limb, and her sorrowful tyrant of an uncle, mutilated of spirit, who can no longer dominate her when she is condemned to crutches and a wheelchair; a little girl in *The Phantom of Liberty* and her parents, searching anxiously for her, calling the police, believing she has been kidnapped, and all the while she is there—we see her but the other characters in the film do not, though she insists, *Hey, look, here I am.*

So, once more, we are startled and dare not come to any conclusions regarding this eternally open and free filmmaker. His last film, *That Obscure Object of Desire* (1977), prevents me from closing the chapter on Buñuel: even if he has died, his films go on displaying their multiple levels of meaning.

In a third film version of the novel by Pierre Louÿs *La Femme et le Pantin*, Buñuel goes beyond the simple dichotomy of the Sternberg and Duvivier versions, where Marlene Dietrich and Brigitte Bardot were supposed to be two different women, angel and devil, Jekyll and Hyde. Buñuel, by casting two different actresses in the role of Conchita the flamenco dancer, shows us that they are really the same woman, although the old lover, Don Mateo, played by Fernando Rey as yet another incarnation of Don Juan, would like to see them as two different beings and Conchita, by offering herself as two, sees herself simply as other: she is not two women, she is another woman.

Desire finds its obscure object: Conchita presents herself as one and then another, and Don Mateo, prisoner of the Socratic universe, cannot cut the knots of the girl's complicated corset with his phallic sword. He cannot accept that, in order to be his, Conchita demands that Don Mateo also become another; he is incapable of transfiguration; he must have Conchita as the object of his desire and can have her only as Don Mateo, a decent, orderly, rich, middle-aged gentleman.

Conchita demands love from Don Mateo, the man of property who would buy the luxury of passion. And her demand inverts the usual roles: Conchita does not deny Don Mateo her love; it is he who denies it to the woman. The object of Don Mateo's desire is to own Conchita; the object of Conchita's desire is to be another in order to be herself. I am I, says the man; I am another, says Conchita, and you must also be another if you are to be *me*.

If Buñuel is perhaps the greatest artist of Surrealism, it is because he assimilates and transcends the two contradictory sides of a movement historically circumscribed but aesthetically unlimited as a permanent activity of the human spirit. Transform the world, change man.

Buñuel never doubted that the internal revolution, the profound liberator of the poetical energy dormant in every individual, is inseparable from an objective transformation of reality, independent of the fact that it may precede, accompany, or follow the latter. The important thing is not to interrupt this activity of the spirit even for a second, in none of its realms, because each and every one of them is the object of desire.

The true mode of this filmmaker is the open ending, the unfinished story, the devolution of responsibility to its purest and most original site: the conscience and the imagination of each filmgoer. This is most beautifully exemplified by the final scene of *Nazarín*, where the young priest, led away by police officers, is offered a most unwieldy gift by a compassionate peasant woman: a pineapple. Nazarín first says no, then accepts, saying, "May God repay you," and walks away, a prisoner carrying the spiked offering of another's compassion. Drums of sacrifice and execution are heard on the sound track. We are left with our own pineapples in our hands.

In Buñuel's artistry, film is freedom as well because it is capable of giving up its unarmed vision unto our own possible freedom. We can then start thinking honestly, not of the artist's responsibility, but of our own responsibility as spectators. If Buñuel were to answer in our name, perhaps he would lose his freedom and we would not have won ours.

I am now going to leave my friend Luis Buñuel as I introduced him to my friend Régis Debray in Paris in 1976. The young philosopher and revolutionary grabbed the old filmmaker by the lapels and shook him in mock anger, accusing him of keeping alive the dogmas and mysteries of the Catholic Church with his obsessions.

And Buñuel laughed helpless tears, and Debray went on: "No one would speak of the Holy Trinity and the Immaculate Conception today if it were not for you, Buñuel!! It's because of your films that religion is still an art!"

I am going to leave him as he celebrated his eightieth birthday and I asked him what he did to keep from being enshrined as a rebel, an agnostic Father of the Church, yet a man who is still attaining youth. He answered: "I know that I would give my life for any man's right to seek out truth, but also that I would fight to the death any man who believes he has found the truth."

I am going to leave him as he packed his bags in a seedy hotel overlooking the Montparnasse Cemetery in Paris, saying: "I am not going to do any more films. I don't want to die between locations, leaving an open script on my night table and a 5 a.m. call. I want to know whose hand will close my eyes."

I am going to leave him as I last saw him, in February of 1984. His wife, Jeanne, and his two sons, Juan Luis and Rafael, were there, and as I looked at them and spoke to them, they looked only at Buñuel. "I'll see you in October," I said. "No," he replied, "we'll never meet again." I am sure this was another of his famous jokes. As a matter of fact, Luis Buñuel is here all the time, even here today, and certainly every time I see one of his films or when I think of his endless art. I have not met another man of such humor, tenderness, intelligence, and passion. I shall miss him very much.

Borges in Action

A neighborhood in Mexico City called Colonia Juárez has given all its streets the names of foreign, mainly European cities. It is an old neighborhood, extensive and populous, formally caught between the boundaries of the two greatest metropolitan avenues, Insurgentes and Reforma.

But something flows out of these municipal frontiers, and it is an avenue surrounding a former racetrack, now a garden of forked paths, which since my childhood has been the most mysterious park in the city: the park of the Colonia Hipódromo, a circular park of broad alleys where you might still hear the pounding of ghostly hoofs, but also of distant feet hurrying over somber, humid pathways that seem to lead from one faraway place to another.

This is perhaps a sensation nurtured by all those signs in the Colonia Juárez reading Rome, London, Geneva, Antwerp, Milan, Warsaw, Prague. It is also an effect of the European migration to its shabbily elegant houses, crowded together in styles going from Parisian Belle Epoque to Barcelona modern to Humphrey Bogart forties to contemporary Las Vegas.

Curiously, most of the Jewish fugitives from Hitler's Europe who came to Mexico settled in this part of town, as did many refugees from Franco's Spain. The rundown cosmopolitanism of the neighborhood is accentuated by a Café Vienna, where you can have Sacher torte and coffee with *Schlag*. There are many kosher delis, German beer gardens, and an international bookstore where you can read the latest issue of *Die Zeit* or buy an Einaudi pocket edition of Italo Svevo or, for that matter, of Italo Calvino.

The old racetrack has been taken over by a winding, circular avenue: Amsterdam Avenue, full of beautiful old trees that seem to survive against the pernicious smog, and cluttered little residences, one hanging for dear life on the shoulders of the next one, as if fearing to fall headfirst into a nonexistent canal.

It is here, walking from the café to the bookstore a few years ago, that I first saw the blind man. I saw him . . . He walked with a white cane, of course, and this gave him away, certainly not the sureness of his gait. He came out of the bookstore and pointed in a certain direction with the cane. I saw his eyes and was mesmerized: he seemed to be literally looking inside himself, as if this were the only thing that counted in matters of sight—seeing outside being a totally frivolous affair. They were frightening eyes because of this interior depth, but kindly eyes because of their innocent dereliction in a city street.

I could not help following him, as his hatless head let a mane of thinning white hair be blown by the Aztec winds, which carry the bones of Moctezuma and Cortés as part of our everyday national asthma. But as he entered Amsterdam Avenue, I could not help feeling that something beyond sight—internal or external—was leading him to his rendezvous. There was a growing tremor in his hands, and his white hair moved with something more than mere motion. It started getting unseasonably cold; I wished for a muffler, and the blind man, indeed, pulled up his collar.

A boy, no more than ten years old, was sleeping next to a tree on the winding central alley of the avenue, and I saw the old man headed straight at him. He was one of the infinitely sad little boys one finds sleeping or crying in the streets of Mexico, destined to grow up swallowing fire at selected intersections during a perpetual rush hour, in exchange for a few copper coins.

I stepped between the blind man and the sleeping child.

He stopped. But he did not see me, I am sure.

He sniffed, he sensed, he grunted like a docile beast. Then he changed course and the child went on sleeping.

The blind old man hurried off, until he came to a halt before a tiny house done in stucco but in the Dutch style, with high pointed roofs, what we call *techos de dos aguas* in Spanish, and wooden lattices closed tight over the window panels. But the fastidious Dutch architect of this Hansel and Gretel abode had of course carved out two hearts in the wood, and now I saw the old man

come close to them, as if he could see inside the house, as he
saw, I am certain, inside himself. I was about to turn away; if he
was not blind, then he was just an ordinary man, a Peeping Tom
perhaps, walking around with a white stick so as to disguise his
vice.

Then the old man extended his arm toward me: he had surely
heard my footsteps, as the blind do, because as I halted he said:

"No, don't stop. Come here and help me. Tell me what you see.
Please."

How was I to refuse this plea? As I said before, he looked
extremely innocent, even childlike, as he gazed blindly on the
world, and only dangerous—how dangerous, I was yet to know—
when he looked inside himself. He needed *me* to look through
those carved Dutch hearts and tell him, somewhat against my better
judgment, that there was a fire, a chimney lit up—this was Mexico
City in June?—and then, and then a big chair, a wing chair, an
old chair—who sits there?—someone with his back to us, I told
the blind man, no, now he shows his hand, a pale bony hand,
there is a book in his hand, a small bound volume, he . . . he has
thrown it into the fire, I exclaimed!

The blind man went into a fury on hearing this. He grabbed my
lapels, almost choked me, screaming: "Don't let him do it, don't
let him burn the book, he will burn the world, he will burn you
and me, he will kill us!" He screamed in such agony that I banged
furiously on the door of the house, only to find that the door gave
way, creaking slightly, against the pounding of my fists. There was
a small foyer, smelling of must and forgotten umbrellas, then the
parlor, then my hand rescuing the volume, the blind man behind
me, panting, muttering ancient words I could not understand, and
before us, sitting in his wing chair, wrapped in velvet ecclesiastical
robes of an intense scarlet, his head covered in a skullcap with
cloth ears dangling like those of a basset hound, a man of infinitely
fine features, with a long thin nose, narrow fleshless lips, and a
penetrating gaze at once merry, disillusioned, astounded, forgiv-
ing, staring at us as he said: "Close the door, please. I hate drafts."

But the blind man did not heed him. He lunged toward my
hands, sniffing the scorched pages, caressing the rescued book.
As he felt its slightly singed corners, he turned on the gracious
gentleman sitting before the fire. "You fool! Why did you do this?"

"Look at it yourself. The book is blank. It is a blind book, don't you see? There are no words on it. Is it simply a fine book for a draftsman? I am not a draftsman. I have had enough portraits made of me. Could I compete with Holbein in drawing myself—or in drawing you?" And he looked at us disdainfully, with an ironical loathing.

"But why destroy the book?" I asked impulsively.

"Because, my friend, I believe that all the wisdom of the world is contained in thirty-two volumes," replied the thin, spiritual man. "When you travel as much as I do, from my native Rotterdam to Basel to Rome to Paris to Hertfordshire, you must be selective in your reading. I have honed my literate appetites down to thirty-two volumes. There is nothing more to know or that is worth learning. Why should I travel around with excess baggage? What use is there in an empty book, a book of white pages with no script?"

Sadly, the old man fingered the singed book and fluttered its pages. As he did so, the book for an instant seemed to catch fire again. No: it was simply, miraculously, that as the wind rushed through these pages, words appeared on one of them, the first page. And these words were a title. The blind man said it aloud, stopping there, on the first page: *The Aleph*. And then he told us this story, as the gentleman in sixteenth-century garb reached with trembling hands toward the fire and I started to feel as cold as he:

"A long time ago, Buenos Aires was melting in the summer heat as I visited a house I had reason to be attached to. It was now occupied by my acquaintance Carlos Argentino Daneri, who called himself a poet. Indeed, he went so far as to emblazon his first volume of verse with the blurb *Daneri Rival of Borges*. Let me tell you: I have yet to publish a book that blurbs: *Borges Rival of Daneri*! This is to tell you with what lack of personal sympathy I arrived at that house on Garay Street—but also what profound reasons I had to go there, in spite of the present occupancy of the house.

"Carlos Argentino Daneri, like most Latin Americans, had the chance to be Columbus *or* Quixote. If the latter, Quixote, he discovers new worlds. If the former, Columbus, he describes them. Hardly had I entered the house (for reasons totally alien to his disagreeable presence) when Daneri, my putative literary rival, assailed me with a description of the poem he was working on.

And hardly a minute had gone by before I realized that this man was not a poet but a land surveyor: he was enamored of space simply because there was so much of it; space, for him, was exact, millimetric, and realistic.

"Daneri had in mind to set to verse the entire face of the planet, and by 1941, when I visited him, he had already dispatched a number of acres of the State of Queensland, nearly a mile in the course run by the river Ob, a gasworks to the north of Veracruz, the leading shops in the Buenos Aires parish of Concepción, the villa of Marian Cambaceres de Alvear in Belgrano, and a Turkish bath establishment not far from the well-known Brighton Aquarium.

"I could not stomach this. Even my passion for being in the house on Garay Street, my memory of the woman who died there on a burning February morning (remember, my Northern friends, that the Austral summer occurs during your winter months) after enduring an agony that never for a single moment gave way to self-pity or fear—this memory of mine could not tolerate his assault on literary intelligence. So this was my rival, not only in literary matters but also, who knows (the ways of the flesh are as mysterious as those of the Lord), for the affection of his first cousin, Beatriz Viterbo—ah, *cousin, cousine*, contiguous flesh, ah, temptation, temptation, thy name is incest, ah, I imagined them together in the flesh whereas *I* had only been her platonic, lonely suitor. I fled, banging the door on Daneri's nose, who thought I was consumed by literary envy of his minuscule descriptions of the Australian hinterland (what a redundancy!) and of his ridiculous substitution of blues for azures, ceruleans, and ultramarines. Bah, let him think what he wished. I fled the house on Garay Street quoting Hamlet to myself: 'Oh God! I could be bounded in a nutshell, and count myself a king of infinite space . . .'

"A king of infinite space: Beatriz Viterbo, my lonely love, had died in 1929. By 1941, her cousin was describing a Mexican gasworks as though it were the Proustian towers of Martinville. But a few days later, this same Carlos Argentino, more anxious than angry, phoned me: he was losing his house—his house! the house of Beatriz! The *pícaro* dared called it his, dared called *her* his, *hissssss*! It was about to be taken over and torn down by a neighboring saloon belonging to a certain pair, Zunino and Zungrí, his landlords.

"I must admit I shared his anguish: Beatriz was dead. Now we were both about to lose the space where Beatriz once sat with a Pekinese lapdog, smiling, hand on her chin . . . But the redoubtable Daneri was not thinking of Cousin Beatriz. He was afraid of losing something, he babbled, *the Aleph*, in the cellar, beneath the dining room; he discovered it as a child, it was his, his, *hissss*; he could not finish his poem without it. It was the only place on earth where all places *are*—seen from every angle, each standing clear, without any confusion or admixture . . .

"I hung up the phone and rushed to the madman Daneri. His craziness filled me with spiteful elation—yet in it I recognized what I was looking for: Cousin Beatriz was a woman, a child, with almost uncanny powers of clairvoyance; but forgetfulness, distractions, contempt, and a streak of cruelty were also part of her. *She had the madness of genius and pain*. Her cousin had only the madness of prideful stupidity and vanity. I could feel contempt for his madness and love for her madness, but what drove me to their house—all right, their house, *yessssss*—was a foreboding that the meeting place of madness and this extravagant Aleph, this place of all places, was called *death*, and that from it the idiotic Daneri was excluded because, like an eternal adolescent, he believed he would never die, whereas, she, she was dead: so she could be, she must be, in a place where he could not see her, but I, who loved her, could. I could because I loved her.

"Let me hasten now: Daneri received me, after making me wait in the living room. He showed me to his cellar, gave me a thread-bare pillow, asked me to lie flat on my back in the darkness and see the Aleph—and if I didn't see it, he said, my incapacity would not invalidate his experience—which, of course, he had transposed to his epic poem describing the world. But he added: 'In a short while, you can babble all of Beatriz's images . . .'

"So, he had seen me as I waited in the parlor for him to receive me. He had seen me sadly kissing the portrait of Beatriz, murmuring imbecilic words of love: 'Beatriz, my darling Beatriz, Beatriz gone forever, it's me, it's Borges . . .'

"Now I was alone; in the dark, facing a blindness called the Aleph, and afraid that Daneri, to keep his madness undetected, would have to kill me. I had fallen into his trap, I . . . I . . .

"I had now met my own despair as a writer. For what my eyes

now beheld was simultaneous, but what I could write about it would have to be successive, because language, alas, is successive. I saw a diameter of little more than an inch, but all space was there, actual and undiminished: each thing (a mirror's face, let us say) was an infinitude of things . . . I saw the teeming seas; I saw daybreak and nightfall; I saw the multitudes of America; I saw a silver cobweb at the center of a black pyramid; I saw a splintered labyrinth (it was London); I saw, close up, unending eyes watching themselves in me as in a mirror . . . I saw bunches of grapes, snow, tobacco, lodes of metal, steam . . . I saw all the ants on the planet . . . I saw in the drawer of a writing table (and the handwriting made me tremble) unbelievable, obscene, detailed letters that Beatriz had written to Carlos Argentino; I saw the dust and bones that had once deliciously been Beatriz Viterbo; I saw the circulation of my own dark blood . . .

"I stopped. I did not see her as I remembered her. I went up the cellar stairs. Carlos Argentino was curious. Had I seen anything? No, I replied. No. So he was not mad. So he was not admirable. So he did not kill me. So he had been with her as I had not.

"I walked out and only then, in the street, did I see what the Aleph had denied me: the spectral image—for it could not have been real, but a reverberation of my dazed eyes in the hot night— of a tall, frail, slightly stooped woman; in her walk there was an uncertain grace, a hint of expectancy . . ."

He paused for a moment and added: "I had seen precisely everything that negated the laborious efforts of Daneri, and seeing it, I understood that he, too, for all his stupidity, was a writer who had to face the seasons of discontent, trying to wrest language out of the order of succession and into the order of simultaneity, where he might contemplate his own creation as if it were a painting. But Daneri did not understand how to apply this to his own telephone-book writing, alphabetical, consultable, like the Yellow Pages perhaps unreadable. So I went home, sorrowful but determined to learn a lesson from the Aleph. Here it is. I carry it with me always; it became my Bible. It is as simple as *taxonomy*: a classification, that is a selection, which is necessarily a representation. Carlos Argentino was defeated by space; I wanted to defeat space. So I wrote:

"There is a certain Chinese encyclopedia in which it is written that animals are divided into the following categories:

    a. Belonging to the Emperor
    b. Embalmed
    c. Tamed
    d. Suckling pigs
    e. Sirens
    f. Fabulous
    g. Stray dogs
    h. Included in the present classification
    i. Frenzied
    j. Innumerable
    k. Drawn with a very fine camel's-hair brush
    l. Et cetera
    m. Having just broken the water pitcher
    n. That from afar look like flies . . ."

As the blind man who called the narrator of his story Borges trailed on into *o, p, q,* et cetera, I, who had fixed my gaze on him, wondering where he would end, if at all, if ever, as if he had now become sick by proxy with Carlos Argentino's mania for extension, now disguised as enumeration, I had not seen what the man in the skullcap now bade me see in the fireplace before him: I turned my hypnotic gaze from the blind man, who so pathetically recalled the act of seeing the world, to the serene man who tugged at my coattail and, without a word, bid me look into the fireplace. Again, words were forming in the fire, a U, then a Q, then a B, then an A, finally an R—UQBAR, this name flashed on the tips of the flames, UQBAR, UQBAR, as the blind man suddenly stopped his enumeration and said: "Space is but a sign referring us to a meaning and a meaning referring us back to its sign: the Earth and the Aleph. Once this significance is understood in all of its in-significance, the writer allows a poisoned orchid to flower between the Earth and the Aleph: the personal history of Beatriz Viterbo. And history is time."

He was silent for a moment, then added: "We have left the world behind."

This occurred as the man in the red robes took my hand and the walls around us disappeared, and the blind man with them, leaving just myself and the cool old Dutchman holding hands, surrounded by a name that had become invisible too, UQBAR, a name searching for a space. So the serene gentleman, who I now realized was a serene fool, took out a little book from the folds of his robes—he and I, you understand, suspended there in a world of glass, boundless—and captured the invisible word UQBAR in the blank pages of his book. I glanced at the title on the spine: *Moriae encomium*. But the pages of the book—I gave a start—were as empty as those of the book he had tried to burn and the blind man urged me to save: *The Praise of Folly*. That name found the space of a book, and a landscape began to grow around us, as if this could be a new space slowly coming into being in place of the Aleph, in place of the name UQBAR shifting like smoke in the pages of *The Praise of Folly*. But what were we to think, this serene fool and I, I ask humbly of you, of a place that was ticking away like a time bomb, for this was all you could hear; there was nothing to see, nothing to smell, just the sound *tick-tock, tick-tock,* and nothing—nothing—as the source of that sound.

Yet, as we peered, overcome by this sensation of floating in a pure vacuum, things started to exist, they came into being: the object only, you see, but not the space that should have surrounded and sustained it.

The man next to me shook violently. Then he tried to kiss my lips. I stepped back (toward what? there was nothing to hold on to) with a grimace of heterosexual disgust; maybe this man thought he was in England, for he was saying: "No, no, do not misunderstand me. My first enthusiasm, you know, was England, going from Holland to England: traveling, I always traveled so much; but only in England was my enthusiasm for being there saluted with kisses. The English greet you with kisses, say goodbye with kisses; everything there is full of kisses: welcome, kiss Erasmus, bye-bye kiss-kiss, Erasmus . . . Now we are coming, my friend, into a country, a country is appearing . . . Look!"

He said this as though, indeed, the world were being born, responding to the blind man's rather intimidating parting phrase: "We have left the world behind."

But I could not see the world again. I looked at the man who called himself Erasmus, peering intently into the vacuum, and I asked my companion in the vortex of the fast-disappearing world of Uqbar: "Tell me the truth: are you simply remembering these things?"

He looked at me without surprise and said yes, I am only remembering.

The man Erasmus flipped his pages. Now the letters were all there, back in the book, but they were illegible because they were juxtaposed, layers of writing resting on previous layers, a palimpsest that seemed to grow in the same way that time grows: remembering and desiring.

So these things we saw were there only because we remembered them, not even because we desired them. Yet the eye of Erasmus alighted on a word in that jumble of words—that verbal jungle of his making: his writing and all the readings his writing had been submitted to had come together at last—and then he pointed at it with a lonely finger and repeated: TLON, T-L-O-N. He said he had never written or read that word; never, he assured me, and then became silent for what seemed a very long time.

"We are simply duplicating things," he said at last. "The only new thing in this book is the name of the time from which we are watching the other place, Uqbar. This must be Tlon because we are looking for Uqbar, which has no space, through another country that does not have space either. But look around you. There is no space, yet there is here everything that makes space possible: a pure serial and temporal reality. Space does not live in pure time, where we now are, my friend. But the objects of space do, because they are supported by memory, which is a temporal fact."

This was all very fine, and I would have accepted the theory with which Erasmus rationalized our situation, if at that moment the blind man had not passed in front of us, hurrying like Alice's rabbit. And we followed him in haste, past a snowstorm and a shower of roses and a hot river and a naked woods, into a library, yes, a library that was simply a mirror, or a mirror, perhaps, that looked like a library, and in this conjunction of both—mirror and library—we saw the two previous worlds, Uqbar and Tlon, being constantly reproduced by images and words, in a silent dialogue.

"Welcome. You have come to Orbis Tertius," murmured the blind old man, with an insecure wave of his hand, as though he were flipping through the pages of books in the air. "From here you can see what you could not while you were there."

This was simply not true: we saw nothing. But we understood that Orbis Tertius was not Tlon or Uqbar: it merely hid them. This

was what the blind man did not know and we did. And if that was
true, then Uqbar also hid Tlon and Orbis Tertius, and Tlon hid
Orbis Tertius and Uqbar. How could this have escaped the blind
poet's attention? Erasmus explained the situation methodically to
the sightless one.

"You are right," the blind man said. "But in the other two
countries no one thought of joining a mirror and a library, so that
only here can we perceive the reproductive existence of the two
other worlds through images and words."

He offered us some very weak tea drawn from old book leaves
and heated to a limp vapor by the reflections of the moon on the
glass, as he spoke on about involuted lands, mutually imbricated
lands, New Worlds that might exist both in time and in language,
although not in space. These New Worlds are only maintained
through imagination in its original form, he said, which is myth.
Only myth, he assured us, permits the verbal and temporal circulation of involuted worlds, for these worlds—his voice became
paler than his tea as he retreated from us slowly into a garden
behind the library-mirror—never say their true name, as this garden—he seemed to disappear into a truly impenetrable dimness—
is not exactly what it seems . . .

"I know this!" Erasmus exclaimed in anger as the blind man
disappeared. "Why, I almost invented the theory of the illusion of
appearance, I was so intent on finding irony behind the dogmas
of faith and reason: everything had to be dual, various, different,
and now this upstart comes and . . ."

In his irritation, Erasmus was rapidly flipping again through his
volume of *The Praise of Folly*, sensitive to the touch of its worn
calf binding and its heavy lettering, almost in relief, as if Latin,
by now, had to be touched to be read: like the blind man's Braille.

We were in the middle of a garden. We had followed in the
blind man's footsteps, unwittingly or unfeelingly, as we talked. It
was a garden of forking paths: a veritable maze. What can you do
in a maze? Either stand still or try to get out. We did not know
what to do. I started some small talk: Hey, Mr. Erasmus, am I
right in surmising that that triple land we just left—Tlon, Uqbar,
Orbis Tertius—is impossible in space but quite possible in time
and language? What three lands? asked Erasmus, spinning on his
heels, irritated by our disorientation. I could not remember. I had

forgotten. I made an effort. Before that . . . we . . . he and I
. . . a fire in the cellar . . . a stooped, elegant woman . . . dead,
was she? . . . bones, a photograph . . . No, of course, we were
lost in the garden of forking paths, and this is where our story
began.

Nothing had happened before—I laughed nervously—nothing
at all. As we walked through the space of this maze, amazed, the
pages of yet another book, written in Chinese characters, fell like
leaves, indeed like the clues of the treasure hunts of our childhood,
and Erasmus and I hurried through the labyrinth of hedges and
rosebushes, oppressive because the cloudless, Magritte-like sky
opened its windows far above our heads, and in the abrupt corners
of this chase we could distinguish well-known, well-worn scenes
of the history of the New World: Columbus landing, Vespucci
naming, Cortés conquering, Pizarro slaying, Almagro mining the
desert, Bolívar plowing the sea, Moctezuma falling stoned to death,
Las Casas denouncing, Atahualpa dying, Tupac Amaru rebelling,
Aleijandinho sculpting, Sor Juana writing—we saw it all, peering
at us as from monstrous flowers with faces, à la Cocteau, until we
were back at the original scene, Columbus landing inside the thorny
capsule of a rose. And I looked, stopping, panting, at Erasmus,
as though incriminating him and his pen pals for inventing the
Myth of the Golden Age in the New World and then deserting us
with our epic violence, and no golden bough, in our hands: a cross
and a sword and our eyes bloodshot through and through, lost in
the garden of forking paths—Queen Isabella's jungle in the New
World.

But like the detective in Poe's "Purloined Letter," the gentleman
from Rotterdam who now lived on Amsterdam Avenue, he as
breathless as I after this runaround, did the one obvious thing. He
picked up one of the sheets that the fleeing blind writer presumably
had been dropping in his wake, and there Erasmus the polyglot
read, translating aloud for my benefit: "He read with precision two
writings of the same epic chapter."

The Dutchman, who obviously had some kind of oral fixation,
kissed this page repeatedly, looked at me with sympathy, yes, but
also with something like a pity I did not urgently desire, and said:
"Come, my friend of the New World, do not accuse me of anything.
History was not closed; the epic can have another ending. We are

being offered by our fleeing blind friend two, and why not three, six, nine, infinite readings of the same text. Do you understand now? Not just your single, fateful past, or your single radiant, utopian future; oh, no—but the infinitely shapable, re-creatable, prefigurable, but also retroactively diversifiable times of freedom . . ."

"Bah"—I shrugged again, full of Hispano-Aztec hubris. "This blind man must be an Argentinian, for he is constantly inventing what he does not have . . ."

Erasmus looked on uncomprehending and said so. "Excuse me, I do not mean to . . . but—"

"I mean," I abruptly said, "that Mexicans descend from the Aztecs, and Argentinians descend from ships."

"Argentinians?" queried Erasmus. "What is that?"

"Yes, you know, the endless wealth of cows and wheat fields, but the poverty of its immediate tradition. Since you don't have the architecture of Florence, not to speak of Oaxaca, you have to build . . ."

"Tlon . . . Uqbar . . . Orbis Tertius . . ." the Dutchman slowly murmured, and I gasped, thrust back into memory, feeling that names were the princes of the art of memory, but the entranced Dutchman went on slowly: "Borgia, Borja, Burgos, what the hell was the name he said? Where had I read it before? Where was it obscurely mentioned, as a mere biographical parenthesis—where? Where?"

He stopped because it was at this very moment that a simple little gate appeared before us, breaking the fatal monotony of the maze, and opening on a space so vast that it seemed actually to be a portrait of the horizon: it was equally monstrous.

"We are in the Pampa," I told my Dutch friend, having the advantage of Mexican grade-school maps in my mind. "We are out of the labyrinth."

"So I would surmise," Erasmus said, looking sadly at the limitless flatland that suddenly became a rushing canvas of war enveloping us frightfully with its proximity of menace and blood and spilled guts. A man fell from his horse into our arms, and Dutch and I, amid the pounding of hoofs, and acrid bursts of artillery, and glistening duels by saber light, embraced the fallen officer, who murmured: "I am a coward. Do not let me die. Please. I need a second chance to prove my courage in this battle."

"It goes on, yes," I said idiotically, "the battle goes on."

"It shall repeat itself." He eyed me, his brow frozen in blood and hatred, and he turned to the strange Dutchman in flowing robes: "Tell them what has happened. Tell them that this second time Pedro Damián was courageous!"

Then he fell quiet. So quiet that we could not tell whether he was dead or alive. The battlefield fled from us: its rampaging fervor moved westward, carrying the broad horizon with it, and only a small hut was left, an isolated dot, along with the loneliness of the ombu tree.

We moved the inert body there. An old gaucho opened the door of the smoke-filled hut. He looked at us as though we were not there. He had eyes only for the man who had called himself Pedro Damián. We asked the gaucho for help.

"He is so heavy, so listless. Is he dead or alive?"

"Put him down there," said the gaucho, pointing to a mat on the earthen floor. Then he bid us take some maté that was brewing on the fire outside and went back into the hut. Erasmus and I, civilized beings that we were, sipped our tea and, looking back on the destiny of Pedro Damián, wondered whether, in effect, acts are our only symbols. No, said the Dutch humanist, probably not. Is Achilles or Hector conscious that he is only a symbol? Of course not! he exclaimed rhetorically, as if addressing a class of not-too-bright students. Then our politeness was shattered by a fearful scream from inside the hut.

We rushed in. The gaucho was there, his hands holding a knife above his head, then plunging it over and over into the writhing, screaming body of the man we had saved, Pedro Damián—and a frightful occurrence: the long blade of the murdered man, as he fell, expiring, went on fighting the blade of the gaucho, who finally let go of it but continued assassinating his victim, the same gestures but with clenched, empty hands. And it was the daggers that now fought, by themselves, as if they had hated each other since they were forged, even before the gaucho ever met his victim Pedro Damián, whom he now addressed, fearful that he might perhaps still be alive, fearful perhaps of the blood hatred of the two au-

tonomous daggers, screaming, oblivious of our presence: "I killed
my father once already! Why did you have to come here and force
me to repeat what I did forty years ago! Damn you, I don't even
know you, damn you, damn you! Why did you give me a second
chance! I, Tadeo Isidoro Cruz, damn you, whoever you are!"

Then, as the two flashing daggers fell on the dust of the pampa,
the man who called himself Tadeo Isidoro Cruz, as if he were going
to say nothing more until he himself died, sat down next to the
sickly hearth of his hut, repeating endlessly: "Any destiny, no
matter how long and complicated, consists of only one moment:
the moment when a man forever knows who he is . . ."

"Knows who he is . . . Knows who he is . . .

"Who he is . . ."

Sitting on three chairs made of skins and hide, we gazed with
him intently at the fire in the hut, and as the walls imperceptibly
thickened, they reintegrated into a cellar whose sides ceased to
be transparent and reappeared simply because we now saw them
again, as if they had always been there. The illusion was strong
in our spirits. Erasmus took my hand, and I, highly suspicious of
his inclinations, wrenched it out of his hold. But I was wrong. He
was not thinking about me, and the mad fire in his eyes only
reflected his desperate search for the in-octavo volume of *The Praise
of Folly*. On finding it, he seized it with a sort of erotic glee. "Here
is my space, at least the space of a book," he said eagerly, laughing.

I tried, halfheartedly, to join in his amusement. But we now
faced, in this cellar, the figure of a bedraggled man, emaciated,
with long hair and beard, somewhat like the Count of Monte Cristo
after a ten-year stay at the Château d'If. He lay there in the cellar,
unaware of us, without a candle, without a book, grunting from
time to time, touching things lightly—in the posture, indeed, of
Adam receiving life, in the Sistine Chapel, from the hands of
Yahweh.

But it was no god, but a strange goddess who finally came down
the cellar stairs into this scene, bearing a tray of limp lettuce and
a dish of water: a dish, not a glass, not even a cup. The prisoner—
what else could he be—lapped it up on all fours, then took the
lettuce between his . . . his paws? and devoured the leaves.

The woman who had come down was frail and slightly stooped.
She sat in front of the man and ate a large sugared cake. She then

told him: "Georgie, you cannot come out yet. The dictator is still in power. You must be patient. Ten years is nothing, do you understand?"

"No . . . not Jorge," he denied vigorously. "Pedro . . . not Georgie . . . Salvadores. Pedro Salvadores is my name . . . you know . . . why do you . . . ?"

"Now, now, Georgie boy, all this darkness can drive a man crazy, I know. But would you prefer a sudden night and a blade seeking your throat?"

"No, no," he said. "Although I dream of that, sometimes, yes."

"I don't know what you dream, little boy George. But it all takes place in this cellar, don't forget that. You just dream things."

"Can I . . . ?" the man said, stretching out his hand.

"No," she said. "No, no longer. You are a coward, you know," she said with a cruel smile. "I don't keep you here. You are not a prisoner. You are afraid, remember that, you are afraid to come out."

"Afraid?" he said. "No, I cannot see you. It is so dark. I can't see you anymore."

We did see her as she walked, stooping, up the stairs: singing "Karma Chameleon." We saw her, forgetful, distracted, contemptuous, beautiful, with that streak of cruelty mixed with clairvoyance . . . and an up-to-date spiked hairdo.

"Beatriz," the blind man managed to say as the cellar door closed on him and plunged him once more into the dream of darkness, from which he was now unable to escape: yes, whatever he dreamed would now take place in that cellar. At first he may have been a hunted man, a man in danger; later, when we saw him, he was more like an animal at peace in its burrow, or perhaps even a sort of dim god, yes . . .

Erasmus and I walked up from that cellar back into his cozy Dutch parlor, where the fire was slowly dying. He rubbed his hands and then went to his shelf of thirty-two books. He chose one and caressed it and opened it, nodding to me all the time: "Yes. You know, my friend, that garden of forking paths was mentioned in this book. But the name of the book—look here—or the name of the garden is never mentioned. Do you know why?"

"Yes," I ventured. "Both were somewhere else."

"No, not somewhere else. They were *something* else. What?"

I resented his questioning and decided not to reply. His eternal snooping attitude, his curiosity disguised as some sort of superior calling: this academic gossipmonger, Erasmus of Rotterdam, indeed!

"I don't know and frankly I don't give an Amster . . ."

He raised a fine, long-boned hand, a Holbein, transparent hand, a veined hand of wax and ink: the hand of Erasmus, bidding me to wait and listen: "Tell me, where were we truly lost? In the maze or in the pampa?" This question stunned me.

"Why, come to think of it, in the pampa. In the labyrinth." I hesitated. "In the maze, I expected to be lost, but it was—you are right—so symmetrical; its sharp turns, its willful design: we were *meant* to be lost . . ."

"So we weren't: the maze is foreseeable," said the Dutchman. "But the pampa isn't. But that is the real labyrinth: the straight line, you see."

"Then you mean, Erasmus, that everything we have seen stands for something else: the maze is simple; the straight line is the true labyrinth, the true mystery . . ."

"And the true name of the garden of Eden, El Dorado, is Time. Do not go away impatiently without understanding this, you above all, you of the New World: you do have something more than an epic fatality; you do have a mythic chance. Come, look at this book, another of my little treasures.

The book he gave me was bound in rough cowhide, like an edition of *Don Segundo Sombra* my father had when I was very young. But this was not the celebrated novel by Güiraldes. It was, of all things, *Don Quixote*. Only, instead of the author's name I expected, Miguel de Cervantes Saavedra, or even as a joke one of its multiple sub-authors or plagiarists—Cide Hamete Benengeli, Avellaneda—I read a name unknown to me: Pierre Ménard.

The book was opened by the bony hands of the Dutchman. "In a certain place of La Mancha, whose name I do not wish to remember, there lived not long ago a gentleman of . . ."

"But this is Cervantes's book!" I exclaimed.

"No," Erasmus said. "The text is the same, but the intention is different."

"What is the intention?" I asked impatiently.

"To confront the mysterious duty of literally reconstructing a spontaneous work," Erasmus said.

"I don't understand," I responded socratically.

Erasmus did not sigh. As a matter of fact, he was quite serious and probing. "We shall never know if all that we have seen is true. But if it is, then this man from Buenos Aires, this Jorge Luis Baroquess, or Borghese or whatever, whom the woman Beatriz Viterbo (if it is indeed she) refused the name Pedro Salvadores, and then this reader of his he was able to mention simply because he knew he was read by him, could also be conceived, you understand, as the writer of everything that has ever been written.

"His name—Burgos—Ménard—Cervantes—Salvadores—Borges—is merely an accident." The Dutchman vigorously nodded. "The sum of all spaces can only be read by one man who is many men, but it could only be written by one writer who was all writers, and his work, in consonance with this principle, could only be one work: one vast narrative in which space has been seen and defeated in and by the Aleph of Literature, an endless, multifarious, multi-cultural time taking over its space: space is only memorable when time occurs in it."

He gasped, and urged me to profit from my chance, our chance: a second chance for our terrible history, an opportunity to refashion time by admitting its polycultural sources. Oh, what a chance that this Borgia or Borja, or George Burke, or Boy George or whatever, was not content with our modernity or with our past or with the promise of our future, unless it included all the wealth of our cultural present, including the present of all our pasts: our modernity is all that we have been, all of it. This is our second history, and Burgos, or Borja, or Berkeley, has written its introduction. We must rewrite our Koran, our Cabala; we must also rewrite the Bill of Rights and the Code Napoléon. We must live them, and in order to do so we need, before, at the same time, later, it does not matter, to reassimilate our ancient myths, our Renaissance epics and utopias; our colonial hunger for the baroque, and our desolate—I looked at him, sinking back into the cave of his time—our desolate Erasmian irony.

Yes: he was now dead to me, he was now back in the cave, having escaped from it: this house, I suddenly realized, was but a cave to which he came back, telling everyone—I saw him, thin and querulous now, a veritable busybody of truths—telling those who remained here that the world outside consisted of realities, not of shadows.

I did not want to see what they did to him; I heard them, the shadows, as I slowly left, shouting back at him that he lied, that their shadows were the only things that existed. And he whispered to me from afar: "They are mad and caught forever in error."

I looked back only once. Erasmus was shrouded in the darkness of the cave. But Borges was balancing himself above the cave on a tight wire, dressed in rags and with a colorful umbrella in his upraised arm.

I left the sudden darkness of the Dutch house and stepped out, back onto Amsterdam Avenue and the glaring sun, the *resolana*, the smells, tortillas burning, gasoline burning, wafts of dead bone borne by the smog, the sound, old clothes, *ropa vieja*, *dulces*, *pirulíes*, knife sharpeners, insulting claxons, a shave and a haircut, *tantararata*, the sights, the dying trees of Mexico City, and the boy still sleeping, still dreaming, at the foot of the tree.

My compassion was aroused at the sight. Should I awaken him, give him a few hundred pesos, perhaps invite him to have some cake in the nice Viennese coffee shop on the corner?

But what if that boy was not really sleeping but being dreamed? I trembled for an instant amid the circular ruins. What if that boy is the child of a man who has dreamed him—a ghost that does not know its name? Wouldn't it be fearful if the boy woke up, his dream interrupted by my Goody Two-shoes humanitarianism— here, boy, take a few pesos, have some Sacher torte—only to discover that he was not a boy but the projection of another man's dream? Perhaps the dream of that prisoner in a cellar?

I saw the blind man fall from his wire if the child awakened.

I saw the old philosopher caught forever in the darkness of his cave—his cellar—his Aleph—his book—if the boy woke up, condemning them both to a realization that they too, terrified and humiliated, were not men but the projection of another man's dream: they, Borges and Erasmus, nothing but dreams of a little Mexican boy being dreamed by them, lying next to a tree on Amsterdam Avenue. I feared what I now knew: a perfect word, a necessary word, is like a dream; once it is said or written, nothing can be added, and what it describes disappears forever—the palace, the desert, the mirror, the library, the compass pass: when they are identical to their word, they disappear forever, they dream forever, they die forever. We must never find the exact identification of word and thing; a mystery, a divorce, a dissonance must remain; then a poem will be written to close the gap, but never achieve the union. A story will be told.

I decided to wake the child up. I shook his shoulder, already dreaming of coffee and cake.

But as he woke up, I wished I hadn't. As his eyes opened, I wished, truly, that I had left well enough alone.

I swear to you: I never intended to wake myself up and see what I am now seeing.

The Other K

In December of 1968, three shivering Latin Americans descended from the train at the Prague terminal. Between Paris and Munich, Cortázar, García Márquez, and I had talked a great deal about detective stories and consumed heroic quantities of beer and frankfurters. As we neared Prague, a spectral silence invited us to share it.

There is no city more beautiful in Europe. Between the High Gothic and the Baroque, its opulence and its sadness consume themselves in a wedding of stone and river. Like the character in Proust, Prague won the face it deserved. It is difficult to return to Prague; it is impossible to forget it. It is true: too many ghosts inhabit it.

The windows of Prague send a shiver down your spine; it is the capital of defenestrations. You look toward the windows and see how they fall, killing themselves on the long and glistening stones of the Mala Strana and the Czernin Palace—the Hussite reformers and the Bohemian agitators, also nineteenth-century nationalists and communists who have yet to find their century. Ours was not the time for Dubček, although it was for the two Masaryks. Between the Golem and Gregor Samsa, between the giant and the beetle, Prague's destiny spans the Vltava River much as the Charles Bridge: heavy with sculptural fatalities, peopled by baroque *comendadores* who perhaps await the hour of the interrupted enchantment in order to move, speak, curse, remember, escape the malefice of Prague. Mozart's *Don Giovanni* opened here, that oratorio of the sacred malediction and the profane joke transcended by grace; from here,

160

Rilke and Werfel fled; here, Kafka remained. Here, Milan Kundera awaited us.

If History has a sense . . .

I had met Milan Kundera the spring of that same year, a spring that would come to have only one name, that of his city. He went to Paris for the publication of *The Joke* and was feted by his publisher, Claude Gallimard, and by the poet Aragon, who wrote the prologue for the French edition of this novel which "explains the unexplainable." The French poet added: "One must read this novel. One must believe in it."

He was introduced to me by our common editor at Gallimard, Ugné Karvelis, who since the early sixties has insisted that the two most urgent centers of contemporary narrative were to be found in Latin America and Eastern Europe. "No, not Eastern Europe, certainly not." Kundera jumped when I used this expression. Hadn't I seen a map of the continent? Prague is in the center, not in the east of Europe; the European east is Russia, Byzantium in Moscovy, Caesaropopism, tsarism, and orthodoxy.

Bohemia and Moravia are the center in more than one sense: lands of the first modern revolts against oppressive hierarchy, elected lands of heresy in its primary sense—to elect freely, to take for one's own; critical spaces, hurried transitions along the dialectical stages—barons vanquished by princes, princes by merchants, merchants by commissaries, commissaries by citizens; heirs to the triple legacy of the modern age—the intellectual revolt, the industrial revolt, and the national revolt.

This triple heritage had given substance to the communist coup of 1948. Czechoslovakia was ripe for the passage from the realm of necessity to the realm of freedom. The Kremlin commissars and the local satraps, for all their science, did not seem to understand that in the Czech and Slovak lands social democracy could arise from civil society and never from bureaucratic tyranny. Because they ignored this, because of their servility before the Soviet model— already set at a distance by Gramsci when he spoke of the absence of an autonomous society in Russia—the party bureaucrats bound Czechoslovakia, strapped her to Stalinist terror, informers, trials of degraded comrades, the execution of the communists of tomorrow by the communists of yesterday.

If history has a sense, Dubček and his communist companions did nothing but afford it one. As of January 1968, from inside the political and bureaucratic machinery of Czech communism, these men took the step forward that, ironically, by making effective the substantive promises of Marxist orthodoxy, rendered useless its formal constructions. If it be true (and it was, and it is) that Czech socialism was the product, not of an underdevelopment hungry for accelerated capitalization in exchange for political numbness, but of an economically and politically fulsome capitalist industrial development, then it was true (and it is, and it will be) that the next step was to admit the gradual withering away of the state as the social groups took on their autonomous functions. Socialist society started to occupy the spaces of communist bureaucracy. Central planning gave way to the initiative of workers' councils; the Prague politburo, to the local political organizations. A fundamental decision was made: at all levels of the party, democracy would express itself through the secret vote.

Undoubtedly, it was this last measure that most irritated the Soviet Union. Nothing was more acrimoniously objected to by the Russian officials against Dubček. In order fully to realize this democratic step, the Czech communists moved forward the date of their congress. The country was politically decentralized but democratically united by one extraordinary fact: the appearance of a free press, a press truly representative of the diverse social groups. The press of the agricultural workers, of the industrial workers, of the students, of the scientific investigators, of the intellectuals and artists, of the small shopkeepers, of the newspapermen themselves, of each and every one of the active components of Czech society. In the socialist democracy of Dubček and his companions, the initiatives of the national state were commented upon, complemented, criticized, and limited by the information of the social groups; conversely, these groups took initiatives that were commented upon and criticized by the official press. This multiplication of powers and opinions within communism was about to be politically translated to the Parliament itself. But first it was necessary to establish democracy within the party. And this is what the U.S.S.R. was not about to accept.

The Ides of August

Kundera gave us an appointment in a sauna near the river to tell us what had happened in Prague. It seems this was one of the few places without ears in the walls. Julio Cortázar preferred to stay at the university lodging where we were living; he had found a shower worthy of himself, undoubtedly designed by his namesake Verne and worthy, also, of adorning the submarine quarters of Captain Nemo: a glass cabin, hermetically sealed, with more faucets than the *Nautilus* and full of oblique and vertical showers aimed straight at the head, the shoulders, the hips, and the knees. This paradise of hydrotherapy became dangerously saturated at a certain height—that of men of regular height such as García Márquez and myself. Only Cortázar, with his more than six and a half feet, could enjoy himself without drowning in the contraption.

Unfortunately, there was no shower in the sauna where Kundera awaited us. After half an hour of intense sweating, we asked for a bath in cold water. We were taken to a door that opened over the frozen river. A hole had been cut in the ice, inviting us to get rid of our discomfort and reactivate our circulation. Milan Kundera softly propelled us toward the inevitable. García Márquez and I sank into these waters, inimical to our tropical essence, and emerged the purple color of certain orchids.

Kundera was bellowing, a Slavic giant with one of those faces you find only east of the Oder River, the cheekbones high and hard, the upturned nose, the close-cropped hair bidding goodbye to the blondness of youth and entering the gray territory of the early forties, a mixture of prizefighter and ascetic, a cross between Max Schmeling and the Polish Pope John Paul II, with the physical frame of a lumberjack, of a mountain climber, the hands of what he is, a writer, the hands of what his father was, a pianist. Eyes like all Slavic eyes: gray, fluid, smiling for an instant as he saw us transformed into Popsicles, the next instant somber—that astonishing transition from one sentiment to another which is the hallmark of the Slavic soul, that crossroads of passions. I saw him laughing; I imagined him as a legendary figure, an ancient huntsman of the Tatra Mountains, bearing on his shoulders the furs he ripped off the bears, so as to look more like them.

Humor and sadness: Kundera, Prague. Anger and tears. The Russians were loved in Prague; they were the liberators of 1945, the vanquishers of Hitlerian satanism. How was one to understand that now they were here entering Prague on their tanks to crush communists in the name of communism, when they should be celebrating the triumph of Czech communism in the name of socialist internationalism? How to understand it? Anger: a girl offers a bouquet of flowers to a Soviet soldier riding atop his tank; the soldier reaches forward to take the bouquet and kiss the girl; the girl spits in the face of the soldier. Astonishment. Where are we? many Soviet soldiers ask themselves. Why are we received this way, with spits, with insults, with flaming barricades, if we came to save communism from an imperialist conspiracy? Where are we? ask the Asian soldiers. They told us we were sent to crush an insurrection in a Soviet republic. Where are we? Where? "We who lived all our lives for the future," says Aragon.

Where? There is anger, but there is also humor, as in the eyes of Kundera. Closely watched trains: the trains that enter Czechoslovakia carrying troops from the Soviet Union blow their whistles, ride and ride, go around and end by coming back to the frontier from which they originally departed. The resistance to the invasion organizes itself by means of underground radios. The Soviet Army faces a gigantic joke: the switchmen sidetrack the military trains; the military trucks obey the erroneous signs on the highways; the radios of Czech resistance cannot be found.

The good soldier Schweik heads the maneuvers against the invader and the invader starts getting nervous. Marshal Grechko, commander of the forces of the Warsaw Pact, senselessly has the façade of the National Museum in Prague machine-gunned; the citizens of Kafka's homeland called it El Grechko's mural. An Asian soldier, who has never seen such a thing before, crashes against the glass partitions of the stores in the underground subway of Wenceslas Square, and Czechs put up a sign on the broken glass: NOTHING STOPS THE SOVIET SOLDIER. The Russian troops enter Marienbad by night, where a cowboy movie is being shown in an outdoor movie house. They hear Gary Cooper shooting and arrive with their machine guns at the ready, firing at the screen. Gary Cooper goes on walking down the empty street of a town in the Far West, forever wounded by the bullets of a bitter joke. The moviegoers of Marienbad pass a sleepless night, and the next day, as in Kundera's *Farewell Party*, they return to take the waters.

Aragon switches on his radio the morning of August 21 and listens to the condemnation of "our perpetual illusions." With him that morning, we all know that, in the name of fraternal assistance, "Czechoslovakia has sunk into servitude."

My Friend Kundera

We were invited by the Union of Czech Writers during that strange period, from the autumn of 1968 to that final spring of 1969. Sartre and Simone de Beauvoir had been to Prague, as well as Nathalie Sarraute and other French novelists; also Günter Grass. The whole point was to make believe that nothing had happened, that although Soviet troops were hiding in the woods near Prague, the Dubček government could still save something, not admit defeat—still make a go of it, with the humorous perseverance of the soldier Schweik.

We, as Latin Americans, had reason to talk of imperialisms, invasions, Davids and Goliaths; we could defend, the law in one hand, history in the other, the principle of non-intervention. We gave a collective interview about these matters for the literary review *Listy*, then directed by our friend Antonin Liehm. It was the last interview to appear in the last issue of the review. We did not talk of Brezhnev in Czechoslovakia, but of Johnson in the Dominican Republic.

It never stopped snowing during the days we were in Prague. We bought ourselves fur hats and boots. Cortázar and García Márquez, who are equally intense music lovers, went out to find recordings of Janáček's operas; Kundera showed us original scores by the great Czech musician that he had found among the papers of the pianist Kundera senior. With Kundera we ate wild boar and knedliks in dill sauce and we drank slivovitz and we formed a friendship that, for me, has grown with time.

Since then I have shared—and I share more and more with the Czech novelist—a certain vision of the novel as an indispensable element, an element not to be sacrificed, of the civilization a Czech and a Mexican can have in common: a way of saying things that could not be said any other way. We talked a lot then and later, in Paris, in Nice—when he traveled with his beautiful wife, Vera, to France and there found a new home because in his "normalized" homeland his novels cannot be published or read.*

One can laugh bitterly. The great literature of a fragile language, ambushed in the heart of Europe, has to be written and published outside its territory. The novel, supposedly in agony, has so much life that it must be murdered. The "exquisite corpse" must be forbidden because, it seems, it is a dangerous corpse. "The novel is as indispensable to man as bread," says Aragon in his prologue to the French edition of *The Joke*. Why? Because in it one will find the key to what the historian, the conquering mythographer, ignores or dissembles.

"The novel is not menaced by exhaustion," says Kundera, "but by the ideological state of the contemporary world. There is nothing more opposed to the spirit of the novel, which is profoundly linked to the discovery of the relativity of the world, than the totalitarian mentality dedicated to the implantation of an only truth."

Can the man who thus speaks then write, in order to oppose one ideology, novels of the opposite ideology? Borges says of the Koran that it is an Arab book because no camels are ever mentioned in it. Elizabeth Pochoda has noted that the longevity of political oppression in Czechoslovakia is witnessed in the novels of Kundera because it is never mentioned.

The condemnation of totalitarianism doesn't deserve a novel, says Kundera. What he finds interesting is the similarity between totalitarianism and "the immemorial and fascinating dream of a harmonious society where private life and public life form but one unity and all are united around one will and one faith. It is not accidental that the most favored genre in the culminating period of Stalinism was the idyll."

The word has been spoken and no one expected it. The word is a scandal. It is comfortable to protect oneself behind the grotesque definition of art offered by Stalin: "Socialist content and national form." It is very amusing and very bitter (the bitter joke is really a structure of the narrative universe of Kundera) to translate this definition into pragmatic terms, as a Prague critic explained it to

---

* In the winter of 1979, Kundera was deprived of his citizenship by the Prague government. He now resides in Paris, where he teaches at the Sorbonne.

Philip Roth: socialist realism consists in writing the praise of the government and the party in such a way that even the government and the party will understand it.

The scandal, the unsuspected truth, is what we hear through the voice of Milan Kundera: totalitarianism is an idyll.

Idyll

Idyll is the name of the terrible, constant, and decomposed wind that blows through the pages of Milan Kundera's books. It is the first thing we must understand. Warm breath of nostalgia, stormy glare of hope: the frozen eye of two movements, one leading us to reconquer the harmonious past of the origin, the other promising the perfect beatitude of the future. They confuse themselves in one movement, one history. Only historical action would offer us, simultaneously, the nostalgia of what we were and the hope of what we shall be. The rub, Kundera tells us, is that between these two movements in the idyllic process of becoming one, history will not let us simply be ourselves in the present. The commerce of history consists in "selling people a future in exchange for a past."

In the famous conference at the University of Jena in 1789, Schiller demanded the future now. In the very year of the French Revolution, the poet refused a promise constantly deferred, so that it would always be a lie without any possible confirmation, thus always a truth, always a promise at the expense of the wholeness of the present. The Enlightenment consummated the secularization of Judeo-Christian millenarianism and for the first time placed the Golden Age not only on earth but in the future. From the most ancient soothsayer to Don Quixote, from Ovid to Erasmus—all of them seated around the same bonfire of goatherds—the time of paradise was in the past. But starting with Condorcet, the idyll only has one time: the future. On its promises the industrial world of the West is built.

The great contribution of Marx and Engels is the recognition that man lives not by the future alone. The luminous future of humanity—a humanity severed by the Enlightenment from all bonds with the past, defined by its philosophers as barbarous and irrational—consists for communism also in restoring the original idyll, the harmonious paradise of communal property, the Eden degraded by private property. Few utopias are more seductive in this sense than that described by Engels in his prologue to *The Dialectics of Nature*.

Capitalism and communism share the vision of the world as a vehicle toward a goal that is deemed identical to happiness. But if capitalism proceeds by way of atomization, convinced that the best way to dominate is to isolate, to pulverize, to augment the necessities and satisfactions—both of them equally artificial—of individuals who need more and feel happier as their isolation grows, communism proceeds by way of total integration.

When capitalism tried to save itself with totalitarian methods, it mobilized the masses, dressed them in boots and uniforms, and put swastikas on their arms. The infernal paraphernalia of fascism violated the operative premises of modern capitalism, whose god-fathers, one in action, the other in theory, were Franklin Delano Roosevelt and John Maynard Keynes. It is difficult to fight a system that always criticizes itself and reforms itself with greater concreteness than is immediately possible for even the most severe of its adversaries. But this same system will lack the seductive force of a doctrine that makes the idyll explicit, that promises not only the restoration of the lost Arcadia but also the construction of the Arcadia-to-come. Totalitarian dreams have nourished the imagination of several generations of young people: diabolically, when the idyll had its heaven in the Wagnerian Valhalla and the operatic legions of the new Scipio, in the spirit of Pound, Céline, and Drieu La Rochelle; angelically, when it could inspire the faith of Romain Rolland and André Malraux, Stephen Spender, W. H. Auden, and André Gide.

The characters in Kundera rotate around this dilemma: to be or not to be in the system of the total idyll—the idyll for all, with no exceptions, with no cracks, an idyll precisely because it no longer admits anything or anybody who could doubt the right of all to happiness in an ubiquitous Arcadia, paradise of the origin and paradise of the future. Not only an idyll, as Kundera underlines in one of his stories, but an idyll for all:

All human beings, since the beginning of time, aspire to the idyll, aspire to this garden where the nightingales sing, this realm of harmony where the world no longer rises alienated against man, and man is alienated against all other men, but where man and men are, on the contrary, made of the same material and where the fire which brightens the sky is the same which brightens the souls. There each individual is a note in a sublime fugue by Bach and whoever would not have it so becomes a black dot, devoid of sense, worthy only of being crushed under the nail like a flea.

Like a flea. Milan Kundera, the other K of Czechoslovakia, has no need for allegory in order to provoke the estrangement and the sense of discomfort with which Franz Kafka flooded, in luminous shadows, the world that already existed without knowing it. Now, the world of Kafka knows it exists. Kundera's characters have no need of awakening transformed into insects, because the history of Central Europe took care to demonstrate that a man need not be an insect in order to be treated as such. Worse: the characters of Milan K live in a world where all the hypotheses of the metamorphosis of Franz K stand unshaken, with one exception: Gregor Samsa, the cockroach, no longer thinks he knows; now he knows he thinks.

He has a human form, he is called Jaromil and he is a poet.

The Holy Child of Prague

During the Second World War, Jaromil's father lost his life because he believed in a concrete absolute; he died to protect a woman, save her from being denounced, tortured, and murdered. That woman was the lover of Jaromil's father. The poet's mother, who feels an equally absolute repugnance toward physical animality as her husband felt toward moral animality, betrays him, not because she is sensuous, but because she is innocent.

When the father dies, the mother comes out of the kingdom of the dead with her son in her arms. She will wait for him outside his school with a great umbrella. She will portray the beauty of sadness in order to invite her son to become with her that untouchable couple: mother and son, frustrated lovers, absolute protection in exchange for absolute renunciation.

This is precisely what Jaromil is going to demand, first of love, then of the revolution, finally of death: absolute surrender in exchange for absolute protection. It is a futile sentiment, that which the serf offered his lord. Jaromil believes it to be a poetic sentiment, *the* poetic sentiment, which permits him to position himself not "outside the limits of his experience but well above it."

Thus, to see it all. To be seen. The messages of the face, the enigmatic looks through a keyhole with the girl Magda in her bathtub (as enigmatic as the encounter of the feet of Julien Sorel and Madame Renal in Stendhal's *Rouge et Noir*), the lyricism of the body, of death, of words, of the city, of other poets (Rimbaud, Mayakovsky, Wolker) make up the original poetic repertory of Jaromil. He does not want to separate it from his life; he wants to be, like Rimbaud, the young poet who sees all and is totally seen before becoming totally invisible and totally blind. All or nothing. He demands it of his love for the redhead. This love must be total or not be at all. And when the lover does not promise him all her life, Jaromil awaits the absolute of death; when the lover does not promise him death, but sadness, she stops having a real existence, an existence corresponding to the absolute interiority of the poet: all or nothing, life or death.

All or nothing. He demands it of his mother beyond the foolish and bitter expectations of the woman who wishes to be the frustrated lover of her son. The varied and ambiguous repertory of the absolutist maternal blackmail, nevertheless, decomposes into too many partial emotions: pity and reproach, hope, anger, seduction. The poet's mother (and Kundera tells us that "in the houses of poets, women reign") cannot be Jocasta and thus becomes Gertrude, believing she gives her son all so that the son may continue to pay her until he pays the impossible; that is, all. Jaromil will not be Oedipus but Hamlet: the poet who sees in his mother not the absolute he longs for but the reduction that murders.

In the most beautiful page of *Life Is Elsewhere* (Chapter 13 of the third part), Kundera places Jaromil in "the land of tenderness, which is the land of the artificial childhood":

Tenderness is born in the instant in which we are pushed toward the threshold of the adult age and realize, with anguish, the advantages of childhood which we did not understand when we were children. Tenderness consists in creating an artificial space where the other person can be treated as a child. Tenderness is also fear of the physical consequences of love; it is an attempt to remove love from the world of the adults and to consider the woman as a child.

This is the impossible tenderness that Jaromil the poet will not be able to find in his mother or in his lover, since both women bear the "insidious, constrictive love, heavy with flesh and responsibility" of the adult age—whether it be the love of the woman for her poet lover or the love of the mother for her grown son. This is the irretrievable idyll in human beings that Jaromil is going to seek and find in the socialist revolution. He needs the absolute in order to be a poet, much as Baudelaire needed, to be a poet, "to exist always in a state of drunkenness, drunk with wine, with poetry or with virtue, as you like it."

The Credulous Poet

Lyricism, Milan Kundera informs us, is a virtue and man becomes drunk in order to confuse himself more easily with the universe. Poetry is the territory where all that is said becomes true. The same can be said of a revolution. It is the sister of poetry. And it saves the young poet from the loss of his tenderness in the adult, relativist world. Poetry and revolution are absolutes; young people are "passionate monists, messengers of the absolute." The poet and the revolutionary embody the unity of the world. Adults laugh at them, and so begins the drama of poetry and revolution.

Revolution then shows the way to poetry. "The revolution does not want to be studied or observed; it wants to become one with her: it is in this sense that it is lyrical and that lyricism is essential to it." Thanks to this lyrical unity, the biggest fear of the young poet is calmed: the future ceases to be a question mark. The future becomes "that miraculous island in the distance" because "the future ceases to be a mystery; the revolutionary knows it by heart." Thus, there shall never be a future; the future shall always be a known yet deferred promise, similar to the life we conceive in the instant of our childhood tenderness.

When he finds this identity (that is, this faith), Jaromil feels freed from the demands of the deceitful Gynaeceum, where feminine love is partial and egotistical but appears pretentiously disguised as an absolute. The uncertainty of revolutionary eras is an advantage for youth, "since it is the world of the fathers which is thrown into uncertainty." Jaromil discovers that his mother was the obstacle in his search for *the* lost mother. This lost mother is the revolution and it demands that we lose all in order to gain all; above all, liberty: "Freedom does not begin there where the fathers are refused or buried, but where they are not. Where man comes into the world without knowing from whom."

The revolutionary idyll substitutes everything, embodies everything; it is at once parasite and new birth, and it demands more than the fathers, more than the lovers: "The glory of duty is born from the severed head of love." The revolution contains the idyllic temptation of appropriating poetry, and the poet accepts it because, thanks to the revolution, he and his poetry will be loved "by the whole world."

This idyll compensates for the insufficiencies of life, of love, of mother, of lover, of childhood itself, elevating them to the lyrical unity of experience, community, action, the future. It is an armed prophecy making an armed prophet of the poet. It is impossible not to surrender before this idyll and offer on its altar all our real actions, actions even more real, more concrete, more revolutionary.

The poet can be an informer. This is the terrible reality stated in *Life Is Elsewhere*. The young poet Jaromil informs in the name of the revolution, condemns the weak, sends them to the gallows, and innocence shows us its bloody smile. "The poet reigns with the hangman" and not, Kundera underlines, because the totalitarian regime has deformed the poet's talent, or because the poet is mediocre and seeks the totalitarian refuge. Jaromil does not inform in spite of his lyrical talent, but, precisely, because of it.

We are not accustomed to hearing something so brutal, and it is necessary to let Kundera speak for himself since he has lived something that we only know secondhand, when he addresses "us":

All the young rebels around you, who can be so sympathetic, would have reacted, in the same situation, in the same manner. If Paul Eluard had been a Czech, he would have been an official poet and his pure and innocent heart would have identified itself perfectly with the regime of the trials and the nooses. I am astonished at the Western incapacity to see its own face in the mirror of our history. The tragicomedy which is being acted out in my country is also that of your ideas, your enthusiasm, your doctrines, your fantasies, your dreams and your cruel innocence.

Kundera is forty-nine years old [at the time of this writing]. At eighty, Aragon could say, "That which we sacrificed in ourselves, that which we tore out of ourselves, out of our past, is something impossible to value, but we did it in the name of the future of all."

The century is going to die without the need to repeat this sacrifice. It is sufficient to die, in our time, to defend the integrity of the present, to defend the integrity of the presence of the human being; he who kills in the name of the future of all is a reactionary.

The Internal Utopia

We cannot evade the burning question in the novels of Milan Kundera. It is a question of our times and it possesses a tragic resonance because it is a fight within ourselves and affects our possible freedom. The question is simply this: How to fight injustice without creating injustice? It is the question of any man who acts in our time. Witnessing this movement, Aristotle limited himself to stating that tragedy is "the imitation of action." What is tragic is neither passive nor fatal, but what acts. Perhaps the answer to Kundera's question, which is our question, is to be found in an order of values capable of absorbing the ethical causality of history, and of elevating it to a conflict, no longer between good and evil, but between two values which perhaps are not good and good, but which will surely not be evil and evil.

The loss of paradise, we read in *Life Is Elsewhere*, only allows us to distinguish beauty from ugliness, not good from evil. Adam and Eve know themselves to be ugly or beautiful, not evil or good. Poetry is next to history, waiting to be discovered, waiting to be invited into history by the poet who confuses the violent idyll of the revolution with the serene tragedy of poetry. Jaromil's problem is Kundera's problem: to discover the invisible avenues that depart from history and then lead to realities we had hardly suspected, hardly imagined, whose modern doors were opened by Franz Kafka.

Coleridge imagined a history told not before or after, above or under, time but in a way next to time, alongside time—the companion and indispensable complement of time. The avenue toward this reality, which completes and makes immediate reality have a sense, is to be found on an extraordinary level in Kundera's novel, where, truly, life is to be found. The opening toward that place where life is (the internal utopia of this novel) has its locus in each and every one of the words which tell us that what we accept as reality is not fully existent because it does not realize that its sister reality, its possible reality, is there beside it, waiting to be seen. More, waiting to be dreamed.

Like Buñuel's films, like Du Maurier's *Peter Ibbetson*, Kundera's novel only exists fully if we can open the windows of the dream it contains. A mystery named Xavier is the protagonist of the dream, which is a dream of the dream, a dream within the dream, a dream whose effects linger while a new dream—the son, the brother, the father of the previous dream—peeks out from it. In this epidemic of dreams, which infect each other, Xavier is the poet that Jaromil could have been, that Jaromil is because he existed next to him, or that perhaps Jaromil will be in the dream of death.

The important thing is that in this dream within a dream—this dream of Russian dolls, similar to the infinitely oracular time of *Tristram Shandy*—everything happens for the first time. Thus, everything occurring outside the dream is a repetition. History, Marx said, first appears as tragedy; its repetition is a farce. Kundera draws us into a history that denies all rights to tragedy and to farce in order to consecrate itself perpetually in the idyll.

When the idyll evaporates and the poet becomes an informer, we are authorized to look for the poet elsewhere: his name is Xavier; he lives in a dream; and there history (not the dream) is a farce, a joke, a comedy. The dream contains this farce because history has expelled it with horror from its deceitful idyll. The dream admits it temporarily, hoping that history will not repeat itself. This shall be the moment in which history ceases to be a farce and can become the place where life can be. Meanwhile, life and the poet are elsewhere, and there they openly reveal the farcical nature of history.

The chapters devoted to Xavier beg the question: Does the poet not exist? And answer with these words: No, the poet is simply elsewhere. And this place where the poet is, but where the poet acts history as a farce, is a comical dream, which, by the way, reveals the vast influence of Milan Kundera as the master of the modern Czech filmmakers. In the seamless passage from one dream to another, history appears as a tearless farce. The melodrama of Balzac's *La Grande Bretèche* is represented by the Marx Brothers, who, as everyone knows, are the fathers of the Marx Sisters, the "Little Daisies" of anarchy in socialism imagined by the filmmaker Vera Chytilova. The perverse dream of the movies is the nightmare and the ambition of Jaromil to be seen by all, to feel "all eyes turned toward him." In the cinema and in the theater, all the others—the world—see us. The undoubted terror of German Expressionist film consists precisely in this possibility of always being seen by another, much as Fritz Lang's Mabuse incessantly sees us from his cell in the madhouse or as Peter Lorre, the vampire of Dusseldorf in *M*, is seen by the thousand eyes of a mendicant night.

That which has been seen by all cannot have any pretenses to originality or, for that matter, virginity. Represented as oneiric theater and rewritten as impossible novel, history always appears as a farce. But if it be only a farce, this is a tragedy—such is the sense of the joke in Kundera. In a world deprived of humor, the joke can only be the refusal of the universe: "a sock in the statue of Apollo," a policeman locked forever in a closet, walled in like a character from Edgar Allan Poe played by Harold Lloyd. Jokes, humor, are exceptional and liberating: they reveal the farce; they mock the law; they essay freedom. Because of this, the law denounces the joke as a crime.

Dura Lex

In both Ks, Kafka and Kundera, a hermetic legality rules. Liberty is no longer possible because liberty is already perfect. Such is the solemn reality of the law. There is no paradox in this statement. Freedom supposes a certain vision of things; it holds the minimal possibility of giving a sense to the world.

But in the world of the penal laws of Kafka and of the scientific socialism of Kundera this is no longer possible. The world already has a sense and this sense is given by the law, says Kafka. And Kundera adds: The world of scientific socialism already has a sense, and revolutionary law, which is nothing but objectified history, common and idyllic, gives it to the world. It is useless to search for another meaning. You insist? Then you will be eliminated in the name of the law, the revolution, and history.

Given this premise, authentic freedom becomes a self-destructive enterprise. The person who defends himself only hurts himself: Joseph K in *The Trial*, the land measurer in *The Castle*, all of Kundera's jokers. Jaromil, on the other hand, not only does not defend himself; he doesn't even offer passive resistance. He enthusiastically joins the political idyll, which is his poetic idyll transformed into historical action. Poetry converts into a farce when it identifies itself with the historical idyll: the subversive poetical act then consists of not taking this history or this law seriously. The poetic act becomes a joke. The leading character of *The Joke*, Ludvik Khan, sends a postcard to his sweetheart, a young communist, serious and jealous, who seems to love ideology more than Ludvik. Since Ludvik does not conceive love without humor, he sends her a postcard with the following message:

> *Optimism is the opium of the people!*
> *Long live Trotsky!*
>> *signed Ludvik*

The joke costs Ludvik his freedom. "But, comrades, it was only a joke," he tries to explain before being sent to a work camp as a coal miner. Yet humor must be paid with humor. The totalitarian state learns to laugh at its victims and perpetrates its own jokes. Is it not a joke that Dubček, for example, should be a trolley-car inspector in Slovakia? If the state is the author of the jokes, it is because it would not leave even this freedom to the citizens, and then the citizens, much as the protagonist of Kundera's story "Edward and God," can exclaim that "life is very sad when one can take nothing seriously."

Such is the final irony of the historic idyll: its ponderous solemnity and its interminable enthusiasm end by devouring everything, even the subversive jokes. Laughter is crushed when the joke is codified by the perfection of the law, which from that moment also says: "This is funny and now you must laugh." I believe there is no image of totalitarianism more terrifying than this one created by Milan Kundera: totalitarianism over laughter, the incorporation of humor into the law, the transformation of the victims into objects of official humor, prescribed and inscribed in vast fantastic constructions, which, like the prison landscapes of Piranesi or the labyrinthine tribunals of Kafka, pretend to control destinies.

The destiny of the young boy Jaromil in *Life Is Elsewhere* exhausts itself with one empty note of salvation: the opposing symmetry with his father's destiny. His father lost his life because he believed in the concrete absolute of saving another person's life. Jaromil lost his life because he believed in the abstract absolute of informing on one person. Jaromil's father acted as he did because he felt that the necessity of history was a critical necessity. Jaromil acted as he did because he felt that the necessity of history was a lyrical necessity. The father died, perhaps without illusions, but also without delusions. Deluded, the son gave himself up to a dialectics in which each joke is transcended and devoured by a superior joke.

Kundera the novelist, a reader of Novalis, searches only for that instance of writing which—relative as all narrative is, risky as all poetry is—can augment the reality of the world while it says that nothing should support the total weight of life, neither history nor sex nor politics nor poetry.

The Corner of Destiny

In April 1969, democratic socialism was formally buried in Czechoslovakia. The Prague Spring, in effect, died two deaths: the first in August 1968, when the Soviet tanks entered so that the elections within the Communist Party would not take place; the second, when the Dubček government, in a country occupied by the "fraternal" invader, desperately looked for the proletarian solution, since it had not been able to apply the armed solution. The Law on Socialist Enterprise created the factory councils as democratic centers for the political initiative of the working class. It was the last straw: the pretension of giving Moscow lessons in proletarian politics. The U.S.S.R. intervened decisively through its local Quislings, Indra and Bilak, to determine the final fall of Alexander Dubček.

Milan Kundera defines democratic socialism in Czechoslovakia as "an attempt to create a socialism without an omnipotent secret police; with freedom of the spoken and written word; with a public opinion of which notice is taken and on which policy is based; with a modern culture freely developing; and with citizens who have lost their fear."

Who wants to laugh? Who wants to cry? Today the joke in Czechoslovakia is made by the state. This it learned from its enemies—humor, albeit a macabre humor. Do you wish to write novels? Then top my joke, a perfectly legal joke, sanctioned and executed in name of the idyll. Two gravediggers, sent by the Prague government, arrive with a coffin on their shoulders at the house of one of the signers of "Charter 77," which demands the implementation in Czechoslovakia of the agreements on Human Rights subscribed to in Helsinki by the Husak regime. The police had informed them that the signer had died. The signer says that he hasn't died. But when they leave and he shuts the door, he waits a moment and asks himself if, in effect, he has not died.

I am soon going to look for my friend Milan and continue talking with him. His shoulders are more burdened, his spirit more introspective, more absent in the profundity of his dark and clear world, where optimism costs dearly because it is much too cheap and where the novel is situated beyond hope and despair in the human territory of moving destinies and relative truths, which is the land of the authors he and I love and read—Cervantes and Kafka, Mann and Broch, Laurence Sterne. For if in history life is elsewhere because in history a man can feel responsible for his destiny but his destiny can feel irresponsible toward him, in literature man and destiny are mutually responsible because one and the other are not a definition or a sermon on any absolute truth, but, quite the contrary, a constant redefinition of each human being as a problem. This is the sense of the destiny of Jaromil in *Life Is Elsewhere*, of Ludvik in *The Joke*, of the nurse Ruzena, the trumpeter Klima and Dr. Skreta, who injects his semen into the hysterically sterile women in the most finished and disquieting of Kundera's novels, *The Farewell Party*. This is the sense of the elegy in his memorable *Book of Laughter and Forgetting*: when we forget we die, because death is not the loss of the future but the loss of the past.

In opposition to the owners of history, Milan Kundera is willing to give it all up for his own destiny and the destiny of his characters outside the "immaculate idyll" that pretends to give all and gives nothing. The illusion of the future has been the idyll of modern history. Kundera dares to say that the future has already taken place, under our noses, and that it stinks.

And if the future has already taken place, only two attitudes are possible. One is to admit to the farce; the other is to start all over again and rethink the problems of human beings. In this final corner of the comical spirit and the tragic wisdom where the idyll cannot penetrate with its historic and histrionic light, Milan Kundera writes some of the great novels of our time.

His corner is not a jail. A jail, Kundera warns us, is but another space of the idyll, which amuses itself in theatrically illuminating even the most impenetrable penal shadows. It is not a circus either. Power has found the means of wiping the smile off the citizens' faces and forcing them to laugh legally.

It is the internal utopia, the real space of the untouchable life, the reign of humor where Plutarch understood the character of history better than in the bloodiest of combats or in the most memorable of sieges.

Gabriel García Márquez
and the Invention
of America

This is a cow. She must be milked every morning so that she will produce milk, and the milk must be boiled in order to be mixed with coffee to make coffee and milk.

I need only, to make them reappear, pronounce the *names*: Balbec, Venice, Florence, within whose syllables had gradually accumulated all the longing inspired in me by the places for which they stood.

"How realities are to be learned or discovered is perhaps too great a question for you or me to determine, Cratylus; but it is worthwhile to have reached even this conclusion, that they are to be learned and sought for, not from *names* but much better through themselves than through names . . ."
    "That is clear, Socrates . . ."

The first of these three quotations is from a famous passage in *One Hundred Years of Solitude*, by Gabriel García Márquez, in which, after a plague of insomnia, the whole village of Macondo is affected by loss of memory, so that Aureliano Buendía devises a saving formula: he marks everything in the village with its name—*table, chair, clock, wall, bed, cow, goat, pig, hen*.

At the beginning of the road into the swamp they put up a sign that said MACONDO and another larger one on the main street that said GOD EXISTS.

In the second quotation, from *Swann's Way*, the Narrator has just accomplished one of the greatest feats of modern fiction: the liberation of time, through the liberation of an instant from time that permits the human person to re-create himself or herself and his or her time. This splendid literary achievement, through which the novel becomes the ideal vehicle for the reintroduction of the human person into time and through time into himself or herself, his or her authenticity, has its fragile but luminescent origin in what is probably a handful of lies: just a few names, Balbec, Guermantes, Venice, Parma, in which the Narrator learns that names forever absorb the image of reality because they are the privileged meeting places of desire; and desire through names can substitute for time itself:

> Even in spring, to come in a book upon the name of Balbec sufficed to awaken in me the desire for storms at sea and for the Norman Gothic.

But Proust's novel, as Roland Barthes warns us, is a voyage of both learning and disillusionment: from an age of words when we think that we create what we name (Parma, Balbec, Guermantes), to an age when the original prestige of names is ruined by contact with the outer world ("So it was this! Madame de Guermantes was only this!") to the age of things, where words manifest themselves as something outside the speaker, as objects (Bloch's anti-Semitic speeches are a rejection of a guilty passion in himself for another: it reveals the truth of the passion as it becomes a thing).

The third quotation is from Plato's *Cratylus*, perhaps the first book of literary theory of the Western world. In it, several attitudes toward names are debated by Socrates and his friends. To Cratylus, names are intrinsic to things: they are natural. To Hermogenes, they are purely conventional: whatever name you give to a thing is its right name. Socrates concedes that an onomastic legislator might give things their fixed or absolute or ideal name; but this substantialist demiurge is soon defeated by history. He makes names, but, alas, the dialectician uses them, and, says Socrates, simply by paying good coin to the Sophists, we will not learn the true name that we come to know dialectically, in its usage, but not originally, in its essence.

Plato, who does not hold the world of letters in high esteem, would not fall into any trap laid by the likes of Marcel Proust (or Gabriel García Márquez). He makes Socrates reveal the deceit of Hermes, which is similar to that of Kafka's messengers: though he is identified with the power of speech, Hermes, the messenger of the word, the purported interpreter of the gods, cannot even give us the true names of the divinities, for it is clear that among themselves the gods address one another in a manner different from our own. They use their true names; we do not.

It is Hermes who is guilty. He circulates words as if they were money and robs them of their permanence, which is the same as their essence; he makes words have a double meaning, sometimes true, sometimes false, always worn thin.

Socrates would then have men of reason dispense with names and rather seek to know things directly, in themselves or through each other, in their relationships. The *Cratylus* is, of course, a polemic against Heraclitus and his philosophy of constant change. It defends a substantialist point of view: if things are always changing, there will always be no knowledge. Names are changing and changeable words, and they belong to the unstable and unessential world where "all things are like leaky pots."

Cratylus is not convinced by Socrates; he prefers to think that Heraclitus's ideas are true. Socrates lets the argument rest. He bids Cratylus come back another time and teach him; and Cratylus leaves hoping that Socrates will also continue to think of these matters. So the dialogue ends on a civilized note of mutual tolerance.

This is America. It is a continent. It is big. It is a place discovered to make the world larger. In it live noble savages. Their time is the Golden Age. America was invented for people to be happy in. You cannot be unhappy in America. It is a sin to have tragedy in America. There is no need for unhappiness in America. America does not need to conquer anything. It is too vast. America is its own frontier. America is its own utopia.

And America is a name.

Gabriel García Márquez is the name of an American writer, a writer of the New World that stretches from pole to pole rather than from sea to shining sea.

America is a name. A name discovered. A name invented. A name desired.

In his classic book *The Invention of America*, the Mexican historian Edmundo O'Gorman maintains that America was invented rather than discovered. If this is true, we must believe that, first of all, it was desired and then imagined. O'Gorman speaks of Europeans who were prisoners of their world, prisoners who could not even call their jail their own.

Geocentrism and scholasticism: two centripetal and hierarchical visions of a perfect, archetypical universe, unchangeable—yet finite because it was the place of the Fall.

The response to this "feeling of enclosure and impotence" was a hunger for space that quickly became identified with a hunger for freedom. Some of the names of this hunger are Nicholas of Cusa and later Giordano Bruno, Luca Signorelli and Piero della Francesca, Ficino and Copernicus, Vasco da Gama and then Columbus. Some of the names of this freedom in its European and American incarnations are:

First, the freedom to act on what is. This is the freedom won by Machiavelli in Europe and acted on by Cortés in America. It is the freedom of an epic world made to the measure of the self-made man, not he who inherits power but he who is capable, with equal measures of will and virtue, of winning it. This is the world, in the Latin American novel, of the descendants of Machiavelli and Cortés in the jungles and plains of the American continent: the Ardavines, the ferocious political bosses of the Venezuelan llanos in Rómulo Gallegos; Pedro Páramo, the fissured Mexican cacique in Juan Rulfo; Facundo, Sarmiento's immortal portrait of the archetypical caudillo. And: Francia, Estrada Cabrera, Porfirio Díaz, Juan Vicente Gómez, Trujillo, and Somoza in the news; and in the novel, Asturias's El Señor Presidente, Carpentier's El Primer Magistrado, Roa Bastos's El Supremo, and, outliving them all, incorporating them all, García Márquez's ageless Patriarch:

"The only thing that gave us security in earth was the certainty that he was there, invulnerable to plague and hurricane . . . invulnerable to time."

The second is the freedom to act on what should be. This is the world of Thomas More in Europe and of Vasco de Quiroga in

America. Discovered because invented because imagined because desired because named, America became the utopia of Europe. The American mission was to be the other version of a European history condemned as corrupt and hypocritical by the humanists of the time. On the contrary, Montaigne in France, Vives in Spain, and the Erasmists all over, saw in America the utopian promise of a New Golden Age, the only chance for Europe to recover, eventually, its moral health as it plunged into the bloody Wars of Religion.

Historically, Father Vasco de Quiroga, the Spanish reader of More's *Utopia*, lived in Mexico in the sixteenth century, arriving only a few years after the Conquest, and created communities totally faithful to the precepts of the English writer. Quiroga— venerated to this day by the Tarascan Indians as "Tata Vasco"— believed that only the utopian commonwealth would save the native inhabitants of America from violence and desperation.

He established the first utopian communities in Mexico City and Michoacán in 1535. That same year, Thomas More was beheaded by order of Henry VIII. So much, one would say, for utopia.

Yet utopia persisted as one of the central strains of the culture of the Americas. We were condemned to utopia by the Old World. What a heavy load! Who could live up to this promise, this demand, this contradiction: to be utopia where utopia was demolished, burned and branded and killed by those who wanted utopia: the epic actors of the Conquest, the awed band of soldiers who entered Tenochtitlán with Cortés in 1519 and discovered the America they had imagined and desired: a New World of enchantment and fantasy only read about, before, in the romances of chivalry. And who were then forced to destroy what they had named in their dreams as utopia.

So Carpentier's narrator in *The Lost Steps* follows the Orinoco River upstream, to its sources, to the Golden Age, to utopia, to

> this living in the present, without possessions, without the chains of yesterday, without thinking of tomorrow . . .

And so the Buendías found a precarious Arcadia in the jungles of Colombia, where not only the virtues of the Golden Age of the past are acclaimed but also those of the coming Utopia of Progress. We realize in García Márquez that, since the Enlightenment, Europe is the utopia of Latin America: law and science and beauty and progress were now a Latin American albatross hung around the neck of Europe: we expected from the West the photograph that finally fixed our image for eternity; or the ice that burns as it cools. But this notion of progress—and the names that accompany it— is to prove illusory:

"It's the largest diamond in the world."
"No," the gypsy countered. "It's ice."

This gypsy leads us to the third aspect of freedom at the root of the name America: the freedom to preserve an ironical smile, a freedom not unlike that won by the first Spanish philosopher, the Stoic from Córdoba, Seneca, but even more rooted in the Renaissance reflection on the duality of truth and on the difference between the appearance and the reality of things. To deny any absolute, be it the absolute of faith before or of reason now; to season all things with the ironic praise of folly and thus appear a madman in the eyes of both Topos and U-Topos: this is the world of Erasmus in Europe and especially in Spain, where Erasmus became, more than a thinker, a banner, an attitude, a persistent intellectual disposition that lives to this day in Borges and Reyes, in Arreola and Paz and Cortázar.

Indeed, Erasmus is the writer of the samizdat of Spanish and Spanish-American literature, the underground courier of so many of our attitudes and words, he who failed externally in Spain only to be victorious eternally forever and ever: Erasmus the father of Don Quixote; the grandfather of Tristram Shandy and Jacques le Fataliste; the great-grandfather of Catherine Moreland and Emma Bovary; the great-uncle of Prince Myshkin; and the revered ancestor of the Nazarín of Pérez Galdós, the Pierre Ménard of Borges, and the Oliveira of Cortázar—but also of the Buendías, who incessantly decipher the signs of the world, those that are put on trees and cows so their names will not be forgotten, or their functions, those signs they have seen behind the world's appearances, those they have read in the chronicles of their own lives, feverishly naming things and people and then feverishly deciphering what they themselves have written. What they have discovered—invented—imagined—desired—named.

> Macondo . . . was built on the bank of a river of clear water that
> ran along a bed of polished stones, which were white and enormous,
> like prehistoric eggs. The world was so recent that many things
> lacked names and in order to indicate them it was necessary to
> point . . .

The invention of America is indistinguishable from the naming of
America. Indeed, Alejo Carpentier gives priority to this function
of the American writer: to baptize things that without him would
be nameless. To discover is to invent is to name. No one dare stop
and reflect whether the names being given to things real and imagined are intrinsical to the named, or merely conventional, certainly
not substantial to them. The invention of America occurs in a pre-
Socratic time, that time whose disappearance Nietzsche lamented;
it happens in a mythical time magically arisen in the midst of the
nascent Age of Reason, as if to warn it, in Erasmian terms, that
reason that knows not its limits is a form of madness.

García Márquez begins his Nobel Lecture by recalling the fabulous things named by the navigator Antonio Pigafetta as he accompanied Magellan on the first circumnavigation of the globe:

> He had seen hogs with navels on their haunches, clawless birds
> whose hens laid eggs on the backs of their mates, and others still,
> resembling tongueless pelicans, with beaks like spoons. He wrote
> of having seen a misbegotten creature with the head and ears of a
> mule, a camel's body, the legs of a deer and the whinny of a horse.
> He described how the first native encountered in Patagonia was
> confronted with a mirror, whereupon that impassioned giant lost
> his senses to the terror of his own image.

This discovery of the marvelous because it is imagined and desired
occurs in many other fantastic chroniclers of the invention of America; but even the more sober, one feels, had to invent in order to
justify their discovery of, even their being in the New World. The
pragmatical Genoese, Christopher Columbus, thinks he can fool
the Queen who sent him off at great expense, by inventing the
existence of gold and species where they do not exist. When at
last he does find gold—in Haiti—he calls the island La Española,
says that there all is "as in Castile," then "better than in Castile,"
and finally, since there is gold, the gold must be the size of beans,
and the nights must be as beautiful as in Andalusia, and the women

whiter than in Spain, and sexual relations much purer (to please the puritanical Queen and not frighten off further appropriations), but there are Amazons as well, and sirens, and a Golden Age, and a good, innocent savage (to please the Queen this time by amazing her). Then the good Genoese merchant reasserts himself: the forests of the Indies where he has landed can be turned into fleets of ships.

So we are still in the East. America has not been named, although its marvels have. Columbus has named what he was sent to find: gold, species, Asia. His biggest invention is finding China and Japan in the New World. For Vespucci, however, the new thing about the New World is its newness. The Golden Age and the Good Savage are here, described and named by him in the New World, as a New Golden Age and a New Good Savage bereft of history, once more in Paradise, discovered before the Fall, untainted by the old. Indeed, we deserve Amerigo's name: he invented our imaginary newness.

For it is this sense of total newness, of primeval appearance, that gives its true tone to names and words in America. The urgency of naming and describing the New World—of naming and describing in the New World—is intimately related to this newness, which is, in effect, the most ancient trait of the New World. Suddenly, here, in the vast reaches of the Amazonian jungle, the Andean heights, or the Patagonian plains, we are again in the very emptiness of terror that Hölderlin spoke of: the terror that strikes us when we feel so close to nature that we fear we shall become one with her, devoured by her, deprived of speech and identity by her; yet equally terrified by our expulsion from nature, our orphanhood outside her warm maternal embrace. Our silence within. Our solitude without.

I will not go into a long discussion of the place of nature in the novel. But in my heart the European fiction of the nineteenth century takes place in cities and in rooms. Donald Fanger has given us a most brilliant discourse on the appearance of the city in Gogol, Balzac, Dickens, and Dostoevsky. Walter Benjamin has reminded us of the existence of nineteenth-century interiors as places where personal property is secure; when it is not, a new hero appears to protect it: the detective of Collins's *Moonstone*, of

Poe's "Purloined Letter," of Conan Doyle's "Bruce-Partington Plans."
And George Steiner has observed that only the literatures of Russia
and the United States reclaim wide spaces—Tolstoy and Turgenev,
Cooper and Melville—without sacrificing the counterpoint of some
of the most suffocating enclosures of all fiction: Poe's nailed coffins
and walled sepulchers, and Dostoevsky's tiny rooms and shadowy
staircases, where Raskolnikov plots and Rogozhin awaits. But perhaps nowhere is the terror of being thrust outside history or into
history as explicitly linked to the act of naming as in the literature
of Latin America. Indeed, the immediacy of the voyages of discovery, written in our own language, is a factor here; John Smith
and the other original wetbacks at Plymouth Rock definitely did
not see mermaids on the coast of Massachusetts.

But again, as I attempted to dramatize in my play *All Cats Are
Grey* (1970), history is most explicitly linked to language in America. The passage of the language of the Aztec nation into a silence
resembling death—or nature—and the passage of the Spanish language into a politically victorious yet culturally suspect and tainted
condition not only is the foundation of the civilization of the New
World: it perpetually questions it as it repeats a history that becomes a myth.

Moctezuma the Aztec emperor refuses to hear the voices of men;
he will listen only to the language of the gods. Cortés the conqueror
is only too ready to listen to the voices of men and turn the complaints against the centralist, patrimonial despot. He even takes
on an interpreter, the Indian princess Marina (La Malinche), whom
he calls Mi Lengua—my tongue—and who bears him a son: the
first Mexican, the first mestizo, a Spanish-speaking native. The
witness to all this is Hermes, the messenger, the writer, under
the guise this time of Bernal Díaz del Castillo. This is his name:
given yet intrinsic, essential yet secondhand, false yet evocative;
changeable yet his destiny. Bernal Díaz del Castillo writes fifty
years after the facts; he can name everything, down to the last
horse and its owner; he can name because he can still desire, like
Marcel Proust, and, like him, searches for lost time. He weeps
over what he had to destroy, and so he is our first novelist, an epic
writer who destroys the chance of utopia in genocide and is then
conquered by the myth of the defeated hero who must now pay in
words his debt to the city he enslaved.

More than four hundred years after the discovery and conquest of America, Rómulo Gallegos writes in his masterpiece, *Canaima*:

> Amanadoma, Yavita, Pimichin, el Casiquiare, el Atabapo, el Guainía: with these names these men did not describe the landscape, they did not reveal the total mystery (of the jungle and the river) into which they had entered; they were only mentioning the places where things happened to them—yet all the jungle, fascinating and terrible, was already throbbing in the power of the words . . .

For, behind these men, if they do not say, name, invent, imagine, discover, desire, lies the "immense mysterious regions where man had not yet penetrated: Venezuela of the unfinished discovery." And there, nameless, the individual may find himself "suddenly absent from himself, at the mercy of the jungle . . ."

Similarly, in Alejo Carpentier, the fascinating, at times even joyous, voyage of discovery up the Orinoco—the voyage to utopia in *The Lost Steps*—suddenly oversteps the limits of the word; in the "vast jungle filling with night terrors," the word splits open, answers itself, pleads, groans, howls:

> But then came the vibration of the tongue between the lips, the indrawn snoring, the panting contrapuntal to the rattle of the maraca . . . As it went on, this outcry over a corpse surrounded by silent dogs became horrible . . . Before the stubbornness of death, which refused to release its prey, the Word suddenly grew faint and disappeared. In the mouth of the Shaman, the Threne gasped and died away convulsively, blinding me with the realization that I had just witnessed the Birth of Music.

In this instant of Dionysiac joy and Proustian liberation Carpentier's Narrator would perhaps like to stand eternally: on the threshold between Music and Word. But the separations unleashed by history have not yet been totally discovered: he is sent spinning off to the very beginning of time, then to the world without word that existed before mankind. It is in this context, in this precarious balance between silence and the word, that the world of Gabriel García Márquez is poised.

Many thought in Latin America, when *One Hundred Years of Solitude* was first published and achieved its enormous and instantaneous success, that its popularity (comparable in the His-

panic world only to that of Cervantes and *Don Quixote*) was due
to the element of immediate recognition present in the book. There
is a joyous rediscovery of identity here, an instant reflex by which
we are presented, in the genealogies of Macondo, to our grandmas,
our sweethearts, our brothers and sisters, our nursemaids. Today,
twenty years after the fact, we can see clearly that there was more
than instant anagnorisis in the García Márquez phenomenon, that
his novel, one of the most amusing ever written, does not exhaust
its meanings in a first reading. This first reading (for amusement
and for recognition) demands a second reading, which becomes,
in effect, the real reading.

That is the secret of this mythical and simultaneous novel: *One
Hundred Years of Solitude* presupposes two readings because it
presupposes two writings. The first reading coincides with the
writing we take as true: a novelist by the name of Gabriel García
Márquez is retelling, chronologically, with biblical—indeed, Ra-
belaisian—hyperbole, the lineages of Macondo; Aureliano son of
José Arcadio son of Aureliano son of José Arcadio. The second
reading begins the moment the first one ends. The chronicle of
Macondo had already been written; it is among the papers of a
gypsy thaumaturge named Melquíades, whose appearance in the
novel one hundred years before, when Macondo was founded, turns
out to be identical to his revelation as the narrator, one hundred
years later. In that instant, the book recommences, but this time
the chronological history of Macondo has been revealed as a mythic
and simultaneous historicity.

Historicity and myth: the second reading of *One Hundred Years
of Solitude* conflates, both factually and fantastically, the order of
what has happened (the chronicle) and the order of what might
have happened (the imagination), with the result that the fatality
of the former is liberated by the desire of the latter. Each historical
act of the Buendías in Macondo is a sort of axis around which
whirl all the possibilities unbeknown to the external chronicler but
which, notwithstanding, are as real as the dreams, the fears, the
madness, the imagination of the actors of the his- or her-story.

One way of seeing Latin American history, then, is as a pilgrimage from a founding utopia to a cruel epic that degrades utopia
if the mythic imagination does not intervene so as to interrupt the
onslaught of fatality and seek to recover the possibilities of freedom.

One of the more extraordinary aspects of García Márquez's novel is that its structure corresponds to the profounder historicity of Latin America: the tension between utopia, epic, and myth. The founding of Macondo is the founding of utopia. José Arcadio Buendía and his family have wandered in the jungle, in circles, until they encounter precisely the place where they can found the New Arcadia, the promised land of origin:

> The men of the expedition felt overwhelmed by their most ancient memories in that paradise of dampness and silence, going back to before original sin, as their boots sank into pools of steaming oil and their machetes destroyed bloody lilies and golden salamanders.

Like More's Utopia, Macondo is an island of the imagination. José Arcadio discovers an enormous Spanish galleon anchored in the middle of the jungle, its hull fastened to a surface of stones, its insides occupied by a thick forest of flowers. He concludes that "Macondo is surrounded by water on all sides."

From this island, José Arcadio invents the world, points things out with his finger, then learns how to name things and, finally, how to forget them, and so is forced to rename, rewrite, remember. But at the very same moment that the founding Buendía realizes "the infinite possibilities of forgetfulness," he must appeal for the first time to the otherwise infinite possibilities of writing. He hangs signs on objects; he discovers reflexive knowledge (he who, before, knew only through divination), and so he feels obliged to dominate the world of science: what he naturally knew before, now he will know only through the help of maps, magnets, and magnifiers.

The utopian founders were soothsayers. They knew how to recognize the language of the world, hidden but preestablished; they had no need to create a second language; they had only to open themselves to the language of what was. How to know this preexisting language that truly names things in their essence and in their true relationships is the Platonic problem, and José Arcadio Buendía, when he abandons divination in favor of science, when he migrates from sacred knowledge to the exercise of hypothesis, opens the doors to the novel's second part: the part that belongs to the epic, which is a historical process in which the utopian foundation of Macondo is denied by the active necessity of linear time. This part, significantly, happens between the thirty-two armed uprisings headed by Colonel Aureliano Buendía, the banana fever, and the final abandonment of Macondo—the founding utopia exploited, degraded, and in the end killed by the epic of activity, commerce, and crime.

The flood—the punishment—leaves behind it a Macondo forgotten even by the birds, where dust and heat have become so tenacious that it is hard to breathe. Who remains there? The survivors, Aureliano and Amaranta Úrsula, hidden away by solitude and love (and by the solitude of love) in a house where it is almost impossible to sleep because of the noise of the red ants. Then the third space of the book opens. This is the mythical space, whose simultaneous and renewable nature will not be understandable until the final paragraphs, when we find out that all this history was in fact already written by the gypsy Melquiades, the seer who accompanied Macondo in its foundation and who, in order to keep Macondo alive, must have recourse to the same trick used by José Arcadio: the trick of writing.

Comparable in this and many other aspects to Cervantes, García Márquez establishes the frontiers of reality within a book and the frontiers of a book within reality. The symbiosis is perfect, and once it takes place, we can begin the mythical reading of this beautiful, joyful, sad book about a town that proliferates, like the flowers inside the stranded Spanish galleon, with the richness of a South American Yoknapatawpha. As in his master William Faulkner, in García Márquez a novel is the fundamental act we call myth: the re-presentation of the founding act. At the mythical level, *One Hundred Years of Solitude* is an incessant interrogation: What does Macondo know of itself? That is, what does Macondo know of its own creation?

The novel is a response to this question. In order to know, Macondo must tell itself all the "real" history and all the "fictitious" history, all the proofs admitted by the court of justice, all the evidence certified by the public accountants, but also all the rumors, legends, gossip, pious lies, exaggerations, and fables that no one has written down, that the old have told the young and the spinsters whispered to the priest: that the sorcerers have invoked in the center of the night and the clowns have acted out in the center of the square. The saga of Macondo and the Buendías thus includes the totality of the oral, legendary past, and with it we are told that we cannot feel satisfied with the official, documented history of the times: that history is also all the things that men and women have dreamed, imagined, desired, and named.

That it understands this is one of the great strengths of Latin American literature, because it reveals a profound perception of Latin American reality: a culture where the mythical constantly speaks through voices of dream and dance, of toy and song, but where nothing is real unless it is set down in writing—in the diaries of Columbus, in the letters of Cortés, in the memoirs of Bernal, in the laws of the Indies, in the constitutions of the independent republics. The struggle between the legal literature and the un-written myths of Latin America is the struggle of our Roman tradition of statutory law, and of the Hapsburg and French traditions of centralism, with our intellectual response to them and ultimately with our perennially undiscovered, inexhaustible, and, we hope, redeemable possibilities as free, unfinished human beings. Legitimacy in Latin America has always depended on who owns the written papers: Mexico's Porfirio Díaz, the aging patriarch who justifies himself as the repository of the Liberal Constitution? Or Emiliano Zapata, who says he owns the original deeds to the land granted by the King of Spain? This is the struggle John Womack has staged superbly in his book on Mexico's agrarian revolution. The truth is that Zapata owns more than a piece of paper: he owns a poem, a dream, a myth.

García Márquez brings to his novels the same distinction and the same approach. The simultaneous nature of his world is inexorably linked to the total culture (dreams, habits, laws, facts, myths: culture in the sense understood by Vico) of Latin America. What is simultaneous in Macondo? First, as in all mythical memories, the recall of Macondo is creation and re-creation at the same time. García Márquez embodies this in an edenic couple, José Arcadio and Úrsula, pilgrims who have fled the original world of their sin and their fear to found a Second Paradise in Macondo. But the foundation—of a town or of its lineage—presupposes the repetition of the act of coupling, of exploitation, of the land or the flesh. In this sense, *One Hundred Years of Solitude* is a long metaphor which merely designates the instantaneous act of carnal love between the first man and the first woman, José Arcadio and Úrsula, who fornicate in fear that the fruit of their union shall be a child with the tail of a pig, but who must nevertheless procreate so that the world shall maintain itself.

Memory repeats the models of the origin, in the same way that, over and over, Colonel Buendía makes golden fish that he then melts in order to make golden fish that he then melts to . . . to . . . to be constantly reborn, desired and desiring, discovering and discovered, inventive and invented, naming and named. *One Hundred Years of Solitude* is a true re-vision and re-creation of the utopias, the epics, and the myths of America. It shows us a group of men and women deciphering a world that might devour them: a surrounding magma. It tells us that nature has domains, but men and women have demons. Bedeviled, like the race of the Buendías, founders and usurpers, creators and destructors, Sartoris and Snopes in one same breed.

But in order to achieve this simultaneity, the myth must have a precise time and a precise writing—or telling—or reading. A Spanish galleon is anchored in the mountain. A freight car full of peasants murdered by the banana company crosses the jungle and the bodies are thrown into the sea. A grandfather ties himself forever to an oak tree until he himself becomes an emblematic trunk, sculptured by storm, wind, and dust. Flowers rain down from the sky. Remedios the Beautiful ascends to this same sky as she spreads out her bedsheets to dry. In each of these acts of fiction, the linear time of the epic dies (this really happened), but the nostalgic time of utopia, past or future, also disappears (this should happen), and the absolute present time of the poetic myth is born (this is happening).

That is the precise time of García Márquez. And the precise writing is the second writing, which, in the second reading, makes us understand the full meaning of the acts of fiction, finally bracketed between the initial fact that one day José Arcadio Buendía decides that from then on it shall always be Monday and the final fact when Úrsula says: "It is as if time had been turning in circles and we had now come back to the beginning." She is wrong. Her time is an illusion; it is the reading that is right as it coincides with the writing. A universal writer, García Márquez is aware that, ever since Joyce, we cannot pretend that the writer isn't there; but also that, ever since Cervantes, we cannot pretend that the reader isn't there; and, moreover, that, ever since Homer, we cannot pretend that the listener isn't there.

We cannot renounce our consciousness of any of these great accomplishments of literature. García Márquez certainly does not give up as he finally integrates his American imagination and his universal imagination in the essential, the artificial, the conventional, the naturally named chronicle of Macondo. Deciphered by several members of the Buendía family, this chronicle is the story of their lives and the prediction that they would spend their lives trying to decipher the chronicle: the lives: the world. Reading and living thus become coexistent; by the same token, so do listening and writing. Aureliano Babilonia, the last male heir of the Buendías, deciphers the instant he is living; he deciphers as he lives it; he prophesies himself in the act of deciphering the last page of the manuscript: as if he were seeing himself in a talking mirror.

> This is a novel. A novel is something that is written. A novel is something that is read. A novel is something that is heard. We must do this so that reality can be remembered. The names in a novel are times and places in the present. There is no other way of truly knowing the relationship between things. The alternative is silence. The alternative is death.

Delivered as the second Allison Peers Lecture
University of Liverpool, March 13, 1987

PART THREE

WE

A Harvard Commencement

Some time ago, I was traveling in the state of Morelos in central Mexico, looking for the birthplace of Emiliano Zapata, the village of Anenecuilco. I stopped and asked a *campesino*, a laborer of the fields, how far it was to that village. He answered: "If you had left at daybreak, you would be there now." This man had an internal clock which marked his own time and that of his culture. For the clocks of all men and women, of all civilizations, are not set at the same hour. One of the wonders of our menaced globe is the variety of its experiences, its memories, and its desire. Any attempt to impose a uniform politics on this diversity is like a prelude to death.

Lech Walesa is a man who started out at daybreak, at the hour when the history of Poland demanded that the people of Poland act to solve the problems that a repressive government and a hollow party no longer knew how to solve. We in Latin America who have practiced solidarity with Solidarity salute Lech Walesa today. The honor done to me by this great center of learning, Harvard University, is augmented by the circumstances in which I receive it. I accept this honor as a citizen of Mexico, and as a writer from Latin America.

Let me speak to you as such. As a Mexican first. The daybreak of a movement of social and political renewal cannot be set by calendars other than those of the people involved. Revolutions cannot be exported. With Walesa and Solidarity, it was the internal clock of the people of Poland that struck the morning hour. So it has always been: with the people of Massachusetts in 1776; with the people of my country during our revolutionary experience; with the people of Central America in the hour we are all living. The dawn of revolution reveals the total history of a community. This is a self-knowledge that a society cannot be deprived of without grave consequences.

The Experience of Mexico

The Mexican Revolution was the object of constant harassment, pressures, menaces, boycotts, and even a couple of armed interventions between 1910 and 1932. It was extremely difficult for the United States administrations of the time to deal with violent and rapid change on the southern border of your country. Calvin Coolidge convened both houses of Congress in 1927 and—talkative for once—denounced Mexico as the source of "Bolshevik" subversion in Central America. This set the scene for the third invasion of Nicaragua by U.S. Marines in this century. We were the first domino. But precisely because of our revolutionary policies (favoring agrarian reform, secular education, collective bargaining, and recovery of natural resources)—all of them opposed by the successive governments in Washington, from Taft to Hoover—Mexico became a modern, contradictory, self-knowing, and self-questioning nation. By the way, she also became the third-largest customer of the United States in the world—and your principal supplier of foreign oil.

The revolution did not make an instant democracy out of my country. But the first revolutionary government, that of Francisco I. Madero, was the most democratic regime we have ever had: Madero respected free elections, a free press, and an unfettered congress. Significantly, Madero was promptly overthrown by a conspiracy of the American ambassador, Henry Lane Wilson, and a group of reactionary generals.

So, before becoming a democracy, Mexico first had to become a nation. What the revolution gave us all was the totality of our history and the possibility of a culture. "The revolution," wrote my compatriot, the great poet Octavio Paz, "is a sudden immersion of Mexico in its own being. In the revolutionary explosion . . . each Mexican . . . finally recognizes, in a mortal embrace, the other Mexican." Paz himself, Diego Rivera and Carlos Chávez,

Mariano Azuela and José Clemente Orozco, Juan Rulfo and Rufino Tamayo: we all exist and work because of the revolutionary experience of our country. How can we stand by as this experience is denied, through ignorance and arrogance, to other people, our brothers, in Central America and the Caribbean?

A great statesman is a pragmatic idealist. Franklin D. Roosevelt had the political imagination and the diplomatic will to respect Mexico when President Lázaro Cárdenas (in the culminating act of the Mexican Revolution) expropriated the nation's oil resources in 1938. Instead of menacing, sanctioning, or invading, Roosevelt negotiated. He did not try to beat history. He joined it. Will no one in this country imitate him today? The lessons applicable to the current situation in Latin America are inscribed in the history— the very difficult history—of Mexican-American relations. Why have they not been learned?

Against Intervention

In today's world, intervention evokes a fearful symmetry. As the United States feels itself authorized to intervene in Central America to put out a fire in your front yard—I'm delighted that we have been promoted from the traditional status of back yard—then the Soviet Union also feels authorized to play the fireman in all of its front and back yards. Intervention damages the fabric of a nation, the chance of resurrecting its history, the wholeness of its cultural identity.

I have witnessed two such examples of wholesale corruption by intervention in my lifetime. One was in Czechoslovakia in the fall of 1968. I was there then to support my friends the writers, students, and statesmen of the Prague Spring. I heard them give thanks, at least, for their few months of freedom as night fell once more upon them: the night of Kafka, where nothing is remembered but nothing is forgiven.

The other time was in Guatemala in 1954, when the democratically elected government was overthrown by a mercenary invasion openly backed by the CIA. The political process of reform and self-recognition in Guatemala was brutally interrupted to no one's benefit. Guatemala was condemned to a vicious circle of repression that continues to this day. John Foster Dulles proclaimed this "a glorious victory for democracy." This is the high noon of Pollyanna: everything is forgiven because everything is forgotten.

Intervention is defined as the actions of the paramount regional power against a smaller state within its so-called sphere of influence. Intervention is defined by its victims. But the difference between the actions of the Soviet Union and the United States in their respective spheres of influence is that the Soviet regime is a tyranny and you are a democracy. Yet more and more, over the past two years, I have heard North Americans in responsible positions speak of not caring whether the United States is loved, but whether it is feared; not whether the rights of others are respected, but whether its own strategic interests are defended. These are inclinations that we have come to associate with the brutal diplomacy of the Soviet Union.

But we, the true friends of your great nation in Latin America, we the admirers of your extraordinary achievements in literature, science, and the arts and of your democratic institutions, of your Congress and your courts, your universities and publishing houses, and your free press—we, your true friends, because we are your friends, will not permit you to conduct yourselves in Latin American affairs as the Soviet Union conducts itself in East European and Central Asian affairs. You are not the Soviet Union. We shall be the custodian of your own true interests by helping you to avoid these mistakes. We have memory on our side. You suffer too much from historical amnesia. You seem to have forgotten that your own republic was born out of the barrel of a gun. We hope to have persuasion on our side, and the help of international and inter-American law.

We also have our own growing apprehension as to whether, under the guise of defending us from remote Soviet menaces and delirious domino effects, the United States would create one vast Latin American protectorate. Meeting at Cancún on April 29 (1983), the presidents of Mexico and Brazil, Miguel de la Madrid and João Figueiredo, agreed that "the Central American crisis has its origin in the economic and social structures prevalent in the region and [that] the efforts to overcome it must . . . avoid the tendency to define it as a chapter in East–West confrontation." And the prime minister of Spain, Felipe González, on the eve of his visit to

Washington, defined U.S. involvements in Central America as "fundamentally harmful" to the nations of the region and damaging to the international standing of the United States.

Yes, your alliances will crumble and your security will be endangered if you do not demonstrate that you are an enlightened, responsible power in your dealings with Latin America. Yes, you must demonstrate your humanity and your intelligence here, in this hemisphere we share, or nowhere shall you be democratically credible. Where are the Franklin Roosevelts, the Sumner Welleses, the George Marshalls, and the Dean Achesons demanded by the times?

Friends and Satellites

The great weakness of the Soviet Union is that it is surrounded by satellites, not by friends. Sooner or later, the rebellion of the outlying nations in the Soviet sphere will eat, more and more deeply, into the innards of what Lord Carrington recently called "a decaying Byzantium." The United States has the great strength of having friends, not satellites, on its borders. Canada and Mexico are two independent nations that disagree on many issues with the United States.

We know that in public life, as in personal life, nothing is more destructive of the self than being surrounded by sycophants. But just as there are yes-men in this world, there are yes-nations. A yes-nation harms itself as much as it harms its powerful protector: it deprives both of dignity, foresight, and the sense of reality. Nevertheless, Mexico has been chosen as a target of "diplomatic isolation" by the National Security Council Document on Policy in Central America and Cuba through fiscal year '84.

We know in Latin America that "isolation" can be a euphemism for destabilization. Indeed, every time a prominent member of the administration in Washington refers to Mexico as the ultimate domino, a prominent member of the administration in Mexico City must stop in his tracks, offer a rebuttal, and consolidate the nationalist legitimization of the Mexican government: Mexico is capable of governing itself without outside interference.

But if Mexico is a domino, then it fears being pushed from the north rather than from the south; such has been our historical experience. This would be the ultimate accomplishment of Washington's penchant for the self-fulfilling prophecy: a Mexico destabilized by American nightmares about Mexico. We should all be warned about this. Far from being "blind" or "complacent," Mexico is offering its friendly hand to the United States to help it avoid the repetition of costly historical mistakes that have deeply hurt us all, North and Latin Americans.

Public opinion in this country shall judge whether Mexico's obvious good faith in this matter is spurned as the United States is driven into a deepening involvement in the Central American swamp: a Vietnam all the more dangerous, indeed, because of its nearness to your national territory, but not for the reasons officially invoked. The turmoil of revolution, if permitted to run its course, promptly finds its institutional channels. But if thwarted by intervention it will plague the United States for decades to come. Central America and the Caribbean will become the Banquo of the United States: an endemic drain on your human and material resources.

The source of change in Latin America is not in Moscow or Havana: it is in history. So let me turn to ourselves, as Latin Americans.

Four Failures of Identification

The failure of your present hemispheric policies is due to a fourfold failure of identification. The first is the failure to identify change in Latin America in its cultural context. The second is the failure to identify nationalism as the historical bearer of change in Latin America. The third is the failure to identify the problems of international redistribution of power as they affect Latin America. The fourth is the failure to identify the grounds for negotiations as these issues create conflict between the United States and Latin America.

The Cultural Context of Latin America

First, the cultural context of change in Latin America. Our societies are marked by cultural continuity and political discontinuity. We are a Balkanized polity, yet we are deeply united by a common cultural experience. We are and we are not of the West. We are Indian, black, and Mediterranean. We received the legacy of the West in an incomplete fashion, deformed by the Spanish monarchy's decision to outlaw unorthodox strains, to mutilate the Iberian tree of its Arab and Jewish branches, heavy with fruit, to defeat the democratic yearnings of its own middle class, and to superimpose the vertical structures of the medieval Imperium on the equally pyramidal configuration of power in the Indian civilizations of the Americas.

The United States is the only major power of the West that was born beyond the Middle Ages, modern at birth. As part of the fortress of the Counter-Reformation, Latin America has had to do constant battle with the past. We did not acquire freedom of speech, freedom of belief, freedom of enterprise as our birthrights, as you did. The complexity of the cultural struggles underlying our political and economic struggles has to do with unresolved tensions, sometimes as old as the conflict between pantheism and monotheism, or as recent as the conflict between tradition and modernity. This is our cultural baggage, both heavy and rich.

The issues we are dealing with, behind the headlines, are very old. They are finally being aired today, but they originated in colonial, sometimes in pre-Conquest, situations, and they are embedded in the culture of Iberian Catholicism and its emphasis on dogma and hierarchy—an intellectual inclination that sometimes drives us from one church to another in search of refuge and certitude. They are bedeviled by patrimonial confusions between private and public rights and forms of sanctified corruption that include nepotism, whim, and the irrational economic decisions made by the head of the clan, untrammeled by checks and balances. The issues have to do with the traditions of paternalistic surrender to the caudillo, the profound faith in ideas over facts, the strength of elitism and personalism, and the weakness of the civil societies—with the struggles between theocracy and political institutions, and between centralism and local government.

Since independence in the 1820s, we have been obsessed with catching up with the Joneses: the West. We created countries legal in appearance but which disguised the real countries abiding—or festering—behind the constitutional façades. Latin America has tried to find solutions to its old problems by exhausting the successive ideologies of the West: liberalism, positivism, and Marxism. Today we are on the verge of transcending this dilemma by recasting it as an opportunity, at last, to be ourselves—societies neither new nor old, but simply, authentically, Latin American, as we sort out, in the excessive glare of instant communications or in the eternal dusk of our isolated villages, the benefits and the disadvantages of a tradition that now seems richer and more acceptable than it did one hundred years of solitude ago.

But we are also forced to contemplate the benefits and disadvantages of a modernity that now seems less promising than it did before economic crisis, the tragic ambiguity of science, and the barbarism of nations and philosophies that were once supposed to represent "progress" all drove us to search for the time and space of culture in ourselves. We are true children of Spain and Portugal. We have compensated for the failures of history with the successes of art. We are now moving to what our best novels and poems and paintings and films and dances and thoughts have announced for so long: the compensation for the failures of history with the successes of politics.

The real struggle for Latin America is then, as always, a struggle with ourselves, within ourselves. We must solve it by ourselves. Nobody else can truly know it: we are living through our family quarrels. We must assimilate this conflicted past. Sometimes we must do it—as has occurred in Mexico, Cuba, El Salvador, and Nicaragua—through violent means. We need time and culture. We also need patience. Both ours and yours.

Nationalism in Latin America

Second, the identification of nationalism as the legitimate bearer of change in Latin America. The cultural conflict I have evoked includes the stubbornness of the minimal popular demands, after all these centuries, which equate freedom with bread, schools, hospitals, national independence, and a sense of dignity. If left to ourselves, we will try to solve these problems by creating national institutions to deal with them. All we ask from you is cooperation, trade, and normal diplomatic relations. Not your absence, but your civilized presence.

We must grow with our own mistakes. Are we to be considered your true friends only if we are ruled by right-wing, anti-communist despotisms? Instability in Latin America—or anywhere in the world, for that matter—comes when societies cannot see themselves reflected in their institutions.

Democracy in Latin America

Change in our societies shall be radical in two dimensions. Externally, it will be more radical the more the United States intervenes against it or helps to postpone it. Internally, it will of necessity be radical in that it must one day face up to the challenges we have so far been unable to meet squarely. We must face democracy along with reform; we must face cultural integrity along with change; we must all, Cubans, Salvadorans, Nicaraguans and Argentines, Mexicans and Colombians, finally face the question that awaits us on the threshold of our true history: Are we capable, with all the instruments of our civilization, of creating free societies, societies that take care of the basic needs of health, education, and labor, but without sacrificing the equally basic needs of debate, criticism, and political and cultural expression?

I know that all of us, without exception, have not truly fulfilled these needs in Latin America. I also know that the transformation of our national movements into pawns of the East–West conflict makes it impossible for us to answer this question: Are we capable of creating free national societies? This is perhaps our severest test.

Rightly or wrongly, many Latin Americans have come to identify the United States with opposition to our national independence. Some perceive in United States policies the proof that the real menace to a great power is not really the other great power but

the independence of the national states. How else to understand
U.S. actions that seem meaninglessly obsessed with discrediting
the national revolutions in Latin America? Some are thankful that
another great power exists, and appeal to it. All this also escalates
and denaturalizes the issues at hand and avoids considering the
third failure I want to deal with today: the failure to understand
redistribution of power in the Western Hemisphere.

Latin America and the Redistribution of Power

It could be debated whether the explosiveness of many Latin American societies is due less to stagnation than to growth, the quickest
growth of any region in the world since 1945. But this has been
rapid growth without equally rapid distribution of the benefits of
growth. And it has coincided, internationally, with rapidly expanding relations between Latin America and new European and
Asian partners in trade, financing, technology, and political support.

Latin America is thus part and parcel of the universal trend
away from bipolar to multipolar or pluralistic structures in international relations. Given this trend, the decline of one superpower
mirrors the decline of the other superpower. This is bound to create
numerous areas of conflict. As former Chancellor Helmut Schmidt
eloquently expressed it from this same rostrum: "We are living in
an economically interdependent world of more than 150 countries—without having enough experience in managing this interdependence." Both superpowers increasingly face a perfectly
logical movement toward national self-assertion accompanied by
growing multilateral relationships beyond the decaying spheres of
influence.

No change comes without tension, and in Latin America this
tension arises as we strive for greater wealth and independence,
but also as we immediately start losing both, because of internal
economic injustice and external economic crisis. The middle classes
we have spawned over the past fifty years are shaken by a revolution
of diminishing expectations—of Balzacian "lost illusions." Modernity and its values are coming under critical fire while the values

of nationalism are discovered to be perfectly identifiable with traditionalist, even conservative, considerations.

The mistaken identification of change in Latin America as somehow manipulated by a Soviet conspiracy not only irritates the nationalism of the left. It also resurrects the nationalist fervors of the
right—where, after all, Latin American nationalism was born in
the early nineteenth century.

You have yet to feel the full force of this backlash—which
reappeared in Argentina and the South Atlantic crisis last year—
in places such as El Salvador and Panama, Peru and Chile, Mexico
and Brazil. A whole continent, in the name of cultural identity,
nationalism and international independence, is capable of uniting
against you. This should not happen. The chance of avoiding this
continental confrontation is in the fourth and final issue I wish to
deal with today, that of negotiations.

Negotiations Before It Is Too Late

Before the United States has to negotiate with extreme cultural,
nationalistic, and internationalist pressures of both the left and the
right in the remotest nations of this hemisphere (Chile and Argentina), in the largest nation (Brazil), and in the closest (Mexico), it
should rapidly, in its own interest as well as ours, negotiate in
Central America and the Caribbean. We consider in Mexico that
each and every one of the points of conflict in the region can be
solved diplomatically, through negotiations, before it is too late.
There is no fatality in politics that says: Given a revolutionary
movement in any country in the region, it will inevitably end up
providing bases for the Soviet Union.

What happens between the daybreak of revolution in a marginal
country and its imagined destiny as a Soviet base? If nothing
happens but harassment, blockades, propaganda, pressures, and
invasions against the revolutionary country, then that prophecy will
become self-fulfilling.

But if power with historical memory and diplomacy with histor-
ical imagination come into play, we, the United States and Latin
America, might end up with something very different: a Latin
America of independent states building institutions of stability,

renewing the culture of national identity, diversifying our economic interdependence, and wearing down the dogmas of two musty nineteenth-century philosophies. And a United States giving the example of a tone in relations that is present, active, cooperative, respectful, aware of cultural differences, and truly proper for a great power unafraid of ideological labels, capable of coexisting with diversity in Latin America as it has learned to coexist with diversity in black Africa.

Precisely twenty years ago, John F. Kennedy said at another commencement ceremony: "If we cannot end now our differences, at least we can help make the world safe for diversity." This, I think, is the greatest legacy of the sacrificed statesman whose death we all mourned. Let us understand that legacy, by which death ceased to be an enigma and became, not a lament for what might have been, but a hope for what can be. This can be.

The longer the situation of war lasts in Central America and the Caribbean, the more difficult it will be to assure a political solution. The more difficult it will be for the Sandinistas to demonstrate good faith in their dealings with the issues of internal democracy, now brutally interrupted by a state of emergency imposed as a response to foreign pressures. The more difficult it will be for the civilian arm of the Salvadoran rebellion to maintain political initiative over the armed factions. The greater the irritation of Panama with its unchosen role as a springboard for a North American war. The greater the danger of a generalized conflict, dragging in Costa Rica and Honduras.

Everything can be negotiated in Central America and the Caribbean, before it is too late. Non-aggression pacts between each and every state. Border patrols. The interdiction of the passage of arms, wherever they may come from, and the interdiction of foreign military advisers, wherever they may come from. The reduction of all the armies in the region. The interdiction, now or ever, of Soviet bases or Soviet offensive capabilities in the area.

What would be the *quid pro quo*? Simply this: the respect of the United States, respect for the integrity and autonomy of all the states in the region, including normalization of relations with all of them. The countries in the region should not be forced to seek solutions to their problems outside themselves.

The problems of Cuba are Cuban and shall be so once more

when the United States understands that by refusing to talk to Cuba on Cuba, it not only weakens Cuba and the United States but strengthens the Soviet Union. The mistake of spurning Cuba's constant offers to negotiate whatever the United States wants to discuss frustrates the forces in Cuba desiring greater internal flexibility and international independence. Is Fidel Castro some sort of superior Machiavelli whom no gringo negotiator can meet at a bargaining table without being bamboozled? I don't believe it.

Nicaragua

The problems of Nicaragua are Nicaraguan, but they will cease to be so if that country is deprived of all possibility for normal survival. Why is the United States so impatient with four years of Sandinismo, when it was so tolerant of forty-five years of Somocismo? Why is it so worried about free elections in Nicaragua, but so indifferent to free elections in Chile? And why, if it respects democracy so much, did the United States not rush to the defense of the democratically elected President of Chile, Salvador Allende, when he was overthrown by the Latin American Jaruzelski, General Augusto Pinochet? How can we live and grow together on the basis of such hypocrisy?

Nicaragua is being attacked and invaded by forces sponsored by the United States. It is being invaded by counterrevolutionary bands led by former commanders of Somoza's national guard who are out to overthrow the revolutionary government and reinstate the old tyranny. Who will stop them from doing so if they win? These are not freedom fighters. They are Benedict Arnolds.

El Salvador

The problems of El Salvador, finally, are Salvadoran. The Salvadoran rebellion did not originate and is not manipulated from outside El Salvador. To believe this is akin to crediting Soviet accusations that the Solidarity movement in Poland is somehow the creature of the United States. The passage of arms from Nicaragua to El Salvador has not been proved; no arms have been intercepted.

The conflict in El Salvador is the indigenous result of a process of political corruption and democratic impossibility that began in 1931 with the overturn of the electoral results by the army and culminated in the electoral fraud of 1972, which deprived the Christian Democrats and the Social Democrats of their victory and forced the sons of the middle class into armed insurrection. The army had exhausted the electoral solution. This army continues to outwit everyone in El Salvador—including the United States. It announces elections after assassinating the political leadership of the opposition, then asks the opposition to come back and participate in these same hastily organized elections—as dead souls, perhaps? This Gogolian scenario means that truly free elections cannot be held in El Salvador as long as the army and the death squads are unrestrained and fueled by U.S. dollars.

Nothing now assures Salvadorans that the army and the death squads can either defeat the rebels or be controlled by political institutions. It is precisely because of the nature of the army that a political settlement must be reached in El Salvador promptly, not only to stop the horrendous death count, not only to restrain both the army and the armed rebels, not only to assure your young people in the United States that they will not be doomed to repeat the horror and futility of Vietnam, but to reconstruct a political initiative of the center-left majority that must now reflect, nevertheless, the need for a reconstructed army. El Salvador cannot be governed with such a heavy burden of crime.

The only other option is to transform the war in El Salvador into an American war. But why should a bad foreign policy be bipartisan? Without the rebels in El Salvador, the United States would never have worried about "democracy" in El Salvador. If the rebels are denied political participation in El Salvador, how long will it be before El Salvador is totally forgotten once more?

Friends, not Satellites

Let us remember, let us imagine, let us reflect. The United States can no longer go it alone in Central America and the Caribbean.

It cannot, in today's world, practice the anachronistic policies of the "big stick." It will only achieve, if it does so, what it cannot truly want. Many of our countries are struggling to cease being banana republics. They do not want to become balalaika republics. Do not force them to choose between appealing to the Soviet Union or capitulating to the United States.

My plea is this: Do not practice negative overlordship in this hemisphere. Practice positive leadership. Join the forces of change and patience and identity in Latin America.

The United States should use the new realities of redistributed world power to its advantage. All the avenues I have been dealing with come together now to form a circle of possible harmony. The United States has true friends in this hemisphere. Friends, not satellites. These friends must negotiate the situations that the United States, while participating in them, cannot possibly negotiate for itself, and the negotiating parties—from Mexico and Venezuela, Panama and Colombia, tomorrow perhaps our great Portuguese-speaking sister, Brazil,* perhaps the new Spanish democracy,

---

* In 1985, Brazil, Argentina, Peru, and Uruguay formed a support group to the original Contadora Four. These eight nations account for 80 percent of the resources, population, and territory of Latin America. Yet their efforts toward a concerted negotiation of peace in Central America have been constantly thwarted by the Reagan Administration's unique obsession with unseating the revolutionary government in Managua through a mercenary group totally dependent on U.S. support and direction. Contadora's diplomatic proposals have not been given a chance. Basically, they consist in reaching agreements on security of borders and the interdiction of passage of arms, foreign military bases and advisers, and support for guerrilla groups. In August 1987, the Central American nations took matters into their own hands: the Arias peace plan is a Central American declaration of independence. The ideal of a neutral, demilitarized Central America is a possibility; but you have to start somewhere. A policy of disregard for inter-American and international law (mining of Nicaraguan harbors, printing booklets with homicidal instructions for use by the contras, terrorism inside Nicaragua, deviation of funds to the contras from arms sales to Iran, etc.) means starting from nowhere and ending in a regional conflagration that can only spell destabilization for Third countries: exactly what U.S. security interests should try to avoid. The Reagan Administration prefers to manipulate its contras than to listen to the continental majority. This scornful attitude has added insult to injury: as the Reagan government went into decline, inter-American relations were in a shambles. We must start thinking of a new, constructive agenda for relations between the U.S. and Latin America, beyond 1988 and into the twenty-first century.—February 1987.

reestablishing the continuum of our Iberian heritage and expanding the Contadora group—these negotiating parties have the intimate knowledge of the underlying cultural problems. And they have the imagination for assuring the inevitable passage from the U.S. sphere of influence, not to the Soviet sphere, but to our own Latin American authenticity in a pluralistic world.

My friend Milan Kundera, the Czech novelist, makes a plea for "the small cultures" from the wounded heart of Central Europe. I have tried to echo it today from the convulsed heart of Latin America. Politicians will disappear. The United States and Latin America will remain. What sort of neighbors will you have? What sort of neighbors will we have? That will depend on the quality of our memory and also of our imagination.

"If we had started out at daybreak, we would be there now." Our times have not coincided. Your daybreak came quickly. Our night has been long. But we can overcome the distance between our times if we can both recognize that the true duration of the human heart is in the present, this present in which we remember and we desire; this present where our past and our future are one.

Reality is not the product of an ideological phantasm. It is the result of history. And history is something we have created ourselves. We are thus responsible for our history. No one was present in the past. But there is no living present with a dead past. No one has been present in the future. But there is no living present without the imagination of a better world. We both made the history of this hemisphere. We must both remember it. We must both imagine it.

We need your memory and your imagination or ours shall never be complete. You need our memory to redeem your past, and our imagination to complete your future. We may be here on this hemisphere for a long time. Let us remember one another. Let us respect one another. Let us walk together outside the night of repression and hunger and intervention, even if for you the sun is at high noon and for us at a quarter to twelve.

June 7, 1983

CPSIA information can be obtained
at www.ICGtesting.com
Printed in the USA
LVOW11s0305120117

520665LV00001B/67/P